Economics and Land Use Planning

Economics and Land Use Planning

Alan W. Evans

Centre for Spatial and Real Estate Economics
University of Reading

Blackwell
Publishing

© 2004 by Alan W. Evans

Editorial offices:
Blackwell Publishing Ltd, 9600 Garsington Road, Oxford OX4 2DQ, UK
  Tel: +44 (0)1865 776868
Blackwell Publishing Inc., 350 Main Street, Malden, MA 02148-5020, USA
  Tel: +1 781 388 8250
Blackwell Publishing Asia Pty Ltd, 550 Swanston Street, Carlton, Victoria 3053, Australia
  Tel: +61 (0)3 8359 1011

First published 2004 by Blackwell Publishing Ltd

Library of Congress Cataloging-in-Publication Data
Evans, Alan W.
  Economics and land use planning/Alan W. Evans.
    p.   cm.
  Includes bibliographical references and index.
  ISBN 1-4051-1861-X (pbk.: alk. paper)
  1. Land use – Great Britain – Planning.   2. Land use – Economic aspects – Great Britain.
  3. Land use – Environmental aspects – Great Britain.   4. Land use, Urban – Government
  policy – Great Britain.   5. City planning – Great Britain   6. Real estate development – Great
  Britain.   7. Economics.
    I. Title.
  HD596.E265   2004
  333.73′0941′091732–dc22
                                                                                    2004001028

ISBN 1-4051-1861-X

A catalogue record for this title is available from the British Library

Set in 10/13pt Trump Mediaeval
by DP Photosetting, Aylesbury, Bucks
Printed and bound in India
by Replika Press Pvt. Ltd, Kundli

The publisher's policy is to use permanent paper from mills that operate a sustainable forestry
policy, and which has been manufactured from pulp processed using acid-free and elementary
chlorine-free practices. Furthermore the publisher ensures that the text paper and cover board
used have met acceptable environmental accreditation standards.

For further information visit our website:
www.thatconstructionsite.com

RICS **FOUNDATION**

The **RICS Foundation** was established by the Royal Institution of Chartered Surveyors to promote and highlight the importance of the built and natural environment. The RICS Foundation supports and develops programmes of research to explore the key issues relevant to the way in which we manage, finance, plan and construct our built and natural environment, to make best and most effective use of the resources available to us.

Real Estate Issues

Series Managing Editors

Stephen Brown RICS Foundation
John Henneberry Department of Town & Regional Planning, University of Sheffield
David Ho School of Design & Environment, National University of Singapore

Real Estate Issues is an international book series presenting the latest thinking into how real estate markets operate. The books have a strong theoretical basis – providing the underpinning for the development of new ideas.

The books are inclusive in nature, drawing both upon established techniques for real estate market analysis and on those from other academic disciplines as appropriate. The series embraces a comparative approach, allowing theory and practice to be put forward and tested for their applicability and relevance to the understanding of new situations. It does not seek to impose solutions, but rather provides a more effective means by which solutions can be found. It will not make any presumptions as to the importance of real estate markets but will uncover and present, through the clarity of the thinking, the real significance of the operation of real estate markets.

Books in the series

To Stephen and Denise,
Christopher and Adrianne,
and their children

Contents

Preface

The aim of this book is to bring together and present systematically work on the economics of land use planning which I and others have carried out over the past 20 or 30 years. The first few chapters of the book set out the economic justification for land use planning, as well as describing economic and other methods of assessing and evaluating planning proposals and controls. These topics are those which were discussed in the most recent book on economics and town planning published in Britain, now over 20 years old (Willis 1980). The second and larger part of the book is an analysis of the economic effects of the system, generally unforeseen, and of what might be called its political economy, why planning takes the form that it does. These are aspects of the planning system which have only been studied by economists since the mid-1980s.

My own understanding of the economics of planning has developed over several years and has been informed by study and experience in a number of ways. My doctoral thesis on the economics of residential location, when it was published, included a chapter which was suggested by the publishers on the economics of green belts (Evans 1973). My first post as an academic, as a Lecturer in Urban Studies at the University of Glasgow, was to research the origins of, and the economic rationale for, planning standards such as those applied to the control of the bulk of office buildings (Evans 1974b). This academic interest in the subject has continued, but over time I have also gathered some practical experience of the operation of the system.

On the one hand I have been involved for the past 20 years in a conservation group in the London suburb in which I live. This has involved looking at planning applications for proposed developments and making representations to the local authority where the group wished to object, either in writing or, on occasion, in person before the authority's planning committee. On the other hand I have for many years been responsible for policy in respect of the Halls of Residence at the University of Reading. In this capacity I have been involved in a number of planning applications put before Reading Council, on occasion appearing before their planning committee to put the University's case, and sometimes chairing meetings to present the University's proposals to local residents. Outside the University, I have also, at various times, been asked to act as a consultant for developers in relation to various aspects of the planning system.

This experience of the practical aspects of what might be called the pro- and anti-development aspects of planning have certainly been useful in increasing my understanding of the system. The arguments have to be presented properly, however, and for their assistance in helping to smooth the rough edges from the arguments in this text I chiefly have to thank the students of the Department of Real Estate and Planning (formerly Land Management) at the University of Reading, where the lectures on which this book is based were first given. Versions of some chapters have been presented at academic seminars and conferences, and some lectures were given to students of planning at the University of Naples. All of the participants in these events, whether students, academics, or practitioners, have asked questions and engaged in discussions which have forced me to rethink or rephrase the arguments, and I have to thank all of them.

For their support in the writing of this book I am grateful to the Leverhulme Trust for their sponsorship of a Fellowship to allow my teaching to be reduced during the period during which most of this book was written. Part of this time was spent as a visiting Research Fellow at the Urban Research Program at the Australian National University, a program which unfortunately no longer exists. Nevertheless I would wish to thank its members, in particular Pat Troy, for their hospitality.

Over the years I have discussed aspects of the planning system with many people, but I should particularly wish to express my thanks to Paul Cheshire, Geoff Keogh, and the late Max Neutze. My wife Jill's responsibility for a series of property developments, and their planning, in her career resulted in many useful and interesting discussions over the dinner table. Her planning consultant, John Lawson, was good enough to read and comment at length on an earlier version of this book from a practitioner's point of view. And, finally, I would wish to thank my colleagues at the Centre for Spatial and Real Estate Economics at Reading – Mark Andrew, Graham Crampton, Eamonn D'Arcy, Alessandra Faggian, Phil McCann, Geoff Meen, Mike Stabler, and, most importantly, our secretary Abi Swinburn. Her help and assistance have made the production of this book possible, just as her cheerfulness and social skills have made life more pleasant for all of us.

1

Introduction

'An honest tale speeds best being plainly told'
(Richard III)

What is planning?

Before we can begin to analyse the economics of land use planning, and the relationship between economics and planning, we need to discuss the aims and objectives of planning. We need to do this for three reasons. First, we need to be able to say whether economic analysis can assist in achieving these aims. Second, we would wish to be able to say whether the aims have been achieved. Third, we want to find out what the unintended consequences of trying to achieve these aims might be. Of course, it might be argued that it is pointless to ask what the aims of land use planning might be, since the answer is obvious – the aim and objective of land use planning must be the planning of the use of land, and this must be so whether it is called land use planning, environmental planning, town and country planning, or urban and regional planning. This is surely true, but there still remain questions as to what are the limits of land use planning and the extent of its objectives. Is the aim aesthetic? Is it efficiency? Is it to ensure equity? Is it sustainability? And if all of these are aims, how should one be balanced against another?

Historically it is clear that the origins of land use planning lie in the work of architects and others concerned with the placing of buildings, with what we would now call civic design, distinguishable from architecture only in that the first was concerned with the location of buildings relative to each other while the second was more concerned with their internal structure and external appearance. The aims were primarily aesthetic, although political and military objectives were sometimes also involved. The aesthetic imperative is most obvious in the great monumental plans carried through in some cities. L'Enfant's design for the city of Washington on the Potomac

River focuses its avenues on the important public buildings and monuments, and these in turn are located on high ground in order to command attention. Burley Griffin's plan for Canberra uses its avenues in a similar way with the difference that the city is built around an artificial lake. Within an existing city Haussmann's boulevards and avenues attempted the same effect in Paris, and here the military factor was also involved since the wide avenues were intended to be less easily blocked by revolutionaries and more easily controlled by military firepower. In Vienna, when the old city walls were finally demolished, the military insisted that the street which circled the city in their place, the Ringstrasse, should be as wide as it is in order 'to maximise mobility for troops and minimise barricading opportunities for potential rebels' (Kostof 1992, p. 54). Here town planning was clearly being used to assist those in power to maintain their hold on power.

Washington and Canberra, Paris and Vienna are instances of town planning in the grand manner, but there are many less familiar examples historically of town planning on a smaller scale. For example, bastides, small new towns to a common pattern, were planted over south-west France by both the English king and the French in the twelfth and thirteenth centuries during the Hundred Years War. They were intended to secure a claim to the land in the area, to house the population and to be defensible. Similar principles were adopted in the Spanish settlements in the New World, with the principal buildings grouped round the Plaza at the centre of the town. Numerous possibilities and patterns exist and they are surveyed in many books on the subject, recently by the late Spiro Kostof in two substantial and well illustrated volumes, *The City Shaped* (1991) and *The City Assembled* (1992).

The civic design element in land use planning is obvious because the design or plan remains, literally, on the ground, at the present day; but other aspects of town planning have also been important in the past, even if there is less evidence of this past concern. Perhaps most obviously there is the problem of infrastructure which becomes increasingly important as a settlement becomes larger. The provision of roads and of water and the removal of sewage are the most obvious and essential elements of this infrastructure. The remains of the aqueducts built by the Romans to bring water to Rome and to some other cities are still standing. The routes of Roman roads are in use today throughout the former empire, and Roman arenas such as that at Verona are standing and in use after two thousand years.

Another fundamental concern of early town planning was public health, and with what an economist would call externalities – the impact of one person's activities on others, otherwise than through the market. For example, if buildings are crowded together and flimsily constructed fire may spread more quickly. Again, if people are badly housed and crowded together disease may spread more quickly. The attempts in the reign of Elizabeth I in 1580, and for nearly a century after, to control and limit the spread of London seem to have arisen from concern about both these 'external diseconomies' (Hibbert 1977, pp. 71–73). It was believed that building outside the walls and therefore outside the control of the Corporation of the City of London would be more likely to allow fire and disease to spread. Thus it was thought that the actions of some inhabitants of the urban area would impact on other inhabitants and therefore must be controlled. A flimsily built structure would be more likely to catch fire and although this might be a private matter as far as it affected the owner and the occupants of the building, it was a public matter if it meant that the houses of others were, in consequence, more likely to be burned. At the present day, of course, building regulations and construction codes try to ensure that the owner is safeguarded against the builder and the tenants against the owner while planning rules and regulations try to ensure that the interests of neighbours are taken into account in what is allowed to be built.

All of these things – civic design, the provision of infrastructure, and the control of environmental externalities – are features of land use planning at the present day, though the latter tends now to be considerably more important than in the past. Perhaps less evident is the military aspect, but political objectives can still affect planning. Sometimes, in extreme cases, they may be explicit, as in the new settlements in the territory occupied by Israel after the 1967 war or the development of South African cities in the apartheid era. More usually the political influences will be less evident, but, as we shall show, may still be present.

The precise characteristics of planning systems will vary from country to country, for cultural and climatic reasons, or for legal and constitutional reasons, or, maybe, because by chance one country adopts one set of rules and ordinances rather than another. In Britain the basis of the modern town planning system was set out more than 50 years ago in the Town and Country Planning Act 1947. The date is important. It means that it was enacted by the Labour government elected at the end of the Second World War, a war fought against Fascism but in alliance with Communism. During the war Britain had been more controlled, more centrally directed, more planned than ever before (or since). It was probably more centrally controlled and planned than the Fascist powers and, it could be argued, was 'more fully socialist than anything achieved by the conscious planners of Soviet Russia' (Taylor 1965, p. 507). Thus, the political environment of the time was largely in favour of controls, of central direction, of planning. There was a belief that planning was good in itself, that a planned environment must necessarily be better than an unplanned environment. There also lingered a view that the individual was relatively unimportant compared with society as a whole. This is evident in statements made at the time. For example, Sir Patrick Abercrombie, the leading British planner of the day, co-author of the County of London Plan and the Greater London Plan, as well as a number of others, such as the Clyde Valley Plan, wrote in an introductory textbook on town planning that an economist 'is a muddler talking about the Law of Supply and Demand and the liberty of the individual' (Abercrombie 1959, p. 27). Whatever may be the truth of the first part of this statement, it is the attitude displayed in the second half that is important here. At a conference in 1944 on the implementation of town planning schemes after the war, one participant, the Borough Surveyor of Tottenham, in north London, commented that 'It seems that the most difficult hurdle to surmount will be the wishes of the people of Tottenham' (Bliss 1945, p. 35). And a contributor to the discussion took a still more totalitarian view: 'Planning means control – you have got to put people out, tell them where to live and if somebody wants to build a factory, you have got to tell them "nothing doing in Tottenham – you must build a factory in so and so".' The contributor concluded by remarking that '[Communist] Russia, [Nazi] Germany and [Fascist] Italy all had planned systems' (Bliss 1945, p. 40).

All of this seems difficult to believe or understand more than 50 years later, but since that time British society has passed through the late 1960s and early 1970s, a period when the social emphasis was on the individual pursuit of happiness and the political emphasis was on participation, and then, in the 1980s, the Thatcher era with its emphasis on the individual pursuit of wealth, and the view expressed by her, at least, that 'there is no such thing as society'. The surprise is that planning in Britain has appeared to change so little over the period.

Prediction or control

In practice, however, planning has changed substantially. One major change resulted from the understandable failure to foresee in the 1940s the economic and social changes which would occur over the following 20 years. When the plan for Greater London was drawn up during the war it was envisaged that the population of Britain would remain more or less constant and might even fall. This, after all, had been the situation between the wars. Apparently the huge growth in population following the Industrial Revolution had come to a halt. While it was realised that there would be an increase in the birth rate after the end of the Second World War, as there had been after the First World War, it was thought that this would be as temporary as the earlier increase. The birth rate duly rose and fell in the late 1940s but then rose continuously for nearly 20 years through to the mid-1960s. The resulting increase in the population was therefore not foreseen and neither was the consequential increase in the demand for housing when these children became adults, forming households and requiring houses of their own. Nor was the level of immigration from the Commonwealth through the 1950s and 1960s and the accompanying need for further additional housing. Nor was the rise in the divorce rate, the increase in the number of single parent families and the increase in the number of elderly people, all changes which meant that households became, on average, smaller so that more actual dwellings were required to accommodate a given population.

Also not foreseen was the increase in incomes. The record for the period between the wars was of economic depression and high levels of unemployment, even if London and southern England had generally prospered. The economic aims for post-war Britain were full employment and a fair distribution of incomes. A doubling and trebling of income levels was not foreseen and, perhaps, could not have been foreseen, neither therefore were the increases in the level of car ownership and the increased demand for larger houses with the consequential impact on the demand for land (Cullingworth 1997).

In the case of London it was expected and consequently planned that the urban area could be defined and bounded by a green belt. It was assumed and planned that the population of London would not grow but that as slums were cleared and densities reduced in the inner areas some of the population, and some of the jobs, could be relocated to new towns beyond this green belt. It was expected that regional policies would effectively discourage movement to London from the regions, and that, if anything, these regional policies would divert 'surplus' growth from London to the regions. As Peter Hall (1982, pp. 120, 123) has pointed out, another implicit assumption was that jobs and employment were determined by the growth and location of manufacturing industry. Also unforeseen, and therefore not planned for, was the growth in employment in 'tertiary' industries, i.e. in offices, retailing, services, education, etc., rather than in 'secondary', manufacturing, industry.

The process of planning tended to treat the plan as a 'once for all' exercise. This was not intended, but was a consequence of the legacy of civic design. Just as L'Enfant set out a plan for Washington, so Abercrombie set out a plan for London. But the architectural design plan for the centre of a future city is substantially different from the plan for the future development of an existing large metropolis. One may set out to construct the first over a period of time and changes in the rest of the world can be treated as irrelevant. This assumption cannot be made when the plan is for an area which is already home to a fifth of the population of the country. The plan is conceptually different because it is a process of planning for future changes not a set of ground plans. So, while one might agree with Abercrombie that a planned environment is likely to be better than an unplanned environment, nevertheless, planning cannot be a once for all exercise – plans must be adjustable, and adjusted, to meet changing circumstances.

What in fact happened was that the population did increase and incomes also increased. Social changes such as a substantially increased divorce rate resulted in many more smaller households being formed. Rising incomes and technological improvements brought car ownership within reach of the majority. The planned character of the London area did not change, however, except that the sizes of some new towns were increased and other newer new towns designated. The green belt remained and was even substantially extended. The result was that, in economic terms, the demand for land increased as the population, the number of households and their incomes grew, while the supply of land did not increase to take account of these changes. The planned allocation of land therefore changed from a prediction of what would be necessary to a restriction on the amount which was to be made available. The nature of planning also changed from predicting change and planning for it to imposing controls and trying to constrain change to fit in with the plan (Cullingworth 1997; Hall 1997).

Another, political, factor helped to change the nature of planning. At the time of the 1947 Town and Country Planning Act, under a Labour Government, it was presumed that most development would be carried out by public authorities of one kind or another, that there would be relatively little development in the private sector (Hall 1982, p. 109). In fact, particularly following the election of a Conservative government in 1951, most development was carried out in the private sector. So, instead of the public sector planning the development that it would itself carry out, the public sector planned for development that might, or might not, be undertaken by the private sector. Since there were no powers to force development to be undertaken, planning became to a large extent negative so far as it affected the private sector. The system could prevent development by refusing planning permission, but it had no positive powers. On the other hand the existence of unsatisfied demand ensured that when land was released for development it was likely to be developed. An imbalance between supply and demand because of constraints on the supply of land therefore tended to ensure that what was permitted by a plan did take place. While this was not, I believe, intended it was one of the factors leading planning into being a constraining and controlling system instead of or as well as a predicting system.

For many years, however, the level of constraint was not recognised because the planners involved believed that the amount of land allocated for development was equal to the demand. It was officially accepted only in the 1990s that there was a shortfall and that the price of land had risen in consequence, an increase which reduced the amount of land demanded and so ensured that demand equalled supply.

Finally, following the Rogers report in 1999, the level of constraint came to be officially regarded as a virtue, as higher densities were seen as necessary to limit car use and save agricultural land. Thus, a system which half a century earlier had planned for lower densities and new houses based on the idea of garden cities, now planned for high densities and apartments, with gardens regarded as a luxury to be permitted as little as possible.

Professional or political?

Another kind of change in the nature of the planning system was a response to social and political changes which occurred in the second half of the twentieth century. The change can be identified with the Report of the Skeffington Committee in 1969 which recommended that there should be more public participation in the planning system. Public participation helped to change the nature of planning. It had been seen as a technocratic exercise in which planners such as Abercrombie used their professional expertise to plan the built environment in accord with what was perceived as best professional practice. It now changed in character as the planning system had to take on board the views of the planned – the wishes of the people of Tottenham were now not to be seen as an obstacle to be overcome but an important input into the planning process.

Alongside this change came a sociological critique of planning, a view of town planning not as a technocratic process outside the political system, but a 'multi-dimensional political act' (Blair 1973, p. 26). 'A new reality showed that town planning was in the much more sordid business of having to undertake an activity in the complex shadowy world of competing interests and power relationships' (Cherry 1996, p. 183). Paradoxically although this critique of planning was, politically, from the left, the effect of 'public participation' was to reinforce the status quo and the position of those in possession.

The consequences of this were important. Among other things, it allowed land use planning to survive the Thatcher era relatively unscathed when one would have thought that the notion of 'planning' would have been a red rag to the libertarian bull. This was because, in practice, public participation was peculiarly imbalanced. If, for example, a housing development was proposed near to a village, the residents of the village could participate in the process (and would inevitably object to the proposal), but the future residents who would live in the houses if the development went ahead did not and could not participate because they were unidentified and unidentifiable. In the language of labour economics there were insiders and outsiders and 'public participation' meant that insiders had more power.

Moreover, these and other changes made it gradually more explicit that planning decisions are made by politicians rather than planners, whether at a local level when planning permission is given or refused by a committee of local councillors, or at a national level where planning policies to guide planning practice are approved by politicians. Although professional planners may advise, and may do the detailed work involved in the operation of the planning system, nevertheless 'the buck stops' with politicians who will inevitably respond to the views expressed by voters.

So, in the 1980s the articulate middle class saw no contradiction in voting for Margaret Thatcher and, by implication, for free market policies, but at the same time using their participative powers locally to try to block development which was seen as inimical to their interests. Or putting pressure on national politicians to leave in place policies which allowed development to be blocked by political pressure. So, as Cherry (1996) states, it became 'clear that the biggest beneficiaries of the planning system were the special interest groups and lobbies, particularly when they were in harmony with environmental values relating to countryside protection. The fact that the same values sought to protect Conservative interests in maintaining residential exclusivity in suburban locations made them extremely powerful' (p. 202). Thus, although some relaxation of controls permitted, among other things, the development of out-of-town supermarkets in the late 1980s and early 1990s, the system remained more or less intact. Indeed the power to block development at a local level was reinforced by the Planning and Compensation Act of 1990.

A clause inserted during the Bill's progress through the House of Commons made the local authority's development plan the material factor in determining what might or might not be permitted. Development control became 'plan led'. This precluded developers from calling in evidence the general unsuitability of a site for housing, or the need for housing in the area. If the local plan did not indicate that the site was suitable, and stated that the other sites available would satisfy demand, then that was, in effect, the end of the matter (Pennington 2000, p. 75).

One side effect was that developers perceived that it was essential to get sites in which they had an interest recognised as suitable for development in the plan. The lawyers who might have been hired to fight planning appeals were instead hired to argue the case before the public inquiry into the development plan (Pennington 2000, p. 82). A second was to increase the amount of legal argument at any appeal that did take place. That is the argument tended to be less about the suitability of a site, more about whether the current procedures had been followed and what sections of the plan could, or could not, be used in evidence.

What ought planning to be: an economic viewpoint

The previous sections indicate the way in which planning in Britain has developed and changed over time, and the way in which it operates and has operated. So, planning has changed over time, for social and political reasons, from a primarily technocratic process to a primarily political process, and from a process designed to plan for future development to one operated largely to constrain and control development. The discussion leaves aside, however, the question of what planning ought to be. Of course, one could simply take the procedural view: 'planning is what planners do'. But, at the least, the discussion above indicates the way in which most planning decisions are in practice taken by politicians, so that planning certainly covers more than merely what planners do.

What, for example, should planning concern itself with? It is obvious, of course, that land use planning is about land use just as, if we use the alternative names, urban planning or town planning is about towns, but is land use or the physical environment all that should be taken into account? Are other matters unimportant even though they may be affected by planning policies? For example, a Committee of Inquiry into the Greater London Development Plan in the 1970s commented that 'we do not accept the statement that the improvement of London depends on the Londoner's well-being' (Foster & Whitehead 1973), with the implication that an improvement of London could take place, presumably of the built environment, which could make Londoners worse off, and which would still be an acceptable planning policy.

Certainly, from an economic viewpoint such a stance would seem surprising. Economics, welfare economics in particular, would hold that policy recommendations should take into account all the changes in economic welfare which might result. (Though even welfare economics is inclined to leave out of account things which others might correctly regard as highly important such as the political organisation of society!) However, the narrower view of planning, the view that it is concerned with the physical environment and nothing else would be acceptable in respect of most other activities. The responsibility of a company is seen, after all, as the provision of a service or product. It is expected that in general the market will look after the interactions with other activities. Should land use planning be any different? In my view the answer should be 'yes'. I suspect that most planners would agree, despite the remark quoted above and whether or not it represented the view of the planning profession in 1973. At the end of the 1990s, the perceived objectives of town planning changed somewhat. First, the Local Government Act 2000 introduced a duty on local planning authorities to have regard to social and economic considerations, as well as environmental issues, though it is still too early to say what effect this injunction may have on the way development plans are implemented. And, second, there is now some agreement that the idea that land use planning should be about 'sustainability' came to the fore as a justification for and aim of the planning system. Though what is meant by 'sustainability' can sometimes be unclear, the fact that it is now regarded as a planning objective serves to negate a view that planning should be about physical land use and nothing else. Thus, we should be concerned not only with the physical effect of a planning decision, of whatever kind, but also with its other effects on people's behaviour and well-being. The sociological critique of planning in the 1970s has given a further non-economic justification for this viewpoint. Following through the interactions with other activities may, however, be difficult, but we can agree they should not be ignored. And most of this book will be concerned with analysing these effects through interactions with other activities and the consequences in the relevant markets.

The problem can be represented in this way. What is the nature of a planning achievement? It has often been said that the green belts or the new towns are the greatest achievements of the post-war British planning system. But it would appear that the criterion of success being used is that they were achieved and maintained. The criterion is the same as that for a work of art. An artistic intention was achieved. Planning is being treated here as civic design. The same criterion is used in other fields, in that of exploration for example. Success is achieved if a rocket is sent to Mars or Saturn and sends back information. Of course, these endeavours are costed beforehand. If they cost too much they would not usually be attempted. But the costs of the achievement of a planning objective may only be discovered afterwards when these economic costs are imposed on others.

An alternative criterion of success would be commercial or economic. That the benefits exceed the costs. In the case of companies in the private sector this criterion becomes that of financial profitability – revenues exceed expenditure. Sometimes the criteria become a little mixed, something may be achieved, like Concorde or the Channel Tunnel, but its commercial success may be questionable. Therefore, according to one criterion the achievement is a matter of congratulation, according to the other it may not be.

It is assumed in this book that the economic factors cannot be ignored, that even if a planning objective is achieved the economic aim should be to indicate the costs and benefits of its achievement, whether directly or through interactions with other activities in the economy.

Some 20 or 30 years ago it was clear how this should be done. The tools of welfare economics should be used to explain the planning system in terms of welfare economics. In the 1970s a number of articles and books developed this theme (for example Evans 1974a; Oxley 1975; Harrison 1977; Willis 1980). They set out the causes of 'market failure' and therefore the reasons why intervention through the planning system could improve economic welfare. In the 1990s a number of authors questioned this. Lai (1994) argued that the basic approach set out by Pigou needed to be modified to take into account the 'transactions costs' of intervention as suggested by Coase (1960), the costs of obtaining the information on which intervention could be based, and the costs of implementing the controls or other form of intervention. The Coasian approach to the analysis of the economy of cities has been followed through in depth by Webster & Lai (2003); in depth because they examine all aspects of the urban economy, not only the planning aspect. With regard to planning, the Coasian approach suggests that since information may often be lacking, and the costs of intervention high, it will frequently be better to leave well alone, letting the market settle the allocation of resources. The welfare economic case for intervention and for non-intervention is set out in the next chapter of this book.

If it is possible, and not prohibitively expensive, the results of planning proposals and policies need to be evaluated. There may be a *prima facie* case for intervention but the costs and benefits of intervention need to be determined, as far as possible, to justify the proposal. The evaluation of policies is discussed in Chapter 3. In Chapters 4 and 5 we consider a number of standard planning policies to try to evaluate them and determine their immediate consequences. Up to this point we have been applying the agenda set out in these earlier papers and articles, modified if necessary by the Coasian view.

In the last half of this book we set out to investigate, from a positive economic point of view, the consequences of intervention in the market through the planning system. Not to investigate what ought to be done but to try to elucidate the economic consequences of what is being done, with the implication that positive economic analysis might suggest ways in which the results of the intervention might be bettered. The analysis in these chapters is modified, however, by a further approach which has become evident, and advocated both implicitly, by Evans (1991) and explicitly, by Poulton (1991a, 1991b, 1997), Webster (1998) and Pennington (2000). This 'public choice' approach suggests that we should look not only at the consequences of what is being done, accepting, implicitly, that planning policies and proposals are intended to improve economic welfare, but also at the political reasons for intervention. How is the planning system operated and on whose behalf? Can the system be manipulated through political pressure to benefit particular groups? An understanding of the political position by the economist and the economics profession helps to explain why, even though it may be demonstrated that a particular planning instrument is not cost effective, economic advice may not be heeded.

In this, therefore, the economic approach to planning may be thought of as catching up with the sociological, neo-Marxist, critique of urban planning in the 1970s. But it must be recognised that the public choice/positive economic approaches do not wholly replace the welfare economic approach, whether Pigovian or Coasian. The analysis of why things are as they are, what the consequences are, and which political groupings benefit from the resulting state of affairs may provide explanations and facts. But the welfare approach can still demonstrate, for example, that the gains to the politically successful group are far outweighed by the losses to the others, so that the situation can be in that sense described as bad. The perennial conflict in the social sciences and in planning between 'what ought to be' and 'what is' is not resolved by any difference in approach.

2

Market Failure and Welfare Economics – A Justification for Intervention

'If to do were as easy as to know what were good to do, chapels had been churches and poor men's cottages princes' palaces' (The Merchant of Venice)

Introduction

Probably the best known comment in the whole of economics is that by Adam Smith on the idea of 'the invisible hand'. If everyone attempts to maximise profits and output, then 'every individual necessarily labours to render the annual revenue of the society as great as he can ... he intends only his own gain, and he is in this, as in many other cases, led by an invisible hand to promote an end which is no part of his intention' (Smith 1776/1960, p. 400). Over the two centuries since the publication of *The Wealth of Nations* economists worked hard to test the validity of this statement, and it is perhaps unfortunate that the qualifications and conditions by which this conclusion is now hedged about are considerably less well known.

So any introductory economics textbook will confirm that economic welfare will be maximised, in some sense, if all the markets in an economy are perfectly competitive. It will define perfectly competitive markets as those in which there are, in each separate market, many buyers, many sellers, and a homogeneous product, and where the buyers and sellers have full information about the alternatives available to them, and each transaction directly affects only the buyer and the seller. If these conditions are fulfilled then perfect competition will lead to a state of affairs which economists describe as Pareto optimal, that is, where one person or household cannot become or be made better off without others becoming or being made worse off.

In this sense, and under these conditions, Adam Smith's conclusion is therefore true. But a further qualification is still necessary. There are, in fact, an infinite number of Pareto optimal states of the economy, depending on the initial distribution of assets in the economy and the resulting distribution of welfare. Pareto optimality, or economic efficiency, does not necessarily mean that the distribution of income and wealth is equitable. Even in an efficient, Pareto optimal, economy intervention may be thought desirable to alter the distribution of welfare.

Of course, no economy is actually perfectly competitive, so that the failure to meet the conditions necessary for Pareto optimality provide other reasons for intervention in order to correct for what is called market failure. Intervention may be thought necessary because there are too few buyers or sellers, the most well known problem being that of monopoly where a single seller, or a group of sellers acting together, can restrict the supply of a good in order to raise the price. Parallel to this is monopsony where a single buyer, or group of buyers, uses market power to offer a lower price for a good or service. Or oligopoly where there are few sellers. Other reasons for intervention might be because of a lack of knowledge and information among market participants. Or it might be that for some reason there is no proper market functioning. For example, it is difficult to set up a market for urban road space so that urban roads have to be provided publicly.

In urban areas the most important reason for intervention is likely to be that the effects of transactions are not felt only by those directly participating. There will be external effects, or externalities, whether external economies or external diseconomies. In much of economics the existence of externalities can be, and is, ignored. It is possible to study economics to degree level, and have very little contact with the notion. Nevertheless it is difficult, if not impossible, in the analysis of cities to ignore their existence. Externalities are endemic in urban areas. Indeed external economies, positive externalities, are one of the reasons why cities exist. As people live and work together in a single place, so the market for the provision of different kinds of goods and services is enlarged. If there are economies of scale in the production of these goods and the provision of these services, and there usually will be, so the cost of the goods and services falls as the market is enlarged. In smaller towns and villages it will not be worthwhile providing some goods and services and they can be obtained, if at all, only from some larger town or city. The larger the town or city, therefore, the wider the range of goods and services provided, thus providing further economic reasons, in the form of these 'agglomeration economies', for people to congregate together in the larger cities.

Extreme examples can be seen in the form of stock exchanges, or theatres, opera houses, jewellers, or major league sports teams, but other, more prosaic, examples exist in the shape of specialist firms of accountants, lawyers, management consultants, etc., all requiring a market of a sufficiently large size to survive.

Negative externalities, external diseconomies, are also endemic in urban areas, if only because activities which would affect no one else in rural areas because there would be no immediate neighbours, will have significant effects in towns and cities where there are neighbours, and the magnitude of the effects will be greater when the neighbours are many. So, the negative effects of noise or of pollution can be ignored in most of economics but not in the economic analysis of urban areas. Further, one form of negative externality, congestion, is irrelevant because non-existent in a rural area but of great importance in cities where many want to use the same road space and reach the same destinations.

And it is these negative externalities which provide the primary economic justification for intervention in the land and property market through the planning system. As we shall show, if an activity such as a factory imposes noise, dirt and pollution on its neighbours, then this may provide a reason for intervention to minimise these externalities. If congestion is created by a shopping centre, if the market would leave too little space for housing or for roads or for recreation, then intervention through the planning system may be used to try to minimise the external diseconomies and to try to maximise economic welfare.

Of course, although welfare economics can provide a justification for intervention, the reasons for intervention in practice are culturally determined. They are relative and not absolute. In the English speaking 'anglo-saxon' countries privacy and quiet are more valued and more valuable, than in, say, many Mediterranean countries. The fact that the English word 'privacy' is used in Italian because no equivalent word exists is, to say the least, indicative. Planning may restrict an activity in one country and encourage it in another. Few better examples of such cultural differences can be found than that reported by Norman Douglas in a book about travel through southern Italy in the early 1900s. He noted that there were no trees planted in the streets to shade the people walking there. 'And who would guess the reason? An Englishman, at least, would never bring himself to believe what is nevertheless a fact, namely, that if the streets were converted into shady boulevards, the rents of houses would immediately fall. When trees are planted the lodgers complain and finally emigrate to other quarters; the experiment has been tried, at Naples and elsewhere, and always with the same result. Up trees, down rents. The tenants refuse to be deprived of the chief pleasure in life – that of gazing at the street passengers' (Douglas 1915/1983, p. 66).

Though watching what goes on in the street is a continuing aspect of Italian life, there are now trees on major thoroughfares in southern Italian towns so, in fairness, one should note that Douglas's observations are not now true. Maybe television provides an alternative to people-watching.

The analysis of external diseconomies

It was stated earlier that intervention may be desirable to minimise externalities, but not necessarily to eliminate them. To show why elimination may be uneconomic we require the use of a diagram to aid the explanation. The economic analysis of external diseconomies is illustrated in Figure 2.1.

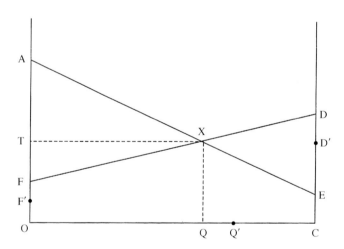

Figure 2.1

An external diseconomy, let us say pollution, is measured along the horizontal axis. If zero pollution is indicated at O, OC is the level of pollution which would be caused by the polluter in the absence of any intervention. Costs, the cost per unit of pollution, are measured on the vertical axis. The upward sloping line, FD, indicates the cost of each additional unit of pollution, that is its marginal cost. The upward slope of the line indicates that each additional unit imposes a higher cost than any previous unit, and the marginal cost of the last unit, at C, is CD. The total cost of all the pollution being caused, the total costs imposed on its neighbours by the factory, is represented in the Figure 2.1 by the area OFDC.

This pollution could, however, be controlled by the firm, but at a cost. The downward sloping line AE represents the cost of this control. Once again it represents the cost of eliminating each further unit of pollution, and it slopes downwards because it can plausibly be assumed that the cost of minimising the effects will be small if very little is done but the cost of eliminating each further unit will increase, and the cost of eliminating all the pollution will be very high indeed. So, at C the cost of elimination is represented by CE and is very low since simple devices may be adequate. However, as the amount of the pollution that has already been controlled increases so the cost of elimination increases. The cost of eliminating the last unit is represented by OA, which is considerably higher than CE. In turn, it follows that the total cost of eliminating all pollution is represented in Figure 2.1 by the area OAEC.

Familiarity with the usual economic approach will suggest to the reader that the social optimum is likely to be given by the intersection of these two cost curves at X with a level of pollution OQ, and this intuition will be correct. The reason why this indicates the optimum is that at this point the marginal cost of pollution is equal to the marginal cost of elimination. At higher levels of pollution than OQ the cost of an additional unit of pollution, the value of the damage caused, is greater than the cost of elimination. It would be socially beneficial to reduce the level of pollution since the (social) benefits would outweigh the (social) costs. On the other hand, at lower levels of pollution, the cost of elimination would be greater than the cost of the damage caused if the pollution were not eliminated. Economically the social benefits of elimination would outweigh the social costs.

This may be the optimum, but how is it to be reached? Can the optimum be reached without government intervention? Is government intervention necessary, and, if so, what form should it take? Following work by Coase, in particular his 1960 paper 'The problem of social cost', it is clear that how the optimum is achieved, and, indeed, whether it is achievable, depends on the legal position, on the ability of those affected to negotiate, and the costs of intervention.

The crux of the matter is that those suffering from the pollution are likely to be for economic purposes separate from the factory that would have to bear the cost of controlling the pollution. They may also be numerous and dispersed and unable, or unwilling, to organise as a group.

Nevertheless, if they are few enough and if they are organised enough to operate as a group, it would be possible for them to approach the firm running the factory and to negotiate with the firm. Negotiation of this kind will lead towards the optimum. At high levels of pollution the cost of the damage suffered by them is greater than the cost of elimination. If the polluter is within his legal rights in allowing the pollution to occur, then the group would be willing to pay the polluter to reduce the level of pollution, and they will be willing to do this so long as the level of pollution exceeds OQ. At this (optimal) point they would be just willing to pay QX to the firm to reduce the level of pollution by one unit and the firm would be just willing to do so. At lower levels of pollution, however, the costs of elimination are greater and the sufferers would not be willing to pay the costs of elimination since these costs will be greater than the cost of the damage they would suffer from the pollution.

If the legal position were different and the polluter were not seen to be in the right, then an alternative form of negotiation might occur in which the polluter offered to pay compensation to those suffering the damage. Once again negotiations would tend towards a result close to the optimum level of pollution OQ, but with the polluting firm paying damage costs, and at the margin paying QX per unit. At higher levels of output compensation would not be paid since it would be cheaper to eliminate the pollution than to pay damages. At lower levels it would be cheaper to pay compensation rather than eliminate the pollution. Although this scenario seems less likely than that set out above it is possible and does happen. Pargal & Wheeler (1996) describe a situation where polluting firms in Indonesia have been forced by political pressure to pay compensation to villages affected by the pollution caused by the operations of the firms.

Usually those affected by an externality will not get together to negotiate with a polluting firm, primarily because there will be too many of them to be able to organise themselves to negotiate as a group. There may then be a case for government intervention. Once again the precise manner in which the optimum may be approached depends upon the legal and/or political position of both the polluter and those suffering the damage. Thus, the optimum can be reached by levying a tax equal to QX per unit of pollution. Alternatively, if the polluter is seen as being in the right, a subsidy may be paid of QX per unit of pollution not emitted. Once again the idea of a subsidy rather than a tax may appear strange, but it is not unusual in agriculture where, for example, British farmers may be paid compensation for not farming areas of land which are designated as Sites of Special Scientific Interest, or, indeed, for not doing a number of things which are seen as environmentally detrimental, but which would increase production and profits if they were to be done (see Bowers & Cheshire 1983; Pennington 1996).

The analysis set out above is the standard analysis in environmental economics of an external diseconomy. The conclusion that can be drawn from it is that there is, economically, an optimal level of an externality, that it may be reached in various ways, but that, contrary to what one might naively presume, complete elimination of an externality may not be socially beneficial. So far as land use planning is concerned, however, a problem is that the discussion is put in terms of money payments, whether these might be taxes or subsidies, compensation for 'polluter' or 'pollutee'. In land use planning direct taxes and subsidies are almost unknown and physical controls are normal. In terms of Figure 2.1, the optimal level of control would obviously be a control limiting the level of pollution to OQ and the presumption would be that the permitted level of pollution is fixed by the regulating authority taking into account information on the damage cost of the pollution and the prevention costs of eliminating it.

There are other possibilities, however, if we assume more flexibility than appears to be permitted by the diagram, in particular if we assume that one of the possible ways to ameliorate the damage caused by the pollution is to alter the location of the factory (or the population being damaged). In terms of Figure 2.1, the line AE indicating the cost of elimination remains the same no matter how many neighbours there are and how close they may be to the factory. But the level and slope of the line FD indicating the damage cost of the pollution will be higher and steeper the greater the number of people affected and the more they are affected. Thus, it will be higher and steeper if the pollution is occurring in a high density residential area and is likely to be lower and flatter the smaller the number of people living nearby. So, if the factory were located in a different area, the line representing the damage cost would fall to F'D', and the optimal output would rise to OQ'.

There is a further possibility, and that is that in practice it is impossible to impose controls or levy taxes in the sophisticated manner envisaged. The alternatives may be either a complete ban or no controls at all. Then the maximisation of economic welfare depends upon a balancing of the costs of total elimination against the damage cost of uncontrolled pollution. In terms of Figure 2.1, on the assumption that the location of the factory cannot be changed, it is a balancing of the area OAEC against the area OFDC. In this instance the former is greater than the latter and no control is better than elimination. A town planning solution, however, would involve the relocation of the factory to another site where the population affected would be smaller and they would be affected less. After such a relocation the total damage costs might be as represented by the area OF'D'C. Since this is even smaller than OFDC, and hence than OAEC, this would be the optimal solution. By ensuring, through zoning or other types of planning controls, that polluting activities were located so as to minimise the damage costs of the pollution, economic welfare is increased.

Politics and the distribution of welfare

The above is a simple analysis of an external diseconomy. It provides some economic justification for the way in which town planning operates through the use of controls regulating the use of land and the location of activities. Of course, the theoretical possibilities and practical remedies envisaged in welfare economic analysis can become much more sophisticated, but it is probably unnecessary at this point to delve further.

One or two further points need to be made, however, before we go on in the next chapter to look at how town planning might be evaluated from an economic point of view. The first is that economists tend, at least in the first instance, to analyse problems in terms of the achievement, or rather the maximisation, of economic efficiency. But any intervention to improve efficiency affects the distribution of welfare, and different forms of intervention have different effects. In the above analysis the optimal level of pollution could be achieved in a number of different ways, through taxes paid by the polluter or through subsidies paid to the polluter, by compensation paid by the polluter to those suffering the damage, or by payments made by those suffering to the polluter, by the imposition of controls or by the relocation of one or other of the parties. But it is obvious that each of these alternative solutions to the problem of efficiency has a different effect on the distribution of welfare to any other solution, and these distributional effects should not be ignored.

For example, we have already noted that in town planning it is everywhere usual to use controls rather than taxes, physical methods rather than fiscal methods. It has been suggested (Webster 1998) that one reason for this is that while subsidies will be expensive for government, the fiscal alternative, taxes, is likely to be bitterly opposed by those, for example, who own buildings which are in what it has been decided is the wrong location. Controls, on the other hand, which give rights to existing 'non-conforming uses', but prevent others competing with them are likely to be supported for this reason by both parties, those suffering from the external effects because no further market entry will be permitted, and those already there for the same reason. The latter then actually gain because the possibility of increased competition is reduced or eliminated.

A further point which needs to be made is that welfare economics tends to try to appear to be neutral as to the kind of institutions which might achieve maximum efficiency, that is, it tends to ignore the fact that people have preferences, sometimes very strong preferences, as to the kind of political institutions that exist. So, in theory, Pareto optimality could be achieved not only in a perfectly competitive economy of the kind described earlier, but also, in theory, in a completely centrally planned economy. Yet these are two diametrically opposed political alternatives, and the economist who presents them simply and neutrally as alternatives is naive. So, if at a different level of institution, taxes, subsidies, bargaining or controls may each possibly help to achieve maximum efficiency, but the means that is chosen will also figure in people's preferences and they may actually prefer that there should be no government intervention rather than the use of any of them.

This view can be justified on economic grounds, on the basis of particular interpretations of economic problems or economic theories outside the mainstream, neoclassical version with which we are primarily concerned. Thus, some have interpreted Coase's analysis mentioned above as justifying an absence of intervention since the parties should sort out the problem for themselves. Some may take what is called an Austrian view of the economy and argue that intervention should be minimised in order that the economy and its participants can operate creatively and with minimal constraint to further economic development. Some might view market imperfections as too small to justify intervention. These philosophical positions are discussed by, for example, Hausman and McPherson (1996).

Nevertheless, the mainstream, neoclassical position in welfare economics is that, in order to maximise economic welfare, interventions should be undertaken where the social benefits exceed the social costs. So, in a planning system where permission has to be given, whether explicitly or implicitly, for any property development to take place, the presumption would be that permission should be given if the total benefits, both private and social, exceed the total costs, both private and social. And if this is not how the system is thought to be being operated, if, for example, proposals are refused where the benefits would exceed the costs, then we have to ask ourselves why. Presumably the reasons will not lie in community preferences for particular institutional forms, as set out above, because, after all the planning system, as an institution, is already in existence and in operation.

One possibility that has been explored in economic analysis over the last 20 years or so, is that any system of regulation may be manipulated to support the interests of a particular group. The libertarian economist might, because of this possibility, prefer no regulation, or at least no government regulation, at all. And others would be concerned to look to see, as we shall later, whether a system of regulation like town planning can be manipulated, and to what extent it has been.

One final point which has to be made about welfare economics and its assumptions is that the assumption is made, implicitly if not explicitly, that people's preferences are fixed and given. The reason for this is methodological. In the analysis of the economic effects of some change, for example a tax rise, it makes sense to start from the assumption that preferences will remain the same. If this assumption is not made, then no sensible answer can be given. But with respect to the natural and physical environment it may be that this assumption is much too strong. Preferences can and do change, and much of the activity of groups such as Greenpeace or Friends of the Earth is intended to try to change people's preferences so that they attribute a greater value to the environment and a greater cost to environmental pollution. Of course, the potential flexibility of preferences is not anything that we can take account of explicitly, but it is as well to be aware of it.

3

Evaluation and Planning

'There is occasions and causes why and wherefore in all things!' (Henry V)

Introduction

The analysis in the previous chapter, and, indeed, much of the analysis that follows assumes that values can be attributed to externalities such as pollution and noise. After all, if the costs of pollution abatement have to be balanced against the costs of damage resulting from the pollution then some estimate of the cost of this damage has to be made even if this estimate is not explicit but only implicit in the decisions made.

Of course, economists have to recognise that many people feel uncomfortable about attributing financial values to things like noise and pollution, and even if they are willing to accept this they may be extremely unhappy about attributing values to things like risks to health and to life. Their view is summed up in the title to an article by John Adams (1974) '... and how much for your grandmother?'. The economists' defence is that it is better to make these values explicit rather than implicit. Suppose, for example, that a decision is made to put a pedestrian subway at some road junction, because the evidence is that there is a 0.5% chance of a fatal accident occurring there in any year, but that it is decided not to put a subway at another location because the probability of a fatal accident there is only one in ten thousand. Then the costs of subway construction are being balanced against the probability of an accident. A valuation is being implicitly attributed to human life, if only through the decision which is being made. The economic view would be that it would be best to make these decisions more rational, that is, more consistent, rather than inconsistent, that is, less rational. Nevertheless, from an economist's point of view, there sometimes appears to be a kind of unholy alliance between the population which, certainly with respect to human life, does not want values to be made explicit because it prefers to believe that life should be literally priceless, and politicians who would prefer the allocation of resources to be wholly determined by political considerations even if this results in inconsistency.

Moreover, there are considerable problems, as we shall show, with what we have called the economists' position. First, it may in practice be very difficult indeed to attribute values to some things. Second, even if values can be attributed, people's preferences may change and so values can change. Nevertheless, the basic position is that decisions should be made on the basis of estimates of the social costs and social benefits attributable to the various options, and that the option should be chosen which maximises the net social benefits. Formally, this approach is called cost–benefit analysis or social cost–benefit analysis and it is with this that we start.

Cost–benefit analysis

One description of the economic problem is that economics is about the allocation of scarce resources among unlimited wants. As we have already noted, welfare can be maximised in an economy in which all the industries are perfectly competitive. In such a competitive economy firms set out to maximise profits but competition ensures that the prices charged just cover costs. In turn, consumers make choices on the basis of their own preferences and the prices charged by firms. In such an economy firms will choose between alternative courses of action on the basis of the costs and revenues expected to result from each alternative. So, if the net income resulting from an investment in a plant will be sufficient to pay off the interest and the capital required to make the investment, then the investment will be seen as profitable, and, unless there is a more profitable alternative available, it will be carried out.

Cost–benefit analysis (CBA) applies the same principles to public investment as in the financial analysis set out above and applied to private investment. The financial analysis is correct, from the viewpoint of welfare maximisation, with respect to a perfectly competitive economy, since then it is known that *all* the costs and *all* the benefits of the investment are priced and borne by or received by the firm. Where there are significant externalities or other forms of market failure, then a purely financial analysis may lead to the wrong decisions being made from a social point of view. For example, the firm may invest in a plant which results in high levels of pollution rather than some less expensive plant which does not. CBA attempts to take these problems of market failure into account.

For example, it is evident that, with a few exceptions when tolls are collected, there is no market in road space, particularly intra-urban road space. So although the capital cost and running cost of some road scheme or road improvement can be easily found, roads are not generally provided by the private sector because there is no revenue associated with the investment, except, as we have said, when tolls can be collected. CBA attempts to replace the financial analysis: the running and construction costs are estimated in the same way, but the benefits (and some other costs) which result from the investment have to be estimated, recognising that they will benefit people who, if there were a market, would be willing to pay to use the road, but because there is no market they will not have to do so, but will harvest all the benefits.

In the case of a road improvement the main benefits will be the time savings accruing to those using the road, but there will also be other changes which can be taken into account in the CBA. For example, there are likely to be changes in the number of road accidents, so that there may be fewer fatalities but more minor injuries. There are also likely to be changes in noise levels and pollution as drivers alter their routes to take advantage of the new road scheme. These changes may be positive at one location and negative at another but need also to be taken into account. The CBA attempts to value all these various costs and benefits, so that the investment which is made maximises the net social benefits, that is the difference between the value of the social benefits and the value of the social costs.

Probably the most thorough cost–benefit analysis carried out was that done for the Roskill Commission on the Third London Airport in the late 1960s (GB Commission 1971). Here the question at issue was that of the location of the airport. Important unpriced factors were the time savings of those travelling to and from the airport, and the impact of the noise of aircraft landing and taking off on those living nearby. The history of the search for the best site for the airport is, however, indicative of the problems of using CBA and of the difficulty in avoiding entanglement in politics. In the late 1960s the then government announced that there was soon going to be a need for a third London airport and that it should be at Stansted, to the north of London, which was already used for cargo. Protests from those living near to Stansted led to the Roskill Commission being set up. This sifted through a number of sites and finally settled on four, which did not include Stansted, and which were its short-list. On the basis of the CBA the recommendation of the Commission was that the airport should be located at Cublington, to the north-west of London, but the government rejected this recommendation and instead opted for a location at Foulness, on the Essex coast, to the east of London, one of the four short-listed by the Commission.

The whole episode illustrates the unavoidability of entanglement in politics, even when one aim in setting up the Commission was presumably to try to remove the problem from the political arena. Wherever it was proposed that the airport should be located, the residents of the area would apply political pressure for it to be located elsewhere, but although the residents likely to suffer from noise may be identifiable and politically represented, the other possible losers or gainers such as the future passengers likely to use the airport are unidentified and unidentifiable and so have considerably less political muscle.

Moreover, in the end technological change altered the balance of advantage. Aircraft size increased substantially so that the existing two airports were better able to cope with the expansion in passenger numbers in the 1970s and 1980s. At the same time aircraft engines were made quieter. The result, in the end, was that no new airport was built, although in the 1980s the existing cargo airport at Stansted was expanded and developed to become, as had originally been proposed 20 years earlier, the third London airport. The history is reported at greater length in Peter Hall's book *Great Planning Disasters* (1980).

The valuation of social costs and benefits

If the social costs and benefits can be identified, how can they be valued? The aim of economists involved in cost–benefit analyses is not to impose values but to find out from people's behaviour how they themselves appear to value the costs and benefits. For example, the value of savings in travel time for those commuting to work may be found from observing their choices when faced with alternative routes. If someone prefers one route which is faster but more expensive over another that is slower but cheaper, then the choice gives an indication of the value which that person puts on his or her time. Studies of the behaviour of large numbers of people give a still better, more accurate, measure of the value of travel time for the population as a whole.

Other kinds of social cost or benefit may be more difficult to evaluate, but with some effort estimates can be made. For example, a number of different ways to measure the costs of pollution have been suggested (Pearce 1978). The first is literally to measure the costs of the damage caused by the pollution. So if pollutants in the air damage the fabric of buildings then the cost of repairing that damage is one possible estimate of the cost of the pollution. The problem here is that all the possible kinds of damage have to be included to accurately measure the cost of the pollution – not only damage to buildings but also damage to other things like clothing and also damage to health, so that there is always a danger of omitting some costs. And people's mere dislike cannot be valued in this way, and in some cases this may be more important than other, more tangible costs. It may be, for example, with respect to noise.

A second approach is through measuring the costs of avoidance. How much are people willing to pay to avoid suffering from some externality. For example, if people live near an airport and suffer from noise, how much are they willing to pay to install double glazing and take other measures to reduce the level of noise within their dwelling. This measure is also unsatisfactory since, first, noise outside the house cannot be eliminated, and, second, it is probable that the market will operate to ensure that those with a high level of tolerance for noise will be those who tend to live at these locations, so that the cost of noise will tend to be undervalued.

The costs of an externality can also be estimated strictly from market behaviour through measuring differences in wage levels and/or property values. The third possible approach is therefore by measuring differences in wage levels. For example, a comparison of wage levels in more polluted and less polluted cities will give an estimate of people's valuation of the cost of the pollution. This assumes, however, that people can freely choose between locations in different cities and although some US economists are willing to make this assumption it is not one which most of the rest of the profession would be willing to rely on (Evans 1990).

A fourth approach compares differences in property values. For example property values in different parts of the same city can be compared to ascertain the impact of pollution or other externalities or environmental attributes on property prices, price differences giving an estimate of the value people put on the externality. For various reasons, such as the relative plausibility of the assumptions that have to be made, the fact that the value obtained does not result in predictable over- or under-counting, and the availability of data on house prices, this approach, called the Hedonic Price Method (HPM) and based primarily on theoretical work by Rosen (1974), is the one which is the most used.

One other approach, the Travel Cost Method (TCM), developed by Clawson and Knetsch (1966), should also be mentioned here. Although it cannot be used to evaluate the costs of externalities such as pollution, it can be used to estimate the value of goods such as recreational areas or scenic landscapes to which people have to travel. Even when entry to the park or other recreational area is free, the cost of travel to the site is implicitly a price which people, in travelling, indicate that they are willing to pay to visit, and so an indicator of the value of the park.

All of these methods can be used because some sort of quasi-market exists. The externality or good to be valued is pervasive enough, and the number of people involved in its consumption is large enough for their behaviour to be analysed and for this behaviour to reveal the value implicitly put on the good. It is when the good is unique, or almost so, and when few people 'consume' it, that is benefit from or suffer from its existence, that difficulties arise. For example, in the case of the Roskill Commission, in the cost–benefit analysis of alternative sites, a cost at one site would have been the loss of a Norman church, while at another a cost would have been the loss of a breeding ground for Brent geese.

Goods such as these are unique and irreproducible. They clearly have a value but what is that value? It is not only the nearby residents or even the visitors to the site who value such things. In the case of extreme examples such as the Taj Mahal, the ruins of Machu Picchu, or the temples of Abu Simbel it is clear that these also have a value to those who may never visit them. In economic jargon there is an 'option' value – a value to those who might wish to visit and who would wish to retain the option to do so, and there is a 'bequest' value – it has a value in that the current generation would wish to bequeath it to future generations. In these sort of cases, whether the sites are globally famous or only known locally, there are severe difficulties in determining a valuation which can plausibly be put upon them.

An approach that had not been developed at the time of the Roskill Commission is the Contingent Valuation Method (CVM) and this has now been considerably refined. The approach differs fundamentally from the methods outlined above. Instead of trying to find out from the way in which people behave what value people implicitly attribute to some good, survey methods are used and people are explicitly asked to attribute a value to a good. The approach was primarily developed to try to value things in the natural environment – parks, forests, landscapes, animal species – but there are now an increasing number of examples of it being used to value aspects of the urban environment. For example, Willis (1994) attempted to assess the value put on a visit to Durham Cathedral. Moreover, comparison of values obtained through the Contingent Valuation Method with those found with the use of other, apparently more objective methods, indicates that the valuations obtained are not dissimilar. Therefore it would appear that in that sense CVM is reliable (Smith 1993).

The approach has, however, been subject to considerable criticism, and it would be unfair not to note that the severest critics have often been those involved in developing the method. Thus, do people give answers which make them feel better? In giving a value are they influenced by the prices suggested as possible answers? Are the answers to the survey influenced by information given in the process of administering the questionnaire? After all, it is perfectly possible that the values obtained through the CVM may be similar to the values obtained by objective methods, when such values are available, because people responding to the survey may be subconsciously aware of these values. Nevertheless, this does not necessarily mean that the valuations obtained with the CVM are accurate when no comparisons are possible.

PBSA/CIA/CIE

An early appreciation both of the need for evaluation in planning and of the valuation problems posed by cost–benefit analysis led the British planner Nathaniel Lichfield to develop methods of evaluation that did not depend upon an attempt to value all the social costs and benefits associated with a proposal. In the first version, the Planning Balance Sheet Approach (PBSA), he suggested that values should only be attributed to those costs and benefits that could be priced easily and without controversy. In the case of other effects consequent on a proposal, the nature of these various effects should be indicated, as to whether they are benefits or costs, but there would be no point in trying to value them, he argued, since any such valuations would only result in controversy (Lichfield 1956).

What was proposed was that a kind of balance sheet should be drawn up in respect of a planning proposal. Costs (liabilities) would be indicated on one side of the balance sheet, and benefits (assets) would be indicated on the other side. There would be no attempt to measure each with a single money measure, however. The planner's job would be to identify the costs and benefits likely to follow from the adoption of a proposal. The results would then be put up to the political body making the decision in the form of a Planning Balance Sheet. The best available description of the costs and benefits, their nature and importance, and where it is thought possible, their value, would appear in this balance sheet and a recommendation might be made to the political body on the basis of this tabulation. In some circumstances, however, the decision might be left to the political authority. In either event the decision would be made with information which was as full as possible, but which stopped short of a complete valuation of all the costs and the benefits.

The reasons for stopping short of a full valuation are threefold. First, as we have already clearly shown, it may be difficult in many cases to attribute a valuation to some costs and benefits which would be generally acceptable. Second, in many cases it would be extremely costly to carry out the research necessary to actually measure and attribute values to all the costs and benefits. The cost of doing so may not be worth the increase in the certainty of the resulting recommendation. Third, it is quite evident that even if a full cost–benefit analysis were expensively and extensively carried out, the political decision makers may set aside the recommendation in favour of one which, to them, makes better political sense. This, after all, is what happened in the case of the third London airport. One interpretation of this is that the valuations put on the various costs and benefits by the politicians may differ from those expensively obtained by the researchers. An alternative interpretation is of more fundamental importance, however. CBA takes no account of the distributional impact of the cost and the benefits, who actually gains and who actually loses, and these redistributive effects are of political and social importance.

CBA depends for its economic justification on what economists call the Hicks–Kaldor criterion, after the two economists who formulated versions of it. Put at its simplest the Hicks–Kaldor criterion states that a proposal or policy is worth carrying out if the gainers can compensate the losers (even though they do not actually do so). The criterion can be put in various ways that may be subtly different. For example, the potential losers must not be able to pay off the potential gainers to prevent the proposal being carried out. There are also various potential problems if the proposal is so substantial as to affect relative prices if it is carried out, but for our purposes, and for most practical purposes, the criterion is that a proposal should be carried out if the potential gainers can, in theory, compensate the potential losers if it is carried out.

Since compensation is usually not paid, but is purely theoretical, in practice some groups will gain from a proposal and some groups will lose. These gains and losses may fall on different income groups so that the effects are on balance either progressive or regressive. The proposal may affect people living in different areas, either positively or negatively. Further, the gainers or losers from a proposal may be easily identifiable or they may be unidentifiable at the time that the proposal is being considered. For example, the construction of a new road may affect those living in the vicinity, either positively if it is, say, a road which bypasses their village, or negatively, if the road runs near their houses and causes noise and pollution. In either case those affected will be aware of the way in which they will be affected and can form action groups, lobby their political representatives etc., to support or oppose the proposal. Others who will be affected by the road, however, such as those who may use it in the future will not be identifiable at the time that the proposal is being considered and so will not lobby. Obviously, in a political system like that in most English speaking countries at least, where councillors and MPs represent people living in specific areas, planning proposals, which by their nature usually affect most obviously those living nearby, are particularly subject to political lobbying.

It is evident that the distributional effects of any proposal can be important and that the political factors increase this importance. To take account of the effects on the distribution of welfare of a proposal, Lichfield further developed the PBSA first into what he called Community Impact Analysis (CIA) (Lichfield 1988), and more recently into what he has called Community Impact Evaluation (CIE) (Lichfield 1996). Here, not only are the various costs and benefits listed as in PBSA, but the impacts on the different groups in the population are also listed. In this way, it is argued, planning decisions, which in the final analysis may be essentially political, can be made with full information as to the expected effects of the proposal. On the other hand, a recommendation based solely on economic considerations is not, in Lichfield's view, possible.

Alternative non-economic approaches

Problems with the economic approach, in particular with the idea that everything can be measured by a single monetary yardstick, and with the difficulty of actually doing the measuring, have led to other alternative methods of evaluation being proposed over the years. An early suggestion was the Goals Achievement Matrix of Morris Hill (1968). Here the primary concern is with the aims or goals of the planning proposal and the extent to which they are achieved by the proposal. Aside from the question of monetary measures it is clear that this approach is fundamentally different from the CBA/PBSA/CIE family of methods. In the latter the objective is to identify the effects of a proposal, whether these are intended or unintended, and to classify these effects as costs and as benefits. The Goals Achievement approach concentrates on the intended effects – the goals – of the planning proposal. In Goals Achievement analysis, 'community goals and sectoral goals are assumed, identified *a priori*, and provide the basis for both plan formulation and the determination of costs and benefits for purposes of plan evaluation. The Planning Balance Sheet emphasises the identification of sectoral objectives in the course of the analysis of costs and benefits' (Lichfield 1996, p. 163).

The problems with the Goals Achievement approach are twofold. First, with its emphasis on the goals of a planning proposal, these goals have not only to be stated beforehand but also to be given weights according to their importance as perceived by the planners or policy makers, whereas CBA allows the weights to be derived, possibly more democratically, from the prices generated from people's preferences. Second, Goals Achievement, as we have already indicated, concentrates on the stated goals of a proposal, while CBA encourages, indeed forces, a consideration of all the consequences of a planning proposal, whether intended goals or unintended effects. As we shall show later in this book, the unintended effects of planning proposals may, in practice, be as important in economic terms as the intended effects. Obviously planning proposals cannot be formulated without some idea of the aims and objectives of the proposal, but these objectives or goals need to be considered as part of the whole, embedded in the total effects, whether physical or economic, of the proposed development of an area.

A successor to the Goals Achievement Matrix, developed more recently, is the Multi Criteria Approach (MCA). In considering alternative planning proposals, the various criteria thought to be relevant are determined, and the alternatives are ranked according to these criteria. The optimal proposal is then the one which most outranks the others, on average. The criteria can be decided on the basis of both the intended goals and the unintended effects of a proposal so that the net is cast wider than with the Goals Achievement Matrix. Nevertheless, the problem of weighting still remains. Unless the best alternative outranks the others on all criteria, then some kind of weight, has either explicitly or implicitly, to be attributed to each criterion and the extent to which it is attained, and this weight must, to some extent at least, be subjective (Buckley 1988).

The Multi Criteria Approach has been developed to facilitate choices between alternatives primarily in the context of environmental choices relating to conservation. In cases such as these, as we have noted earlier, there may well be a lack of market or quasi-market data so that the attribution of financial values or prices to goods would be, in all probability, highly speculative. It would therefore be difficult if not actually misleading to use a full cost–benefit analysis in these circumstances, and the listing approach of PBSA/CIE might be preferable. The MCA, however, goes further than listing, since it relies on the attribution of weights arriving at some 'grand index', and so it too may be misleading if these weights are not arrived at consensually with the population as a whole but are imposed by the policy maker, the planner, or, worst of all, the technical expert who understands the methodology of the approach.

One feature of the MCA, and indeed of the CIE/PBSA, should be particularly noted. The MCA was formulated as a method of coping with the problem of uncertainty when the evaluation of a number of alternative policies is being carried out before a decision is made. It has to be recognised that CBA may be less suitable for providing an answer to this kind of question than for answering the question as to whether a policy which has already been carried out has been successful, i.e. whether the benefits outweigh the costs.

An analogy can be made with deciding which horse to back in a race. This will involve the consideration of all sorts of criteria, some of which may be explicitly financial, such as the amount of the bet, the type of bet (win, place or show), and the odds available, and some of which may be definitely non-financial, such as the form of the horse, the jockey, the going on the course. All of this information may be evaluated by the punter before the bet is placed, and making the right decision is difficult. That is the nature of choices *ex ante*. Once the race has been run, however, deciding whether the right bet has been placed is easy, and the process of evaluation is based solely on financial information – the money won or lost.

Similarly, a cost–benefit analysis of the gains and losses, expressed in monetary terms, may be the best way of deciding whether a planning policy or proposal was correct, after it has been carried out. On the other hand, methods such as PBSA/CIE or the MCA may be more suitable to evaluate alternative proposals since they are designed to deal with the problems of uncertainty and lack of information which exist when proposals are at the planning stage.

Dealing with the problem of uncertainty was even more explicitly the intention of the Analytical Hierarchy Process, developed as a mathematical approach to decision making in the absence of full information by Saaty (1980, see Zahedi 1986). The approach has been used in Italy for the evaluation of alternative proposals for the conservation and restoration of buildings and areas (Lombardi & Sirchia 1990; Roscelli & Zorzi 1990). But the approach, while being mathematically sophisticated, has both the advantages and disadvantages of the Multi Criteria Analysis; it can be used in the absence of full information, but, at the same time, because of the absence of full information as to the costs, benefits, and implications of the alternative proposals, the approach may result in decisions being made which would not have been made if better information had been available. And this argument applies not only to the consequences of the alternative chosen, which could not have been completely predicted. It also applies to the weights which should have been attached to the different criteria, which might not be the same as the weights implicitly accepted by the population which might also be different.

Economic evaluation and political choice

In the end there are two factors which will determine the extent of any evaluation that is carried out whether after or before a decision is made. The first is the cost of carrying out an evaluation. If the cost of evaluating alternatives is high, then, at the least, many of the alternatives will be ruled out through a preliminary screening. This will be as true in the private sector as it is in the public sector, for example, it is known that a firm choosing to relocate a factory or office will make its final choice from a very short short-list.

The extent of the evaluation that is made will depend upon the cost of carrying it out: there will necessarily be some kind of trade-off between this cost and the perceived benefit of further information. It will also depend on the degree to which the process of evaluation has become routine. For example, road improvements of one kind or another are carried out constantly, so that carrying out a social cost–benefit analysis may become routine, as it has in the UK. Proposals which might be of a similar financial magnitude, but which are less frequent, even rare, may have to be decided on the basis of less information and less sophisticated techniques of analysis simply because the cost of devising the techniques to be used in the evaluation would have to be borne by only one project rather than many.

The second factor is the extent to which the process of decision making is explicitly political rather than intended to be quasi-independent. As we have already pointed out, in the case of the most well known and expensive cost–benefit analysis ever carried out, that for the Roskill Commission on the Third London Airport, the recommendation of the Commission, based on the results of the CBA, was ignored by the then government which instead opted for the recommendation of the single dissentient. If an evaluation is likely to be ignored for political reasons then there is little point in expensively surveying the costs and benefits of alternatives.

Although this view may seem cynical, it is also realistic. Nor is it intended to be an economist's negative view of politics. When CBA was being developed as a decision-making tool in the 1960s, it was suggested that it would become a way of making political decisions in a rational way. But for this to be true, for CBA to be widely used and its results accepted, first, the Hicks–Kaldor criterion has to be generally agreed to be an appropriate decision-making criterion, and, as we have pointed out earlier, if only because of the way that it ignores distributional effects, this may not be so. Second, the values or prices, whether market prices or quasi-market prices obtained through surveys, have to be generally accepted as 'true' values of the costs and the benefits.

The difficulties of obtaining acceptance of CBA in this way can be illustrated by an example of a problem which most people would not think susceptible to economic analysis of this kind at all. Two authors, Meeks (1990) and Posner (1992), published cost–benefit analyses of a policy of legalising abortion. Their methodological assumptions were questioned by Julianne Nelson (1993) and their findings (that legalised abortion was economically inefficient) do not concern us anyway. The point is that most people would regard this as an ethical problem not susceptible to economic evaluation. That is, at the least, as Nelson argues, most people would not accept that the Hicks–Kaldor criterion is an acceptable criterion to decide such questions, on whichever side of the debate they might stand.

There is, however, a second problem. The prices and values used in a CBA are assumed to be fixed and unchanging because it is assumed that these values are derived from people's preferences and that these preferences do not change. But it is clear, both intuitively and from experimental evidence, that people's preferences do change. Furthermore, much political activity is designed precisely to change these preferences. On one view political lobbying, demonstrations, etc., can be seen as attempts to change preferences so that prices and values would be changed, and so the results of any CBA.

Good examples of this were the demonstrations mounted in the 1990s by protesters against a number of transport projects in the UK. The demonstrators camped in trees, in tunnels, and on the ground in the path of the earth movers in order to hinder the projects. The protesters were not open to the argument that the road proposals had been exhaustively examined in public inquiries and that cost–benefit analyses had clearly shown them to be economically beneficial. Their view was that road construction (or in one case the construction of an airport runway) was in some sense morally wrong, and that the CBAs were wrong or irrelevant because the analyses either failed to take into account environmental factors, or that the costs had been understated because people failed to realise, and therefore did not properly value, in their view, environmental costs such as the impact on global warming of increased road traffic. Since public opinion and political sentiment have moved against further road construction, this political activity would appear to have been politically successful.

The point which I am trying to make here is that economic evaluation is merely an input into the political process, not a means of taking decisions out of politics, of replacing political decision making. But this is not to concede that whatever political decision might be made is right, whatever the conclusions might be of an economic evaluation. Political decisions may be made in the interests of a particular person, group, or class, and may still be economically wrong on the evidence available. Decisions that continually advance the interests of a particular group in this way, but which continually result in decisions that in total reduce the total wealth of society (since the gainers could not compensate the losers) must in the end be wrong. What is important, however, is the tension between economic evaluation and political decision making. This tension is part of the planning process. It is a theme which will recur throughout this book.

4

Controlling the Density of Development

'Past and to come seem best: things present worst'
(Henry IV Pt II)

Introduction

In the preceding chapters we have set out the way in which land use planning may be justified in the light of welfare economic analysis, why intervention in the market for land and property may be justified by perceived market failure. The discussion has been relatively general, however. In the next few chapters we will look at some specific planning instruments in order to see whether their use can be justified, specifically, rather than generally, from a welfare economic point of view. Do the benefits of intervention exceed the costs?

Often these controls are used with little discussion as to the intended effects; their use seems often to be almost intuitive – 'This is what one does as part of a plan'. To try to give an economic interpretation it is therefore sometimes necessary to try to set out what the effects which are intended might be, and then also to set out the unintended effects, those which occur through the market as a consequence of the operation of the control. A knowledge of these effects then allows an assessment of the benefits and the costs. The analysis is sometimes theoretical and sometimes dependent on empirical evidence. Different planning controls have to be interpreted in different ways.

We start by looking at two forms of planning control which would appear, on the face of it, to be very similar, the control of residential density and the control of the density of development of office buildings through controls on the amount of floor space which would be allowed on a given site. We shall find, however, that their economic effects are different, and so, therefore, must their analysis be.

Residential density controls

Residential density controls, in one form or another exist in most planning systems, although the controls can be expressed in many different ways. Maximum densities may be expressed in terms of dwellings per acre or in terms of bed spaces per acre, that is in terms of the population expected to live on the site. In the United States, in particular in the suburbs of the cities and towns, the control may be put in terms of a minimum lot size per dwelling. One thing that is clear is there is no maximum density which it is generally agreed should not be exceeded. Permitted densities vary considerably between countries and cities, but this variation can, of course, be explained in terms of cultural or income differences. Nevertheless, even within a given city, within a given culture, permitted densities are likely to be higher in the inner areas than in the suburbs. So, in the original County of London Development Plan of 1951 the proposed residential densities were of 200 persons per acre in the central area, 136 per acre in the area surrounding it, and 100 per acre in the rest of the County north of the Thames but 70 per acre south of the Thames (London County Council 1951, p. 43).

There are very clear reasons why some kinds of very high densities should not be permitted. High densities in insanitary, overcrowded or badly constructed dwellings make for the rapid spread of disease and illness, and also for both the rapid spread of fire and greater loss of life from any fire. In developed economies where building regulations ensure at the least that buildings are well constructed and sanitary, and where higher incomes mean that overcrowding of any dwelling is less likely, these are not likely to be the problems resulting from a high density of development in terms of dwellings per acre.

One possible justification for restricting the density of residential development would depend on the fact that, at least in the English speaking countries, people prefer living at lower densities to higher. Thus, the empirical evidence suggests that, other things being equal, any given house will sell at a higher price if the density of development of the surrounding area is lower (Ball 1973).

If this is so then it can be shown that if an area is developed in a piecemeal, competitive, fashion, then from a welfare economic point of view the density of development may be too high. There is therefore a case for controls to limit the density of development. If, on the other hand, the area is developed under the control of a single developer, then the density of development will be close to the level allowed by the control, that is to the optimum. This is because, as we shall show, the single developer would take into account the effects of higher densities in determining the optimal density, in the same way as the local authority would be expected to do.

This argument can be developed formally using the diagram in Figure 4.1. Costs and prices are represented on the vertical axis and density is measured along the horizontal axis. The downward sloping line, AR, indicates the schedule of prices which would be paid for a (standard) dwelling in the area, as a function of the residential density. The line slopes downward because it is expected that the price which would be paid will be lower when the density of the surrounding area is higher.

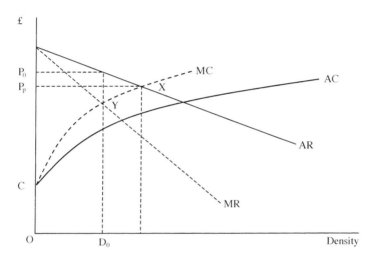

Figure 4.1

The cost of construction of housing is also represented in the figure. The average cost of construction of a dwelling is indicated by the upward sloping line marked AC. The curve slopes upward because it can be presumed that the cost of construction will be higher at higher densities, as would certainly be true if the higher densities have to be achieved by building higher. In determining the most profitable density of construction any developer would have to take account of the additional cost of any increase in development, the marginal cost of a dwelling. The relationship between marginal cost and density is indicated by the dashed line, MC. This shows, as a function of density, the additional cost of increasing the density by one dwelling unit. The curve lies above the average cost curve because a further dwelling has to be constructed, at the average cost, but also imposes further costs elsewhere. So when the additional unit has to be accommodated by building higher, the cost of the additional unit is not just the cost of constructing its floor space alone, but also includes the costs of strengthening the lower floors and walls to support the additional weight.

If development were to occur piecemeal, in the absence of any intervention, with the numerous owners of sites in the area developing each site in competition with each other, then the density of development would be indicated in Figure 4.1 by the intersection of the marginal cost curve, MC, and the price curve or average revenue curve marked AR, shown in the figure by the point X. Each developer would build to the density at which the price of the dwelling constructed was equal to the marginal cost. Since at lower densities price would be greater than marginal cost it would be profitable to increase the density of development of the site, but at higher densities it would be unprofitable since the additional construction cost would be greater than the revenue obtained from the sale.

What would be the optimal density? To determine this we have to take into account the fact that increases in density on a site have external effects. These 'negative externalities' are indicated by a fall in the price of housing in the area as the density increases. To determine the optimal density using Figure 4.1 we have to construct the downward sloping line marked MR. This 'marginal revenue' curve defines the additional revenue that would accrue to a firm, acting on its own, developing the area as a whole, if an additional unit were constructed. This is lower than AR, the curve indicating, as a function of density, the average price at which a unit can be sold, because an increase in density through constructing one additional house results in a fall in the price of all the other houses. The reduction in the revenue accruing to the developer through this fall is represented by the vertical distance between the average revenue curve, AR, and the lower, marginal revenue curve, MR.

The optimal density is indicated at Y by the intersection of the marginal cost curve, MC, and the marginal revenue curve, MR. This is the density at which the whole area would be developed if this development were carried out by a single developer. Such a firm would take into account the fact that an increase in the number of dwellings would cause a fall in the price of all the others and so would maximise its profits from the development at the density D_o. At higher densities the construction of another house would yield a price greater than the marginal cost of the house, it is true, but this additional revenue would be reduced by the fall in the price caused by the increase in the density of development. Thus, marginal cost equals marginal revenue indicates the profit maximising density for a single firm developing the whole area. In economic terms the externalities have been internalised.

Two conclusions result from this analysis. The first is that there is an optimal density which is lower than the density reached through competition between small land owners and developers. Second, when large areas are developed by single land owners the density of development is likely to be lower than if development is piecemeal. Evidence of this can be seen in the West End of London where, when the area was developed in the eighteenth century, a small number of land owners controlled large areas of land. Land owners such as the Duke of Bedford were able to leave a number of areas vacant as 'squares', open green areas surrounded by houses. Their calculation was, presumably, that the price of the surrounding houses would be higher because of the improved environment, and that this would more than make up for the loss of revenue in respect of the houses that were not built on the sites occupied by the squares. On the other hand, there can be no doubt that if the land occupied by the squares were in the hands of different land owners who did not own the land occupied by the surrounding houses, then these squares would have been built over.

If development is carried out piecemeal by a number of firms, as it often is, each one developing a single site, or a small number of sites, an increase in density on one site remains an externality for all the others, and the density of development will be too great. One solution is therefore to impose controls to limit the possible density of development to D_o. There is, thus, an economic justification for controls on residential density. The analysis also suggests that the optimal density will be higher, the greater is the demand for housing in the area. If demand is higher, for example towards the centre of a large city, so that house prices and rents are higher, in Figure 4.1 the lines AR and MR would be higher and the intersection of MR with MC would be that much further to the right, that is, the optimal density would be higher. Thus, the economic analysis can also suggest an explanation for the fact that the densities permitted by residential density controls tend to be highest near the centre of large urban areas, and to decline with distance from the centre, as rents and house prices also tend to decline.

It might be noted that since about 1999 British planning policy has gone into reverse. While before densities were to be kept low, now higher densities are to be encouraged wherever possible. The rationale for this is that higher densities will discourage the use of cars and will also save land. Both these things will, it is argued, assist global sustainability. Thus, in contrast to the analysis set out above, which assumes that the local environment is what matters, and the impact of local externalities, the presumption in PPG 3 (one of a series of Planning Policy Guidance Notes issued by the Department of the Environment to guide the development of local plans by local planning authorities) is that the externalities of low density are global in character.

Control of office floor space

Controls are often used to limit the amount of office space which can be built on a site. These controls operate by limiting the ratio of the area of floor space which can be built on the site to the ground area of the site or plot. As such they are called Plot Ratio Controls in the United Kingdom and Floor Area Controls in the United States, both being shorthand for the floor area to plot ratio. At first sight one might think that the analysis applied above to residential controls could also be applied to the analysis of office space. After all, since in both cases the aim is to restrict the density of development, intuitively one might think that the same kinds of external diseconomies are being controlled. This intuition is incorrect, however, and, as we shall show, it is more difficult to provide a similar economic justification for controls which limit the density of development of office buildings.

In the first place, while we have noted that house prices appear to be higher if the density of development in the surrounding area is lower, it would not be true to say that the rent of office space is lower if there is less office space in the surrounding area. Rather the reverse. The evidence would suggest that office rents are higher the greater the amount of office space there is nearby. People in offices depend upon contact with others. At one level this is very obvious. There is a high demand for office space at the centre of a city and the rent of office space at such a location will be higher than elsewhere. Although it is difficult to abstract from location, the position would appear to be that the greater the amount of office space which is nearby, and therefore the greater the number of possible contacts, the higher the rent which can be obtained.

Repeating the previous form of analysis would therefore suggest that the density of development, if development is piecemeal, would be too low rather than too high, because there are external economies of density with office developments, rather than external diseconomies, as with residential development. But the planning arguments for controls do not depend on this sort of argument but on aesthetics and the control of congestion. If one looks at what is written about floor area:plot ratios, the intention seems to be, first, to control the mass of buildings for aesthetic reasons, and, second, to limit the number of trips or journeys which will begin or end at buildings in order to control congestion (Evans 1974b). As we shall see it is difficult to justify the blanket use of controls for either reason.

As regards aesthetics it is very evident that there are both significant buildings, in architectural terms, with extremely high floor area:plot ratios, and important commercial areas where all the buildings have high ratios. Obvious examples are Manhattan island, in particular the southern end around Wall Street and the mid-town area where the Empire State and Chrysler buildings are located, the harbour side of Hong Kong island (the Hong Kong and Shanghai Bank building), the Loop district of Chicago, or the commercial centre of Sydney south of Circular Quay. In each of these cases, of course, the height and mass of the buildings is made more visible and dramatic by the fact that they can be seen across water, whether the sea, a harbour or a lake. Nevertheless, the examples cited demonstrate that the blanket use of controls to limit the mass of buildings is not necessary for aesthetic reasons.

Different factors are evident in cities such as Paris or Rome, where the historic skylines of the old city centre have been maintained although larger and taller buildings have been allowed outside the city centre, most notably at La Défense to the west of the centre of Paris. Aesthetically it is difficult to argue that the compromise which has occurred in London has been as successful as any of the examples cited above. Some taller buildings have been built where developers have either put together a large enough site or have manipulated the situation by trading floor space for something else. The result, a scatter of tall buildings, has been compared to a failed crop of asparagus, and it could be argued that it would have been better either to maintain the historic skyline in the city centre, as in Paris, and as has partially been done in the area between St Paul's and the Thames, or to have allowed the greater massing which would have been justified by the demand for space, in the financial district of the City of London in particular.

Indeed, in early 2001 the Mayor of London, Ken Livingstone, argued that London should have more tall buildings, in order, apparently, to assert its position as a major financial centre. Events on September 11th of that year, however, provided further argument against the construction of conspicuous office buildings. Nevertheless in November 2003 planning permission was given for the construction of the tallest building in Europe at London Bridge, on the south bank of the Thames opposite the City.

Of course, the problem with arguments about aesthetics is that there is, as is well known, no 'right' answer, each person's taste is different – *chacun à son goût* – and there is no point in arguing about this – *de gustibus non disputandum est*. But, because there is no right answer, and because the evidence provides examples of large buildings which are not aesthetically displeasing, the argument for maintaining density controls on office floor space cannot only depend on a view that large buildings are visually displeasing.

It follows that the use of floor area:plot ratio controls to limit the size of office buildings cannot depend upon aesthetic arguments alone. Moreover, as was noted earlier, their use cannot be defended by any evidence with respect to rents of the kind used to support the application of residential density controls. The other argument that is used relates, instead, to the effects of large buildings on congestion. If greater massing of tall buildings had been allowed in the City of London, it can be argued, although the visual effect might be more dramatic, the resulting congestion would be insupportable.

The argument from congestion depends upon false premises, however. The implicit assumption is that there is a constant linear relationship between the floor area of a building and the number of trips beginning and ending at its location by private transport. In fact, the relationship is certainly not linear and constant. Trips may be generated not only by people coming to work and going home, but also during the working day by people travelling to make contact with others working in other offices. Offices are, after all, about the processing and exchange of information. An office located in a city's central area is there because of ease of access both for people travelling to work but also because people will travel between it and other offices. If this were not so there would be no reason for it to be located in a city centre and the higher rents payable there could be avoided.

If a building is small, then trips to other offices must largely take place outside the building, to other buildings at other locations, but if the building is large then the larger it is the more probable it is that the destination for any journey will be within the building. This is made even more likely by the tendency for commercial activities of the same kind to gather at the same location, and therefore often in the same building. As, for example, the editorial offices of the national newspapers migrated in the 1980s from Fleet Street to Docklands to the east of the City, with three being located in the same building, the tower at Canary Wharf. As the number of possible destinations in a building increases, so the proportion of the total number of trips staying within the building tends to increase. Moreover, communication is made easier as the possible origins and destinations are stacked vertically above each other, with a consequent reduction in the distances which would have to be travelled if they were spatially separated on the ground in different buildings.

Thus, journeys which might take place between buildings using public or private transport take place within buildings on foot, using lifts and esca-lators. Moreover, the massing together of a number of large buildings increases the number of destinations within walking distance. Therefore, a higher floor area:plot ratio in a commercial area does not necessarily create excessive vehicular congestion, since journeys take place on foot which might in a more spread out city centre take place by other means, whether by taxi, public transport, or private car.

Furthermore, the concentration together of a large number of workers, rather than their dispersion over a larger area, means that public transport, which needs economies of scale to keep costs down, becomes much more competitive with private transport. The latter, in turn becomes uncompe-titive, particularly with respect to the journey to work, and the high density of potential users means that subways and underground railways come into their own.

For the reasons outlined above, the intuitive, simplistic, argument that lower plot ratio controls will reduce congestion is simply wrong. By dis-persing office uses over a wider area, journeys on foot are discouraged, public transport made less economic, and motor vehicle use encouraged. In addition, of course, the whole office complex is made less efficient as communication, the economic reason for the grouping together of office uses, is made more costly.

The essential arbitrariness of plot ratio controls was exemplified by events in London in the 1980s. At the beginning of the decade, the Docklands 'Enterprise Zone' was designated in an area to the east of the City where containerisation had led to the abandonment of the nineteenth century port facilities located there. To encourage redevelopment of these derelict industrial sites, planning controls were lifted for a period of ten years, and tax incentives were given. One consequence was the construction of the Canary Wharf development, the largest office building in Europe. The City of London reacted competitively to this perceived threat to its dominance of the office market in London, indeed in Britain. It modified the plot ratio controls which were operative there, so that, for example, only actual usable floor space counted, measurements being taken net, that is from the inner edges of walls, rather than gross, from the outer edges. Although the actual ratios were not changed, this and other changes substantially increased the amount of space which could be constructed on a site.

The relaxation of the controls occurred at a time of an increasing demand for office space in the city immediately after the 'Big Bang' of October 1986 when trading was made easier (Inwood 1998, p. 91). The two things together

induced a major construction boom which, it is said, resulted in the redevelopment of a third of the office space in the City (Diamond 1991).
Unfortunately most of this space came onto the market after the end of the
boom when the demand for office space in the City fell at the end of the
1980s. The point, so far as we are concerned, is, however, that plot ratio
controls could be arbitrarily modified in this way. What, after all, was the
justification for the original ratios? What had changed from a planning point
of view that allowed these ratios to be altered? Why was it possible to
change the method of calculation of the plot ratios?

This brief history illustrates the difficulty in finding an economic justification for floor area:plot ratio controls. The aesthetic arguments regarding
the mass of a building and the massing of buildings seem to be culturally
determined if not arbitrary. The arguments regarding congestion are
intuitive and do not stand up to critical scrutiny. The only other possible
argument also relates to travel, and that is that the control is used to limit
the number of journeys beginning and ending at a location to the level
which can be served by the existing transport system. But this is a recipe for
stagnation. Cities develop and change, as technology changes and as their
economies change. It would, in almost all circumstances, be better to adjust
the transport system in response to the changes in demand than to attempt
to freeze the level of demand to the capacity of the system. The Canary
Wharf episode is again a useful example. In this case the development
occurred alongside the construction of a surface railway system and stimulated the development of an underground railway to serve the new office
complex.

Moreover, freezing the area of office space may itself be an inefficient
method of limiting the number of people working there. If the demand for
space increases, but the quantity of space available is limited then the rent
which has to be paid per square foot will increase. If the cost of space
increases then it will be used more intensively than if the cost of space were
lower. A consequence is that the number of people working in the area will
increase and the transport system will have to cope with the increased
numbers anyway, so that both travel to work and the workplaces themselves will be more congested than they would have been if the controls had
not been operating.

Conclusion

In this chapter we have looked at two planning instruments used to control
the density of development. In the case of residential density controls we

have shown that a *prima facie* economic case can be drawn up to explain and justify their use to limit residential densities. On the other hand, in the case of floor area:plot ratio controls it is more difficult to develop an economic defence. In some cases their use to limit the amount of office space that can be constructed on a site may serve an aesthetic purpose, as in the historic centres of some European cities. In other cases, however, where the reason for using controls would seem to be to try to limit congestion it is difficult to find any economic justification for their use. Indeed the position may be made worse, as rents increase and workplace conditions decline as the demand for space increases but the available space does not, resulting, if and when the controls are relaxed, in a building boom and bust.

5

Zoning and Conservation

'Praising what is lost makes the remembrance dear'
(All's Well That Ends Well)

Introduction

Under the system used to control development in the United Kingdom, every proposal, with very few exceptions, has to be put to the local planning authority and be given permission for it to go ahead. Only some very small changes in use do not require this. For example, an extension of an existing house by up to 10% would not usually require permission, although any second extension which would take the increase in area over the 10% limit would require permission. The expected land use for an area may be designated in the local plan, but such designation does not mean that a proposal in accordance with the plan will automatically be given permission.

The system used in the United States and in much of the rest of the world involves the designation, or 'zoning', of areas as suitable for a particular kind of development, with the explicit undertaking that development in accord with that designation is automatically permitted. Zoning in this way necessarily means the separation of different types of land use into different areas or zones. This is likely, indeed probable, under the British system, but is not, in the same way, a necessary consequence of the system, since uses which do not conform can be given permission, just as uses which do may not be.

One way in which a kind of zoning is used in the British planning system is in the designation of areas that have already been developed as 'Conservation Areas', areas which because of their architectural or historic interest, should be conserved, and in the second part of this chapter we look at the economics of this kind of designation.

Zoning

As we have already noted, zoning involves the physical separation of different land uses. The economic implication of this is that the 'non-conforming uses' impose external diseconomies on the permitted land uses. It is implied that the separation of the different land uses or activities will increase economic welfare in the manner suggested in the analysis of externalities in Chapter 2. By ensuring that, say, apartment blocks or commercial activities are not located in areas zoned for single family housing, the welfare of residents of these areas will be increased. It is also implied that the welfare of others will not be reduced to the same extent, if zoning increases economic welfare.

Considerable empirical work has been carried out by American and Canadian economists to discover whether these externalities are significant, and so whether zoning, in fact, increases welfare. Virtually all of this work has been carried out using Hedonic Price Methods, that is analyses of differences in house prices. The impetus for this work was provided by a study by Crecine *et al.* (1967) who, using data on house prices in Philadelphia, could find no significant statistical evidence of the existence of external diseconomies sufficient to justify zoning. The numerous studies that followed these negative results, surveyed by Fischel (1989, 1990), Pogodzinski & Sass (1991), and Evans (1999), also often found it difficult to identify any significant externalities. There were several possible conclusions from this absence of evidence. First, and most obvious, it was possible to conclude that externalities were, in practice, unimportant, so that zoning, and, by implication, land use planning, did not serve any useful economic purpose. Second, however, it was also possible to conclude that since zoning had been operative for many years in the areas studied, planning had, in fact, been very successful in reducing the negative impact of the externalities. Third, it might alternatively be possible to conclude that the negative impacts of any non-conforming use were only felt in a very small area, an area much smaller than the area likely to be zoned for a use. It would therefore have been difficult to identify any negative impacts with the available data since these tended to be for larger rather than smaller areas.

The solution to the problem was indicated in a study by Li & Brown (1980), which tended to confirm the third of the possible hypotheses outlined above. They used micro-level data and demonstrated that the external diseconomies of proximity to a non-conforming use were difficult to identify because there were often both advantages and disadvantages to proximity. So, the price of a property could be both raised and lowered by proximity and the balance of forces would depend upon the property's distance from the non-conforming use.

The nature of the problem can be demonstrated using Figure 5.1. A commercial shopping centre is used as an example of a use which might generate externalities. Distance from the commercial centre is indicated on the horizontal axis. The variation in the price of housing that arises from proximity to the shopping centre is measured on the vertical axis. The price of housing might be expected to be reduced near the centre because of negative externalities – congestion, difficulty in parking, noise, and litter. The way in which these negative effects might vary with distance is shown by the curved line in the lower half of the diagram. The negative externalities may be expected to be large close to the centre, but to diminish rapidly with distance, albeit at a declining rate. On the other hand, it is to be expected that the price of housing will be raised near the shopping centre because the households living there have better access and shorter shopping journeys. It is to be expected that these positive effects will decline with distance, but less rapidly than the negative effects, and it is assumed that they will decline linearly. These assumptions are indicated in the upper half of the diagram where the solid line slopes downwards. Taking the two together suggests that the negative effects will outweigh the positive near the shopping centre but that the positive will outweigh the negative slightly further away.

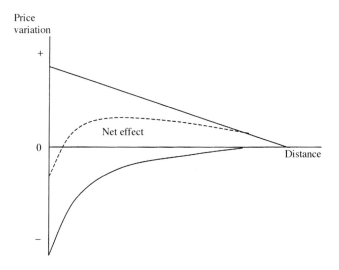

Figure 5.1

Net relationships of this sort could be identified by Li & Brown from their data. Using micro-level data it is possible to identify the existence of external diseconomies arising from non-conforming uses of this sort. Thus the empirical evidence provides some justification for zoning. On the other hand, the evidence also suggests that the negative externalities, such as they are, are not very great, and it would appear that small numbers of shops, industrial units or apartment buildings in an area otherwise zoned for single family housing would seem to have few negative effects, if any.

Mixed land uses of this kind are not encouraged by zoning systems, however. A reason for this may lie in the nature of zoning. The pattern of land uses resulting from a system of zoning will, necessarily, be simpler than the one which results solely through the interaction of market forces. This is likely to be so however excellent the planning system may be within which the zones are defined. As the experience of the planned economies of eastern Europe showed, it may be impossible for a planning system to cope with the multifarious nature of consumer demand. The wide range of products and consumer choice in the market economies was necessarily reduced and simplified in order for a centrally planned economy to be able to cope. The presence of externalities provides an economic justification for government intervention that does not exist in the case of the whole economy, but the method of intervention will still necessarily result in a simplification of the land use pattern.

Another reason may lie in the limits of political ability. It is easier to zone an area so as to exclude all non-conforming uses, considerably more difficult to zone in such a way as to allow very few such uses, since their existence constitutes the thin end of a wedge, a precedent for further such intrusion. The fact that any at all have been allowed leaves the planning authority open to the argument that there seems no reason why one more should not be allowed. So far as the residents and the local authority are concerned, the aim of zoning may be to avoid this slippery slope, to create certainty, the certainty that none will be allowed.

The problem of certainty and uncertainty may be a factor underlying the results of a study of alternative modes of land use control in the city of Houston in Texas. Much of that city is not zoned, although development is still regulated, but by means of 'covenants' or legal agreements, voluntarily entered into by those owning or buying property in the area. Such covenants do exist in England, in some private estates, or in Scotland as a consequence of the property holding system where, even in the case of land held apparently in perpetuity, there may be a 'feu holder' to whom an annual payment or 'feu' must be paid, and with whom legal agreements may be made as to what can and cannot be done on an estate.

The position in Houston has been described in some detail by Siegan (1972). He argued that the Houston example demonstrated that government intervention in the land market through zoning ordinances was unnecessary since the problem of externalities could be taken care of through the market. An alternative possibility has been suggested in a recent study by Speyrer (1989). She noted that though the greater part of Houston was covered by covenants, some parts of the city were zoned, and other parts were neither zoned nor covenanted. A comparison of house prices in the three different areas showed that prices in the areas that were uncontrolled were lower than prices in the other two areas. There was, moreover, no significant difference between prices in the zoned and covenanted areas. It would appear from this that there is a benefit provided by land use control, whether freedom from negative externalities now or the security of freedom from future negative externalities. This benefit, whether obtained through zoning or through covenants, is of financial value to residents who have willingly paid a premium to live in controlled areas.

There is a problem with this interpretation which has been noted by McDonald (1995). Referendums have been held in Houston and the majority of residents have voted against the introduction of zoning controls. It would seem odd that they should do so if it would apparently result in an increase in the value of their properties, whether this increase would be immediate or occur in the future. An alternative explanation depends upon a political rather than an economic interpretation of zoning. McDonald notes that, according to the evidence available, it was the poorer areas which voted against zoning. He argues that this was because of a belief that zoning is used by the better off to exclude poorer households, and that therefore zoning would not benefit the residents of these areas but might in practice disadvantage them.

The Houston case therefore remains unsettled, but it is certainly true that zoning can be and has been used for political purposes. Pogodzinski & Sass (1991) in their survey of the zoning literature note three different motives for zoning. There is externalities zoning – zoning to reduce the negative effects of external diseconomies, which we have extensively discussed. But there is also exclusionary zoning – zoning to exclude lower income groups, possibly also particular racial groups. Thus, it is customary to lay down a minimum lot size for single family housing, and to exclude multi-family housing. The effect is to ensure that house prices everywhere in the area remain above a certain minimum level so that lower income families are excluded because there is no housing in the area which they could afford.

A further motive for zoning cited in the literature is fiscal zoning – trying to ensure that the land uses allowed in the area generate high property tax payments while, as far as possible, resulting in low levels of local government expenditure. On this basis some industrial use can be allowed, even encouraged, since industrial property may generate low demands for services relative to the taxes paid on the property. On the other hand, fiscal arguments suggest that higher income households will try to prevent poorer families moving in to their area, since the property taxes paid by the poorer families will be lower but their demands for services will be at least as high.

Note that both exclusionary zoning and fiscal zoning are motivated by the wishes of those who already live in an area. A majority of the residents in an area may be able to manipulate the political system to maximise their own welfare. While our analysis of externalities zoning assumed that the benefits to one group would outweigh the losses to another, this is not so in the case of exclusionary and fiscal zoning. The presumption here is that the system is being manipulated in the interests of a particular group and that the gains to this group are lower than the losses to other groups.

Fiscal zoning implies that there may be an interaction between the operation of the zoning system and the levels of taxes charged. This is an area of current research in the United States. Lenon *et al.* (1996), looking at towns in Connecticut, found evidence of considerable interdependence between zoning, taxing and spending levels, both within towns, and between nearby, and therefore competing, towns.

The political element in zoning decisions has led some US economists to suggest that in practice the pattern of land use is very little altered by the institution of zoning. Wallace (1988) and McMillen & McDonald (1991) have suggested that 'zoning follows the market'. The argument is that any intervention which substantially changed land and property values in an area would encounter significant political resistance and so would not be put into effect. This conclusion is certainly supported by the evidence they produce. So, McMillen & McDonald (1993) investigated the way in which the city of Chicago was zoned in the 1920s and found that, in practice, the zones followed the uses which had already been established. So, for example, land alongside railroads was zoned for industrial use but these areas were already mainly used by industry. They still found, nevertheless, the zoned pattern of land use was rather tidier. So, even if, in general, zoning followed the market it would still also be true that zoning excluded non-conforming uses, and created an environment with more certainty and less uncertainty about what might or might not be constructed in the neighbourhood.

While it might be reasonable to suppose that any newly instituted zoning system would tend to be adapted to existing land uses, it still does not necessarily follow that the pattern of zoning would be adapted to respond to changes in market forces. For this to occur any economic and social changes which meant that property values in an area would be increased by rezoning would result in political pressure to rezone. The argument must be that since voters in other areas have no reason to oppose the change the rezoning is likely to take place. This is not necessarily true, however, since the land owners who might benefit from rezoning may be few and the other voters may see reasons to oppose the change. Certainly, as we shall show later there is evidence that attempts to control and limit urban growth have resulted in differences in land values which have not been eliminated by rezoning.

Heritage, historic districts and conservation

One form of zoning which is used within the UK planning system, within the US system, and in many other countries is the declaration of parts of an urban area as worthy of preservation or conservation (Greffe 1990). The implications of such a declaration vary considerably, however, from one country to another. In the UK it has been possible, since 1967, to designate such areas as 'Conservation Areas'. Within a Conservation Area permission has to be obtained to demolish a building as well as permission to construct one, so that, in effect, any redevelopment requires two kinds of planning permission. Individual buildings can also be 'listed' as of particular historic or architectural interest and the same rules apply, that is permission has to be obtained to demolish as well as to alter or reconstruct. In both cases there is a presumption that changes will not be permitted unless they would in some way enhance or improve either the area or the building.

The externality that is believed here to require government intervention in the property market is of a particular and peculiar kind. After all, similar rules do not apply to works of art which may also be unique and worthy of preservation. Although one might wish that they should be conserved for the future, similar rules do not apply. Antique furniture or works of art in private hands are not similarly surveyed and listed. The only roughly similar condition is that some countries restrict the export of certain works of art, which may, for example, have to be offered to a public art gallery or museum to purchase before there is a possibility that permission might be given for their export.

The presumption seems to be that it is expected that the owner of a valuable work of art will naturally wish to preserve it, while this is not true of a historic building. The problems appear to be twofold. First, the owners of buildings expect to obtain some return from their use other than simply contemplating their aesthetic merits, and people also generally expect buildings to be in use rather than lie empty. However, technological and social change may make a building obsolete in a way that is impossible for a work of art. Second, the owner of a listed building owns two things, one is the building but the other is the site. The building cannot (usually) be moved to another location, but the site might be more valuable, because of economic change, with another building. So, while the owner of a work of art would not wish to destroy his asset, the owner of a historic building might easily find it profitable to demolish it and build something else. Thus, special provisions have been thought necessary to preserve buildings which have not been thought to be necessary for other kinds of works of art. In the case of both listed buildings and Conservation Areas, the value to society of the properties is implicitly thought to be greater than the value to the owners.

Nevertheless, there is an economic distinction to be made between conservation areas and listed buildings. Particularly in the case of residential areas, the owners of buildings within a Conservation Area may gain from its designation while the owners of listed buildings are unlikely to do so. This is because the economic implications of the listing of a building would appear to be almost wholly negative. Although it is possible that the building may gain some increase in value from its explicit recognition as being of architectural or historic interest, this effect is likely to be of small importance compared to the negative effect of the owner's (virtual) inability to demolish the building, and the considerable restrictions on the ability to change, extend, or otherwise alter the building. Economically and mathematically, the imposition of a constraint on the owner's ability to maximise the value of the property cannot increase its value but can only leave it the same or reduced.

For the owners of buildings in Conservation Areas, the negative effects of restrictions on the ability to change the property do operate, but there is also the possibility of a positive effect. This can happen because the properties are likely to gain some of their value from the character of the surrounding area, from their environment. Designation of this area as a Conservation Area is intended to ensure that the character of this surrounding area will not change, and so it makes it less likely that it will. Thus, the value of a property may be reduced by the owner's inability to change it, but it is increased by the parallel inability of other, neighbouring, property owners to change theirs. The net effect of the designation of a Conservation Area may therefore be to increase property values in the area. Moreover, the net effect is more likely to be positive in the case of residential areas than commercial areas. The quality of the environment is less likely to be capitalised into the value of a factory or shop, unless, in the case of the latter, the environment is itself a reason why people visit the area. Even in residential areas the net effect will differ from property to property. For example, in an area where the environment is valued because of its low density and general greenness, a house that has already been extended may increase in value, while a house on a substantial plot that has not yet been extended may decrease in value because the opportunity for extension of the house or development of the site has been closed.

Anecdotal evidence suggests, moreover, that the residents of possible conservation areas will lobby for their area to be designated, indicating that the majority view tends to be that they will gain. On the other hand, anecdotal evidence certainly suggests that the owners of commercial buildings regard designation as reducing its value. Indeed, in one notorious case, that of the Art Deco-style Firestone factory to the west of London, the owners arranged for the building to be vandalised, quickly, over a weekend, when they believed it was about to be listed.

There is some empirical evidence of the effects of designation as a 'Historic District' in the United States, but the effects are found to be small and difficult to quantify, possibly, as indicated above, because of the contradictory effects of listing, which mean that the net result may be small. The effects also depend on the differing tax position. Schaeffer & Millerick (1991) found that, in respect of an area to the west of the centre of Chicago designated as a 'National Historic District', property values seemed to be higher than in the surrounding area. However, this increase seemed to be largely a consequence of the tax advantages of designation, and by the fact that there was little associated increase in the stringency of the planning controls. On the other hand, two smaller areas within the National Historic District were designated as 'Chicago Historic Districts', which were subject to significantly stronger controls, but gained no further tax advantages. Property prices in these two areas were lower than in the surrounding National Historic District, as one might expect, although they were still probably higher than in the 'unhistoric' surrounding area.

Conclusions

What we can conclude from this discussion of the economics of two forms of zoning is that the evidence does seem to confirm the intuitive view that some types of land use have external effects, and that it is possible that intervention in the market may therefore improve welfare. It does not necessarily follow that welfare actually is increased by zoning. There is also evidence that zoning is used as a political instrument, particularly by higher income groups, both to exclude others from their residential areas, and to try to minimise the property tax burden.

With respect to designation of areas as Conservation Areas it would seem that this too is subject to manipulation, although since some aesthetic judgement must be exercised by outside experts the possibilities are more limited. The 'listing' of individual buildings, however, seems to be something which is almost wholly to the detriment of the owner, and therefore any political lobbying is likely to be negative.

6

Green Belts, Growth Controls and Urban Growth Boundaries

'Which serves it in the office of a wall
Or as a moat defensive to a house,
Against the envy of less happier lands'
(King Richard II)

Introduction

In the preceding chapters we have primarily discussed the allocation of land uses within urban areas. But land use planning is also concerned with the allocation of land between urban and rural uses. In Britain one of the main concerns leading to the creation of a comprehensive planning system was the way in which the private car allowed development to occur outside the boundaries of existing built-up areas. For the first time, people other than the very rich did not have to live within walking distance of jobs, shops, or public transport. Evidence of this concern was the Restriction of Ribbon Development Act of 1935, the very title of the Act in itself indicating 'the sense of panic which engendered it' (Buchanan 1958), the aim being to prevent development spreading along not only existing roads, but also the newly built bypasses and arterial roads.

The attitude to urban development in previously rural areas has varied from country to country. Varying degrees of concern have been expressed at what has been called urban sprawl. Sometimes the aim has been to contain urban growth, sometimes the aim has been to control, to restrain, or to delimit it. Britain and South Korea have designated 'green belts' which have stringently contained development. Such a degree of constraint is rare, but Urban Control Areas have been defined in Japan, and Urban Growth Boundaries and other forms of growth control have been used in the United

States. The differences between countries in their attitudes seem to depend on cultural and legal differences as well as the general perception of the amount of land available for development. In England farming communities have historically been contained within villages, as urban communities have been contained in towns, so that the English countryside has appeared relatively empty. In France and Italy, on the other hand, the dwellings of the peasants and farmers have been scattered across a more fertile and more intensively farmed landscape. Since buildings have been distributed across the landscape, either it has not been felt that more houses would be an environmental intrusion, or it has been seen as difficult to prevent further development when so much was already in existence. Socio-legal reasons have also affected the extent of the constraint which could be imposed. The Fifth Amendment to the Constitution of the United States prevents the taking of land without due compensation. The designation of land as part of a 'green belt' where no form of urban development would be allowed in future would be regarded as 'taking', so that full compensation would have to be paid. Not surprisingly city and state authorities have therefore been unwilling to designate green belts. Other methods of controlling development have been used instead, where it has been thought desirable by local governments, methods which stop short of an outright ban on development on large areas of land.

The economics of a green belt

The probable economic effects of designating a green belt around a city where the population is expanding can be demonstrated very simply using Figure 6.1. Distance from a city centre is shown along the horizontal axis and the price of land is shown on the vertical axis. The initial situation, before the designation of the green belt, is indicated by the line ABA' which shows the relationship between the price of land and distance from the city centre. AB is the land value gradient within the city, with the price falling with distance from the city centre. BA' indicates the value of agricultural land outside the urban area and it is assumed that it varies little, if at all, with distance from the urban area. Where the value of land in an urban use is greater than its agricultural value, it will be developed, and so the point B represents the limit of the city's built-up area, and the radius of the city is indicated on the horizontal axis as OX.

Suppose that there is no green belt and that the demand for space in the city continues to grow, either because people want to move to the city or because the incomes of the existing population increase. Then the price of land within the city will rise and the result will be a new land value gradient

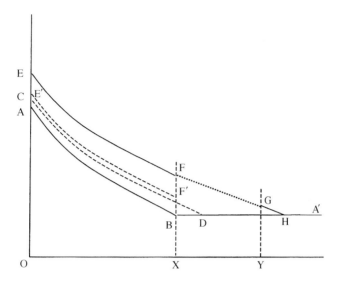

Figure 6.1

such as might be shown by the line CD in the figure. Another possibility would be that rising car ownership or improvements in public transport make it cheaper or faster to travel between the city centre and the suburbs. In that event land prices would tend to fall near the centre and increase near the edge of the city. The new land value gradient would have a lower slope than AB or CD but might still cut the line BA' at a point such as D. In both these cases the changes in the demand for land would lead to development beyond the edge of the existing built-up area, since the value of the agricultural land there would be higher if it were developed.

Suppose now that a green belt had been designated beyond the boundary of the existing built-up area. In Figure 6.1 the width of this belt of land is represented on the horizontal axis by XY. The enforcement of the green belt prevents the urban expansion which would otherwise have taken place, and so no new development is allowed to take place within the green belt. The demand for space has nevertheless risen, and must be accommodated in some way. If the increase in demand results from an increasing population the new residents still have to be housed. If it is the result of rising incomes, rising prices must somehow choke off the increased demand for space. In the absence of a green belt some new land would be developed, between B and D in the diagram, while within the existing built-up area higher rents and land values would lead to land being used more intensively and the redevelopment of sites to provide more space on the existing land. The existence of the green belt means that no new housing space can be supplied within the green belt. The supply restriction means that prices will rise further than they otherwise would and a new land value gradient, at E'F', say, higher than CD, will be the result. If an increased population has to be catered for, the further increase in land values and property prices will lead to more redevelopment and a still more intensive use of the land that is available. If the increase in demand is because incomes have increased, then in part the increase in demand will be choked off by the rise in the price of land, but in part the increased demand will be accommodated by redevelopment as larger houses and flats are built on the existing sites, and built space substitutes for land.

If the increases in incomes or population or other changes are large enough, or go on long enough, while the green belt remains sacrosanct, then the further increases in demand will result in still higher prices. If the increase in land values within the existing built-up area is large enough then one possibility is indicated in Figure 6.1 by the broken solid line EFGH. The increase in prices and land values has made the price of housing within the urban area so high that it becomes worthwhile for people to pay substantially higher travel costs and live on the further side of the green belt and commute across it. On the far side development is not prevented and the price of housing which can be built there will be substantially lower than the price of housing in the urban area. Thus enforcement of a green belt is likely to lead to substantial commuting across it.

Green belts in Britain

Over the last 50 years green belts have been designated, and in some cases, extended around a number of British towns and cities. The aims of these green belts in physical planning terms have been stated in PPG 2, one of a series of Planning Policy Guidance Notes issued by central government to guide the development of local plans by local planning authorities, and to ensure consistency in these plans.

In PPG 2 the stated aims of the green belts are:

- To check urban sprawl
- To safeguard the surrounding countryside
- To prevent towns merging
- To preserve the character of historic towns
- To assist in urban regeneration.

Can these aims be analysed economically? Clearly the achievement of the first objective depends simply upon the preservation of an open, undeveloped, area beyond the existing area in the manner described in the previous section. Note that if there is no increase in demand for land at the edge of the city because of increases in population, increases in incomes or improvements in transport, then designation of a green belt would be superfluous. It would be unnecessary, except possibly to tidy up the periphery of the city, and therefore would have no economic effects.

If, on the other hand, it is not superfluous, if the green belt is successful in preventing urban development which would otherwise have occurred, then it will have the economic effects described in the previous section. The necessary results of a green belt achieving its desired aims are the various economic consequences outlined.

The first and most important result will be that land and property values within the urban area will be higher than they otherwise would be. A consequence of this will be an increase in the density of development within the existing urban area as the increased demand for land, particularly towards the edge of the city, results in the substitution of capital for land and the extension and redevelopment of existing properties. In addition there will be pressure to 'infill' existing open space within the urban area because of the perceived shortage of land for development.

With time we would also expect that there would be two further consequences of a green belt that was successful in achieving the aims set out above. These would be an increase in the amount of development on the further side of the designated green belt, and a consequent increase in the amount of commuting across it. Thus, the prevention of urban sprawl may paradoxically result in a more dispersed urban area, if the urban area is not defined merely as a contiguous built-up area, but in a sense, whether economic or geographic, which regards the suburbs from which people commute as part of the same urban area as the workplaces to which they commute. Another economic consequence is likely to flow from the increased probability that the area designated as green belt will remain 'green'. This increase in certainty will be capitalised into higher prices for pieces of properties on the edge of the green belt or located within it.

Another consequence of a green belt, in Britain at least, will be distributional. The economic effects will almost certainly be regressive. Those who benefit most from the achievement of the green belt's aims are those living towards the edge of the urban area and within it, since as we have said, the values of the properties that they own are likely to rise more than those elsewhere. In Britain, the people living in these areas will tend to be middle and higher income households. Those who benefit least are those living towards the centre of the city who will tend to be, in Britain, lower income households. The environmental benefit to them of the existence of the green belt is small, and probably negative. To the extent that the density of development is increased by the infilling of existing urban open space, their immediate environment is likely to be worsened, while, on the other hand, the environmental benefit to them that there is farmland 10 miles away rather than 11 is negligible. Or as Stephen Inwood puts it in his history of London 'Children playing in London's increasingly busy streets, and without most of the new local parks that [the Abercrombie Plan for Greater London] had promised, could console themselves with the thought that 10 or 15 miles away there was a belt of agricultural land that they would never be able to spoil' (Inwood 1998, p. 834).

In much of continental Europe the wealthy are more likely to live near the city centre than in Britain, and the poor are more likely to be living near the periphery. With this pattern of residential location the distribution of the environmental benefits of a green belt is also likely to be different, the poor are more likely to gain and the rich more likely to lose. Given the distribution of political power green belts are less likely to be enacted in such countries.

The regressive nature of the economic consequences are exacerbated by the character of property ownership. Higher and middle income households are more likely to own houses and property, while lower income households are more likely to rent. The former therefore gain from the increase in property values which occurs throughout the urban area, while the latter are made worse off by the increase in the rents that have to be paid. These distributional consequences have political consequences. Middle and higher income groups will tend to be strong defenders of the green belt and to resist any change through political pressure groups, whether local or national.

So far we have the economic consequences of achieving the first three of the stated aims of a British green belt, that is, to check urban sprawl, to safeguard the surrounding countryside, and to prevent towns merging. But what of the fourth and fifth aims, to preserve the character of historic towns and to assist in urban regeneration.

With respect to the last of these the belief would appear to be that if development is not permitted outside the urban area then it will occur within the urban area. There appears to be an assumption implicit in this that there is an economic advantage to location in the urban area, so that development which is discouraged in the green belt will not simply go elsewhere. The explicit assumption is that development which is discouraged in the green belt will take place in the urban area, and, in particular, that it will occur in those parts of the inner city where factories and plants have become obsolescent and derelict. Of course, in practice one site is not like another, and the reasons why plants have closed down in the inner city may be precisely the reasons why other plants do not wish to locate there – the existing buildings may be obsolescent and expensive to clear, the sites may be less accessible by road than exurban sites, and the available sites may be too small for modern factories and processes. Nevertheless, through the economic system and through changes in prices resulting from market forces, the enforcement of a green belt can be shown to aid the achievement of the aim of urban regeneration, but at a cost.

As the economic analysis in the preceding section demonstrated, a green belt which successfully constrains the physical growth of an urban area will result in increase in land and property values within the existing built-up area. As the demand for space within the city has increased, so land values have increased by more than they otherwise would have done, and it has become more worthwhile to use space intensively. This increase in value also affects sites in the inner city. The greater value of the land makes it worthwhile demolishing the existing derelict buildings, because the cost of clearing the site has become a smaller proportion of the total value of the site. The opposite is true in a completely unconstrained urban area. There, lack of growth coupled with low land values make it possible that the cost of clearing a site might be higher than the value of the cleared land. This can lead to the abandonment of both sites and buildings, as has occurred at times in some US urban areas (Leven *et al.*, 1976), and can frequently happen in rural areas where a barn or, say, a filling station on a former main road may simply be abandoned. In an urban area where growth is constrained abandonment becomes less and less possible as an option since it becomes less economically rational to walk away from a site as it becomes more valuable.

Thus, the aim of assisting urban regeneration is achieved through the operation of the market – the cost of land is increased by the constraint and this ensures that it is used intensively rather than extensively. There is, however, a cost. The price of land is raised throughout the urban area and not just within the districts that might be thought to be in need of regeneration. In consequence the pressure to use land intensively applies across the whole area enclosed by the green belt. As a means of achieving urban regeneration it is a scatter gun rather than a rifle shot approach. The pressure to use land intensively applies not only where there is dereliction and the danger of abandonment, but in other areas where, not only is there no danger of abandonment but it is planning policy to try to resist development, within urban conservation areas for example. As a means of assisting urban regeneration it is clear that other policies might be as effective and efficient and better targeted. For example, the Enterprise Zones designated in Britain in the early 1980s used tax incentives together with the relaxation of planning controls to stimulate the redevelopment of derelict areas, most successfully in the London Docklands but also elsewhere. These tax incentives were, however, a direct cost to the taxpayer. Planning controls such as green belts have no such direct cost. But as we have indicated above and as we shall demonstrate further in later chapters there are nevertheless indirect costs as the effects of the constraint on the supply of land work their way through the economic system.

Discussion of the remaining aim of the British green belts, the preservation of the character of historic towns, is more problematic. If what appears to be intended is achieved then this will involve some costs and some conflicts. From a physical planning point of view, the aim is presumably that cities and towns such as Oxford, Cambridge or York should not expand but should remain at their present size. In virtually all cases, the exception would seem to be Bath, the rural area surrounding the town does not provide a backdrop to the historic centre, so that the preservation of such a backdrop would not seem to be the objective.

As we pointed out earlier, if there is in fact no increase in the demand for space in the town or city, then a constraint on its physical expansion is largely unnecessary. If, however, there is an increased demand for space in a historic town, and its green belt successfully constrains its physical growth, one result will be that property values within the urban area will be raised to a level higher than they otherwise would be. And a consequence of this will be increased economic pressure to use more intensively all the land within the area enclosed by the green belt. Thus, success in achieving the aim of 'preserving the character of a historic town' is likely to be pressure to redevelop and use land more intensively within the city. Paradoxically, therefore, successful physical constraint is itself likely to threaten the character of such a town through the economic forces which it sets in motion.

These effects, however, are not likely to be so intense in a small town as they might be in a large. The width of the green belt is not likely to be great and so commuting across it is more feasible, and the increase in land values stimulated by the green belt will not be very large. Moreover, given that there may be other locations in other similar, but unhistoric, towns nearby, firms will tend to avoid the higher cost of location in the historic town and locate elsewhere. In the case of a larger city alternative, equivalent, locations may not be so easily available.

The green belt in South Korea

The two countries in the world in which green belts have been imposed and enforced most strongly have been Britain and South Korea. The aims of the Korean green belt would appear to be more or less the same as the first three stated aims of the British green belts.

> The green belt is a form of restrictive land-use control in Korea. Green belts are designed to prevent the uncontrolled physical expansion of cities, thereby protecting the environment and securing national defence. Within the green belts the Urban Planning Law of Korea prohibits land-use conversion and construction activities other than rebuilding or altering an existing structure. Land within the belts is made up of forest and arable land. (Huh & Kwak 1997, p. 990)

Even though South Korea is one of the most densely populated countries in the world, the amount of land available for urban development is severely restricted. The result of the very stringent controls has been that only about five per cent of the land surface is in any urban use, whether housing, commerce, or anything else (Kim & Kim 2000, p. 1162).

The economic results have been as might be expected, although within a different form of market economy to the British. Pressure for development within the major urban area, Seoul, has increased and to ease this pressure new towns have been built on the other side of its green belt, although these in turn have been developed at a relatively high density. It has been estimated that, in 1987, some 600 000 people commuted across the green belt to work in Seoul, and that the additional cost of these longer journeys to work was about one million pounds per day (Kim 1993, p. 65).

The constraint on the availability of land for development has, of course, had an impact on the price of land and housing. 'The land prices for Korea's 12 largest cities between 1962 and 1993 increased 791 times, a compound average growth of 21.5 per cent. Part of this extraordinary gain is the result of inflation. In that period [there was] an average compound inflation rate of 10.2 per cent [and] these data imply that the average annual inflation-adjusted increase in urban land values in Korea was 11.3

per cent – a return that is in addition to annual land rents' (Lee 1997, p. 1072).

The increase in land values is, of course, associated with a high price for housing. 'Given an average urban income of about 5.4 m won in 1988, the average value of a traditional urban single-family Korean home (165 sq m) – about 83m won (US$120 000) – would be approximately 15 years' income. By comparison the price of a typical new Japanese home is about eight times annual income' (Lee 1997, p. 1072f).

Of course, a major factor distinguishing South Korea from the countries of Western Europe, particularly Britain, has been its rapid economic growth. The rate of growth of GNP has been above 5% per annum in every year, except 1980, between 1963 and 1994 and frequently above 10%. This rapid rate of economic development has been associated with industrialisation and urbanisation, with consequent immigration to the cities from the countryside. This means that the increase in the demand for housing in the cities, both because of increases in income and increases in population, has been much greater than would have occurred in a city in one of the developed economies. This increase in demand has come up against the stringent land use controls and the effects have consequently been greater than they would have been elsewhere. The distributional impact of increases in property values has also been very great.

> Approximately 11m Korean individuals own land, their holdings being about 66.1 per cent of the total. An additional 24.3 per cent of the land is owned by the public sector and 4.1 per cent by corporations. Statistics from 1988 report that the top 5 per cent of individual landowners own 65.2 per cent of the total land area owned by individuals, with the top 10 per cent of land owners owning 76.9 per cent. The ownership of land is much more concentrated than that of financial assets and the size distribution of income in Korea. Thus, rapidly rising land values make income and wealth distribution less equal in Korea. (Lee 1997, p. 1074)

Of course, it is possible that these statistics may overstate the problem. Since much of the land is not allowed to be developed, its value is lower than it otherwise would be. In practice the distributional effect depends on what land is owned as well as by whom it is owned.

As we have shown earlier, restrictions on the availability for development of land outside the city will tend to result in a density of development within the contained urban area which is higher than it would be in the absence of such constraints. It is evident that Korean housing is high

instead occur in suburb X nearby or city Y further away (Levine 1999). This is a different situation to that existing in Korea or Britain where the physical growth of the capital city is constrained and there is clearly no equivalent in the country, let alone nearby. If suburb X is small, and can accommodate only a small proportion of the population in its region, the constraint on growth may be effective without causing higher house prices, since prices in the constrained area must remain competitive with prices in the suburbs where growth is unconstrained. Moreover, even if it were observed that house prices were somewhat higher in the area where growth was constrained, it might still be possible that prices are higher because growth control has resulted in an environmental improvement for which people are willing to pay, and which has therefore been capitalised into higher house prices.

Some fairly sophisticated economic and econometric analysis has consequently been required to try to distinguish the negative from the positive consequences of growth controls. The conclusion has been that growth controls have resulted in higher house prices and that these higher prices are only partly, if at all, a consequence of an environmental improvement caused by the controls (Fischel 1990). The difficulty in determining the exact effects of growth controls has probably been eased over the last 20 years or so as an increasing number of cities, particularly in California, have chosen to adopt forms of growth control. The higher the proportion of an area that is subject to growth controls, the greater is likely to be effect on prices of the constraint on the supply of land and housing.

With respect to the application of the urban growth boundary in Oregon, the empirical evidence is that although there was no initial impact on prices, about four years after designation the price of land contained within the boundary, and therefore developable in the short run, was higher than the price of land outwith the boundary. At first sight it is not obvious why this should have been so. After all there would apparently still have been 16 years supply of land available at that time. The explanation has to do with the operation of the land market and the role of land owners. As we shall discuss further in the next chapter, land owners do not immediately sell their land when the price rises. In this case many who are farming the land may be unwilling to sell because they wish to continue farming in that area and have no wish to move. They may also believe that prices will rise rather than fall so that there is little to lose and a possible gain in not selling. This behaviour is, after all, the reason why urban sprawl occurs in the first place. Those owning land adjacent to the existing built-up area may be unwilling to sell, while others some distance away are willing to do so, possibly because they wish to retire from farming. The urban growth boundary limits urban sprawl and limits the market for would-be developers. Land which they might have been able to buy beyond the urban growth boundary is not available so that they have to pay a higher price for land within it (Evans 1983, 1985, 2004).

Thus, as we have indicated, the evidence shows that the price of land and housing was higher within the area contained by the UGB. Further, land prices within the belt of land outwith the UGB, in effect within the 'green belt', were lower than they otherwise would be, and there is also some evidence that the price of land on the other side of this 'belt' was higher than within it. In other words the UGB was operating as a green belt might, with development being diverted across the 'green belt' to its further side, an implication being that commuting from longer distances had been increased (Nelson 1988).

Evaluation

Unlike most other types of planning policy, some attempts have been made to evaluate the economic costs and benefits of green belts. The major difficulty has been that although it is relatively easy to identify the economic costs, it is more difficult to identify and evaluate the economic benefits. As we have shown, the costs come in the form of higher house and property prices, and, possibly, longer journeys to work for some people. To evaluate these costs the easiest method is to try to assess current house prices. In a large city this can be identified with the house price gradient, the rate at which house prices decline with distance from the city centre, and this gradient can be compared with an estimate of what the gradient would have been if land in the green belt had been available to be built on.

An attempt to estimate the benefits of the London green belt was made by Willis & Whitby (1985). They based their work on an earlier study by Wabe (1971) which assumed that the value of the green belt was environmental and benefited only those living close to it. It was therefore assumed that the benefits of the green belt were capitalised into the value of the houses adjacent to it. The benefits of the green belt were then estimated as the amount by which the prices of properties in or near to the green belt were above the price that it was estimated they would otherwise have been.

The trouble with this kind of approach is that the intention in defining a green belt is presumably to benefit the residents of the city as a whole, not only those living near it. An alternative approach was used by Willis (1982) in a study of the costs and benefits of the Tyne and Wear green belt, the major city in this conurbation being Newcastle-upon-Tyne. In this study he used the Contingent Valuation Method to evaluate the benefits. As we indicated in Chapter 3, this approach involves using survey methods to ask people directly to put a value on the environmental attribute, in this case the green belt. The question can be posed in two different ways. They can either be asked how much they would be willing to pay to preserve in existence the thing evaluated (Willingness To Pay – WTP), or they can be asked by how much they would have to be compensated if the thing evaluated were to cease to exist, in effect how much they would sell it for (Willingness To Accept – WTA). As might be expected, questions as to willingness to pay tend to give values which are lower than questions as to people's willingness to accept. In this case Willis & Whitby asked residents of Tyne and Wear questions regarding their willingness to accept, so that the results obtained would tend to inflate the estimated value of the Tyne and Wear green belt relative to results that might have been obtained using 'willingness to pay' questions.

Even with the higher figures which resulted from using WTA questions, the estimated benefits of the green belt, as it existed at the time of the survey, were found to just cover the estimated increases in the costs of property resulting from the existence of the green belt. An extension of the Tyne and Wear green belt was proposed at the time, but only later put into effect. The costs and benefits of this proposed extension were also estimated and it was found that the estimated costs of the extended green belt exceeded the estimated benefits.

Conclusions

In this chapter we have looked at the economic consequences of planning controls which constrain the physical growth of urban areas, in particular the effects of green belts. We have shown that an effective green belt in planning terms will have predictable economic consequences, in particular it will cause both the value of land and the price of housing to rise within the contained urban area. It will also probably result in an increase in the length of some commuter journeys as people are forced, by the high price of housing in the city, to live on the other side of the green belt and to commute across it to work. There will be economic pressure to use the land which is available for development more intensively, leading to some increase in the density of development within the urban area.

We have also shown that the empirical evidence seems to demonstrate that the lighter controls on growth adopted in some US cities have similar effects, in particular increases in the price of land and housing. We have attempted briefly to explain that this is a consequence of the way in which the land market functions, so that even a partial restraint will have an economic effect. The way in which the land market works is important to an understanding of the effects of planning controls, however, so in the next chapter we look at the economics of the land market.

7

Planning and the Land Market

'There's place and means for every man alive'
(All's Well That Ends Well)

Introduction

The objective of land use planning is primarily, as we discussed in Chapter 1, to determine, or failing that, to influence, the use of land. In doing so it affects the price of land, through the operation of the market. The price of some land will be higher than it otherwise would be, and the price of some other land will be lower than it otherwise would be. Predominantly the effect will be to raise the price of land, however. The price of land is lowest in agricultural use and, in all but the smallest city states, most of the land in a country is in agricultural use. As a result the relative supply of agricultural land will be affected to only a minuscule extent by changes in the amount of land in urban use. The price of agricultural land is determined primarily by agricultural policies, the demand for food and the price of imported food. Therefore if the urban areas are restricted, the price of urban land will rise but the price of agricultural land will not change to any noticeable extent. It is nevertheless true that the price of some agricultural land on the urban fringe which might otherwise have been developed will be lower than it would have been if development had taken place. The precise consequences of planning controls on land prices will, in practice, depend upon the particular characteristics of the land market and the nature of the controls. How then does the market for land operate?

The author has written on this at length in another volume (Evans 2004). The object of the discussion in this chapter is to set out the essentials of the analysis to provide a basic understanding of the economics of the land market, an understanding which is necessary to understand the effects of planning controls.

Ricardian theory

A basic theory of the land market was set out by David Ricardo in 1815 in his *Principles of Political Economy and Taxation*. The elements of the theory can be explained using Figure 7.1. Quantity of land is indicated on the horizontal axis and the price of land is indicated on the vertical axis. There is a downward sloping demand curve for land, DD' in the figure. In Ricardo's original analysis he was trying to represent a whole national economy in which the demand for land was determined by the price of corn, or, in effect, food, since this is the sole product of the agricultural sector. Since he was trying to analyse a simple model of a complete national economy, he could, with some justification, assume that the supply of land was fixed. In Figure 7.1 this fixed supply of land is indicated as OS on the horizontal axis, so that the supply curve for land is the vertical line RS. The intersection of the demand curve, DD', and the supply curve, RS, marks the equilibrium price of land indicated by OP on the vertical axis.

At the time that Ricardo was writing there was controversy over the question as to whether the price of food was being pushed up by landlords asking for higher and higher rents, or whether other factors, in particular the Corn Laws restricting the import of food, caused the price of corn to be high, and this in turn resulted in higher rents as tenants competed for land. His analysis demonstrated that the high price of land was indeed the result of the high price of corn rather than the cause. Since the supply of land is fixed, it can be seen from Figure 7.1 that the price of land can change only because

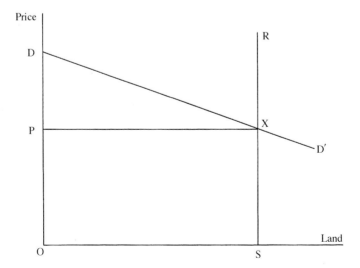

Figure 7.1

of shifts in the demand curve. Since the demand for land, in his analysis, is derived from the demand for corn, his conclusion was that the price of 'corn is not high because a rent is paid but a rent is paid because [the price of] corn is high' (Ricardo 1815, p. 38).

This conclusion depends upon and results from the Ricardian assumptions, in particular the assumption that the supply of land is fixed. If the supply of land can be changed, then changes in the supply of land as well as changes in the demand for land will affect its price. In Figure 7.1 a shift to the right of the vertical supply curve RS, i.e. an increase in the supply of land, will cause a fall in the price of land, a shift to the left – a reduction in supply, will cause an increase in price. And increases in the supply of land do occur, even at the level of the national economy. Marshy land may be drained, as with the Marsica in central Italy or the Fens in central England. Land may be reclaimed from the sea, as in The Netherlands. Where land is expensive it may be obtained by filling in shallow water. So, according to a recent estimate, 33% of the land in Macau, 10% in Singapore, and 5% in Hong Kong was new land formed in this way (Glaser *et al.*, 1991).

Another assumption that Ricardo made was that land had only one use, to grow corn. If land use is unplanned, then, as we shall show, this assumption too will be unrealistic and misleading, but in an economy subject to stringent land use controls, in which a piece of land may only be used for one designated purpose, then the Ricardian analysis may still be useful. Turning again to Figure 7.1, in effect the horizontal axis shows the amount of land available for a particular use and the vertical axis shows the price of land in that use. The demand curve, DD', shows the derived demand for land for that use, while OS on the horizontal axis and the vertical supply curve, RS, indicate the amount of land which has been allocated for that use by the planning process. In this case, of course, the supply is very clearly not immutable but can be changed through the planning system.

In fact, of course, there are virtually no cases where there is only one use for an area of land, and the situation is better illustrated if it is assumed that there are two uses rather than one. Suppose that there are two uses for an area of land, an urban use, say housing, and a rural use, say agriculture. The situation may be represented as in Figure 7.2. The total amount of land in an area is indicated by the length of the horizontal axis, OS. Of this, OX is assumed to be allocated for housing and XS is used for agriculture. As before the price of land is shown on the horizontal axis. The price of agricultural land is taken as given, within the economy, by agricultural policies and the price of imports. Thus the demand curve for agricultural land is the hor-

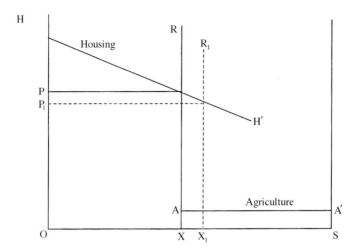

Figure 7.2

izontal line AA′ and the price of agricultural land is A′S = AX in the figure. The demand for housing is represented by the downward sloping line HH′. The vertical line RX defines the supply of land for each of the two uses, and its intersection with the demand curve for housing land determines the price of housing land as OP, just as its intersection with the demand curve for agricultural land indicates its price AX.

A reallocation of land from agriculture to housing, by, for example, the grant of planning permission for housing on an area of farmland, is marked in the figure by a shift in the vertical supply curve from RX to R_1X_1. If the demand for housing land remains the same then it is clear from the figure that the price of housing land would fall from OP to OP_1.

It is necessary to stress this because, at the end of the 1980s it was forcefully argued that the price of land in southern England was high because the price of housing was high and not vice versa. The argument was based on a faulty recollection of Ricardo's conclusions regarding the price of corn and the price of land. It was then wrongly argued that the amount of land made available for housing was immaterial and any increase would not affect either the price of land or the price of housing. That is, Ricardo's conclusion was remembered but not the assumption, that the supply of land was unalterable, on which his conclusion was based (Grigson 1986; Evans 1987). As we have shown, the price of land for housing, and the price of housing, depend upon both the demand for housing, as determined by incomes, interest rates etc., and the supply of land for housing determined through the planning system. Further, as we shall show later in this chapter, the supply of land will be also affected by the willingness and ability of land owners to sell their land for some other use.

An alternative (neoclassical) view

The model of the land market outlined above is probably a fairly realistic representation of the situation in Britain, in southern England at least. Evidence for this view is provided by the large differences that frequently exist between the prices of pieces of land with planning permission for different uses. For example, Cheshire *et al.* (1985) quoted representative prices per acre for land in and around Reading in southern England in 1983 as being £3000 for agriculture, £0.6 m–£2.5 m for residential use, £0.4–£0.5 m for industrial use, £2.5 m–£3.4 m for retail, and £0.6–£13 m for offices. In the same year, representative prices for land in Stockton, California, were £86 k for industrial use, £139 k for retail and £83 k for offices, that is, considerably lower and with much less variation.

At different times and in different places, however, a different situation may prevail because planning constraints, for whatever reason, are less binding. Then the marginalist or neoclassical theory of the land market, put forward around 1870 would be the operative model, and it certainly would be in the absence of any intervention through the planning system to try to control the supply of land to particular uses. The Ricardian model was an extreme simplification of the situation in its day since it was assumed that there was only one use for land. This simplifying assumption was made by Ricardo because he was trying to construct a model of a whole economy and his main concern was with the distribution of income between the different classes of nineteenth century society, land owners, workers and capitalists. The marginalists were less concerned with the distribution of income and more with the determination of the prices of different goods and factors of production. The marginalist model therefore treats land like any other factor of production in that it is assumed that there are alternative uses, and not just one (Buchanan 1929)

A model of the situation is represented in Figure 7.3. The area of land available at a location, an area which can be taken to be fixed, is represented along the horizontal axis OQ. Price is represented on the vertical axis. To simplify the situation in order to represent it in a figure we assume that there are two possible uses for this land, residential use and commercial use. The derived demand for land for commerce is shown conventionally by the downward sloping line CC'. The amount of land used for commerce is therefore measured along the horizontal axis rightward from O. Since the

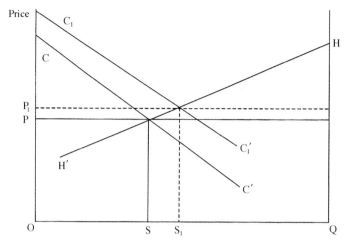

Figure 7.3

available land can be used either for commerce or for housing (or left vacant), the amount of land used for housing can best be represented along the horizontal axis leftward from Q. The derived demand for land for housing is therefore represented in a slightly unconventional way by a line, HH', which slopes downward, but from the right-hand vertical axis. Measuring from the right therefore, if the price is high little is used and as the price falls more and more land is used for housing. Equilibrium is indicated in the figure by the intersection of the two demand curves. In Figure 7.3 equilibrium would exist if the price of land were OP with the amount of land being used for commerce being represented by OS and the amount of land used for housing by SQ. This is the equilibrium price because if the price were higher it can be seen that the total amount of land used for housing and commerce would be less than the total available. Some would be vacant and unlet so that the price would fall as the owners of this land competed for tenants. On the other hand if the price were lower than OP the total amount of land demanded for each use would be greater than the total available and competition between possible users would cause the price to rise. Finally, it is clear that the price of land must be the same for each use 'at the margin', since, if it were not, land owners would try to transfer their land from the lower price use to the higher price use.

Changes in demand will result in changes in the price of land and changes in the use of some pieces of land. Suppose that for some reason the demand for land for commerce rises. In Figure 7.3 this is represented by an upward shift in the demand curve CC' to a new position indicated by the line C_1C_1'. A new higher equilibrium price is shown as OP_1, and there is a new allocation of land between the two uses with OS_1 being used for commerce and S_1Q for housing. The increased demand for land for commerce has resulted in an increase in the amount of land being used for commerce, as one might expect, and a consequential decrease in the amount of land used for housing.

This reduction in the amount of land available for housing and an increase in its price will necessarily result in an increase in the price of housing, both to reduce the demand, since less land is available, and because the price of one of its production inputs, land, has risen. Thus, when there are alternative uses, it is entirely possible for 'the price of housing to be high because the price of land is high' and so for the Ricardian conclusion that this was impossible to be wrong. The price of land and of housing may change as the market transmits the effects of shifts in demand for different goods. In this case the price of housing is higher so that less land is demanded for housing because more land is required for commerce because of an increase in the demand for that use.

Either the Ricardian or the marginalist theory of the determination of the price of land may be correct, depending on the extent and the degree of enforcement of planning controls. If they are rigidly enforced then Ricardian theory will be a better representation of the situation. If they are inoperative, either because they do not exist or because they are enforced laxly, then marginalist theory is applicable and the price of land in different uses will be equalised at the margin. What is also possible is that shifts in demand may change the situation.

Suppose, for example, that the construction of commercial buildings is constrained because it is thought that they would impose social costs on people living in the area. This initial situation may be as represented in Figure 7.4. As in Figure 7.3, the quantity of land in the area, OQ, is indicated on the horizontal axis, and the demand for commercial land is represented by the demand curve, CC', sloping downward from the left. The demand for land for housing is again represented by a demand curve sloping downward from the right, HH'. The area of land allocated for commercial use is indicated on the horizontal axis as OX. Because the amount allowed for commercial use is limited, the price of land for commerce, OP_c, is higher than the price of housing land, OP_H. Suppose now that the demand for housing increases substantially, say because of reductions in interest rates or increases in incomes or increases in tax incentives. This increase in demand is represented in the figure by the shift in the demand curve for housing land to the position indicated by the dotted line H_1H_1'. If the planned allocation of the available land between the two uses remained the same the result

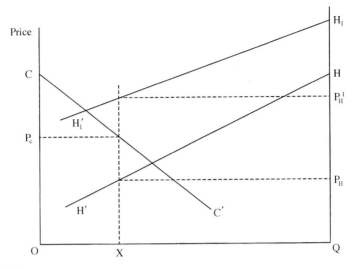

Figure 7.4

would be that the price of land for commerce would also remain the same, but the price of land for housing would increase, to QP_H' in the figure, a price above the price of land for commerce. But although there is a constraint on the amount of land available for commerce, it is not obvious that the constraint would be intended to operate to limit the amount of land available for housing. Thus, it might be expected that planning permission would be given for the construction of housing on land previously allocated for commercial use. The price of land for housing would then become the same as the price of commercial land, which would itself be higher than before, the amount of land used for commerce would decrease, and the amount of land used for housing would increase. Thus, economic changes may cause the marginalist model to become a more accurate representation of the situation than the Ricardian model, or, of course, vice versa.

The supply of land for a particular use

There is an implicit assumption in the above analysis that the owners of land have no role to play. While employees may choose between alternative jobs and capitalists may choose where to invest their capital, land owners apparently are thought to have no individual ideas of their own. They behave like automata, selling or renting out their land for the use which currently yields the highest income.

In fact, as we pointed out in the previous chapter in the discussion of growth controls and urban growth boundaries, land owners can and do behave differently. That is to say they may choose to use their land, or to allow it to be used, for an activity which yields a lower income than is available in other activities.

Three reasons have been identified as to why this might occur (Neutze 1987). The first is the most obvious. Owners may take the view that a higher price may be obtained in the future than is available now, and so they would rather hold on to the land than sell it, in other words they may take a speculative position, literally speculating as to what the future might hold. Unfortunately 'speculation' is a word with negative emotive connotations. Speculation is usually thought to be something which is in itself bad. This is not necessarily true, however. For example, a land owner may feel that it would not be a good idea to sell off land for housing now, but that it would be better to wait until the population of the area has increased and to sell it for retail use. The process of development of the land may be similar to what happens if a planner designates land on the plan for a new town for commercial use, but plans for the retail facilities to be built somewhat later than the housing. The one is a market response, the other a planning response. The one is not necessarily good, nor the other necessarily bad. Again, it is usual for the owners of large sites to plan for their development to take place over a number of years. I have seen, for example, the proposals for the development of a large industrial estate which had a planning horizon of 20 years, rather longer than that of the local authority in which the land was located. Such a planned development might be expected to function better and to look better than if the owner of the land did not 'speculate', but sold off all the sites for immediate development by a number of different firms.

A second reason for holding on to land rather than selling it immediately is uncertainty about the future (Titman 1985). Ownership of a site can be regarded as, in a sense, ownership of an option. Development of a site, being irreversible except at very great cost, closes that option, as, of course, does sale of the site which is completely irreversible. There will often be uncertainty as to what the most profitable form of development would be, both now and in the future. Land owners will therefore often be unwilling to exercise their option, i.e. to sell or develop a site, before that uncertainty is clarified. Titman himself motivates his analysis by observing that vacant but valuable sites in Los Angeles seem sometimes not to be immediately redeveloped as one might expect but are used temporarily for car parking.

A third possible reason why the owners of land may be unwilling to sell, most especially if they are owner occupiers, whether farmers or home owners, is because of their attachment of the site, in particular to their home (Evans 1983). Having lived somewhere for many years they may be unwilling to sell unless fully compensated for the disruption to their lives caused by the move. Indeed, in a survey carried out in the early 1970s to find out the level of compensation that home owners might require (GB Commission on the Third London Airport 1970), a proportion of those asked said that they would be unwilling to move however much was offered and the compensation required by most of the rest was substantial relative to the value of their homes. That people may be reluctant to move even if offered large sums for their properties is demonstrated by the occasional situation where a development has to take account of the absolute refusal to sell by the owner or owners of a property that is part of the proposed site. Often, of course, the owners will be elderly people who see no reason to move from a house that they may have occupied for much of their lives, and who have no particular use for extra capital or income.

All of these reasons suggest that the usual representation of the supply of land as determined solely by a desire on the part of land owners to obtain the highest current income from a site may be misleading. If we consider the supply of land for a particular use in a period, then the supply curve may be represented as conventionally upward sloping, as with any other commodity, that is the supply is neither completely inelastic nor completely elastic.

The position is represented in Figure 7.5. Once again we represent an area of land, OQ, along the horizontal axis. In this case let us assume that this is an area of agricultural land just outside an urban area. The price of land for agricultural use is indicated as OP on the vertical axis. This is assumed to be given since it will be unaffected by variations in the amount of agricultural land available in this small part of the national market. The supply of land to the market in the period is indicated by the upward sloping line SXS'. It is assumed that the land is farmed by owner occupiers. Some of these farmers would be unwilling to sell at the current price for agricultural land, but the schedule of prices at which they would sell is represented by the section of the supply curve XS'. Some are willing to sell however. They are 'in the market'. Maybe they wish to leave farming for another occupation, or maybe they wish to retire, or maybe the owner has died and the estate is in the hands of an executor, who must sell. In the absence of any demand for land for any non-agricultural use, some of the land will be sold in the period OR on the horizontal axis to others who wish to farm the land, while some, RQ on the horizontal axis, will not be sold but will remain in the hands of the existing owners.

Suppose that there is now some demand for land for urban development, because this area of land is just beyond the existing built-up area and the economy of the city is growing. This can be represented by a conventional downward sloping demand curve. One is drawn as a dashed line, UU, in Figure 7.5. This represents an initial situation when the demand for land for urban development is low. The downward slope indicates that developers would be willing to pay a premium over the agricultural use price for land for development, but that the price they would pay is lower the more land is made available to them. This demand curve intersects the horizontal line indicating the agricultural land price at V. This means that they will not have to pay a premium. The price of land will remain its price in agricultural use. Only some of the land that comes on to the market will be sold for urban use, OW on the horizontal axis, and the rest will still be sold for agricultural use, WR on the horizontal axis. There will as a result be some scattered development.

The more usual situation is also represented in Figure 7.5. The demand for land for urban development has become greater and is indicated by the downward sloping demand curve $U_1 U_1$. The demand curve now intersects the upward sloping supply curve. Equilibrium is indicated by the intersection of the two at Z. The amount demanded will equal the amount paid only if the price paid for land is higher than the agricultural use price. The premium being paid will encourage more owners to sell who would not otherwise have done so. All the land that is sold, OT in the figure, is bought for urban uses. Nevertheless some land, TQ on the horizontal axis, will

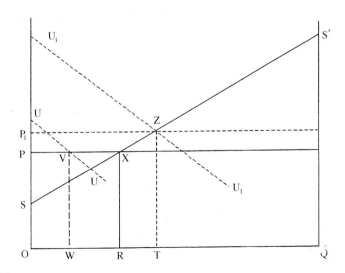

Figure 7.5

remain in the hands of the farmers, since the amount offered is still not enough to induce them to sell.

What will be the effect of imposing a constraint on development so that, say, only half the land in this area is allowed to be sold for development? Figure 7.6 shows the area divided into two halves, each with a horizontal axis equal to half the length of OQ in Figure 7.5. Suppose, since we have no reason to suppose otherwise, that the land owners are randomly and equally divided between the two halves. We can then represent their preferences by two identical supply curves, one in each half of the diagram. Similar premiums are demanded by similar land owners in each half of the market, but there are half as many in each as in the full market shown in Figure 7.5. In consequence the slopes of the two supply curves are twice as steep. So O_AS_A equals Q_AS_B in Figure 7.6, and both are equal to OS in Figure 7.5. Similarly Q_AS_A' equals Q_BS_B' in Figure 7.6 and both equal QS in Figure 7.5. However, since development is not allowed in the area represented by part (b) of the figure, the demand curve for land for urban development remains the same as in Figure 7.5, but relates solely to the land represented in part (a).

The implications of the analysis are clear. The intersection of the demand curve with the steeper supply curve in part (a) indicates that the price of land for development will be higher. A higher price will have to be paid to induce those land owners who are allowed to sell to do so. Nevertheless, even though the price is higher, substantially less land is sold for develop-

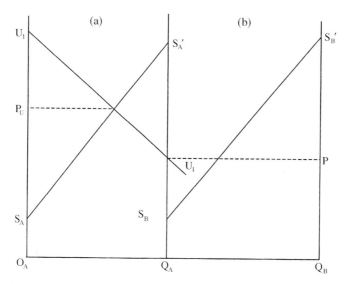

Figure 7.6

ment as was presumably the intention of those imposing the constraint. But the model shows that not all the land which is allowed to be developed will actually be developed in the period. The higher premium is still not high enough to induce all the land owners allowed to sell to do so. Thus higher land prices, prices substantially greater than the price of land in agricultural use, can coexist with land remaining undeveloped when there is no bar to its development. Planning constraints can cause land prices (and property prices) to be higher even when the situation in the land market might suggest that the constraint is relatively loose. It is not necessary for a green belt or growth boundary to be drawn tightly around the built-up area of a city for the constriction to result in higher land and property prices. As we noted in the previous chapter, empirical evidence for this conclusion is provided by the studies of the effects of Urban Growth Boundaries in Oregon.

Conclusions

The aim of this chapter is to set out the way in which the land market works, and the way in which planning controls may affect land prices through the market. It is clear from the discussion in this chapter, and that in the preceding chapter, that planning controls, if they are enforced and effective, will result in some land prices and property prices being higher than they otherwise would be. In the next few chapters we will explore the consequences of this, both as they affect the land and property market, and as they also affect the planning system itself.

8

The Division of the Spoils: Profits, Planning Gain, Premium Seeking and Taxation

'I have bought golden opinions from all sorts of people'
(Macbeth)

Introduction

As the analysis in the previous chapters shows, the effective implementation of physical planning constraints results in the value of most urban land and some rural land being different to what it would have been if the land market operated without any government intervention. The value of some of the urban land is higher and the value of the rest is lower. This has an important implication – the value of some land could be increased if a change in use were permitted. It follows that the owners of this land are likely to try to change its use, by one means or another. So, the successful application of a set of physical planning constraints brings into operation forces which seek to reduce this effectiveness. The differences in land values induce owners, or would-be owners, either to seek to obtain planning permission for some alternative use, or to lobby to seek to change the use for which their land is zoned, depending on the planning system in force.

Put bluntly, planning permission, or rezoning, becomes a valuable commodity which people are willing to spend money and resources to obtain. Furthermore, the ability to allow this change of use is in the hands of the planning authority, usually at a local level, but sometimes at a state, regional or central government level. The realisation that this ability is valuable may induce planning authorities to seek some recompense for allowing such a change of use.

The way in which these political and market forces operate, if they do, will differ from country to country because of differences in the legal position and the social climate, and they will also differ within countries because of economic and social differences between areas. For example, in some countries the development rights attached to some pieces of land may be sold by the owner of that property and used elsewhere. In this chapter we look at the situation in Britain where the development rights, or the lack of them, cannot be detached from the land. The question at issue then becomes one of how the increase in the value of the land resulting from permitting a change of use is divided up – who gets what – and that is the central concern of this chapter.

A diagrammatic analysis

In Britain it is by now generally accepted that the planning system con-strains the development of land and that these constraints mean that the value of developed land is raised above the value of undeveloped land. The difference in value varies from one part of the country to another, however, since it depends on the demand for developed land relative to its supply. As a result the difference is greatest in the south-east and tends to decline as one travels northward and, to a lesser extent, westward. Differences also exist between the price of land in one kind of use, say offices, and that in another, say housing. Nevertheless in this chapter we will mainly consider the difference between the value of undeveloped land and the value of developed land, particularly land which might be used for housing.

The question at issue is whom this increase in values benefits, and the impact of the difference in values on the planning process. For, as we have stressed, as a result of the constraint, planning permission may be of sub-stantial value. Indeed, in southern England the value of planning permission may be substantially greater than the value of the land in its current use, although, of course, in practice the two cannot be sold separately. (In this the British system differs from that of some other countries such as Greece, Spain, or the USA, where, in some cases and in some areas, the development rights for one site may be sold and transferred to another site.) For example, the value of a hectare of agricultural land in the vicinity of Reading, to the west of London, in 2003 would have been about £5000, but the value of the same land with planning permission for residential development would be well over £1 million, possibly over £2 million, depending on the site and the character of the housing for which permission was given.

In economic terms the situation may be as illustrated in Figure 8.1. An area of land, OQ, is indicated along the horizontal axis, and the price of land on

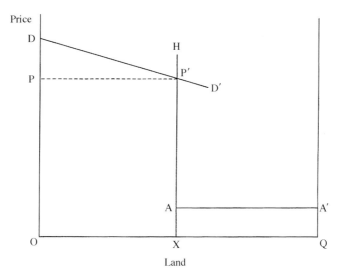

Figure 8.1

the vertical axis. Part of this land has been allowed to be developed, and is represented as OX, and a part has not, XQ. The static supply curve of developable land as given by the planning system is indicated by the vertical line, HX, through X. The price of agricultural land is indicated by the horizontal line AA'. The line is horizontal since it is assumed that there is a very large supply of alternative agricultural land elsewhere. Any change in the quantity of land used for agriculture at this location will not therefore affect its price, which anyway will be primarily determined by agricultural policies.

The demand for land for housing is indicated by the line DD' sloping downward from the left-hand axis. It slopes conventionally downward since it is assumed that housing in other parts of the country is not a perfect substitute for land in this area, adjacent to this town, so that an increase in the area of land for housing there will result in a fall in price. Since, however, the supply of land is fixed, the price, in the diagram, is determined by the intersection of the demand curve DD' with the supply curve HX at P', and indicated on the left-hand vertical axis by OP. Therefore in this diagram the value of planning permission for housing is marked by the difference between OA and OP shown on the line HX by A'P'.

The reasons for the constraint on the availability of land for housing are irrelevant, so far as the analysis in this chapter is concerned. It might be that there are considered to be negative externalities attached to housing, that rural land has a social value many times greater than its value for housing, and that A'P' is an accurate indicator of the extent of these externalities so far as the population is concerned. On the other hand, it might be that there are no net social costs but that the supply of land for housing results from a balancing of the various political pressures involving central government, local politicians, local planning officers, and local and national pressure groups. For the purposes of this chapter it suffices only that planning permission becomes a valuable commodity because of this constraint. Moreover, since planning permission is attached to a piece of land and that land is saleable, then planning permission is not only a valuable commodity but it is also a saleable commodity.

Figure 8.1 shows only the position at a point in time. During the next period the situation will change. In particular, it is likely that the demand for housing land will increase because of rising incomes, a growing population, and reductions in household size resulting in an increasing number of households. In England the Department of the Environment in its various forms has in the past attempted to forecast the increase in the total number of households requiring dwellings (Breheny 1999). Then the expected number of households in each region has also been forecast and, through a process, which is in part political bargaining, the increase in the number of households that each county must plan for has been forecast. It has then been necessary for the counties to indicate to the Department how it is planned that these households will be accommodated. Whether the houses will be provided through the redevelopment of existing urban sites, or through the infilling of open areas within towns, or through new development on agricultural or other rural land.

The position is shown diagrammatically in Figure 8.2. Compared with the initial situation shown in Figure 8.1, the demand curve has now shifted upwards to D_1D_1'. We assume that the local authority agrees that to accommodate the increased number of households an area of rural land should be allowed to be developed, represented in the figure by XY on the horizontal axis. If this is done then balancing the increased demand against the increased supply will result in an increase in the price of land for residential development to OP_1. This increase in price is plausible but not necessary. If more land had been allocated, relative to demand, the price might have fallen, or might even have remained constant.

The position is then that in this period the quantity of land to be made available for residential development is given, in the diagram, by XY, and the price at which it can be sold with planning permission is OP_1. The price at which similar land could be sold for agricultural use, without planning permission for residential use, is, in the diagram, QA. The total value of the

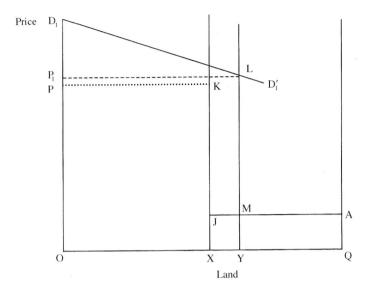

Figure 8.2

planning permissions likely to be granted is therefore equal to this increase in price multiplied by the amount of land released for development. In Figure 8.2 this is indicated by the rectangle JKLM. The land which has already been developed will also increase in value in this case but that is irrelevant to the argument here.

The beneficiaries

The question at issue here is how JKLM, representing the increase in the value of the land released for development, is to be distributed. To whom does this increase in wealth accrue? There are, of course, a number of possibilities, since there are a number of economic actors who may be involved in the relevant transactions. The most obvious beneficiary, according to conventional economic theory, would be the owner of the land. The company that is the actual developer of the site would also seem to be entitled to a share and although it may sometimes be the original owner of the site, this is not necessarily the case. A third possible beneficiary is local government. It is, after all, the economic actor that actually possesses the power to give planning permission in the first instance, and basic economics suggests that it will wish to obtain something in return. Fourth, central government will certainly take the view, if the profits are substantial, that some of this profit, as with any other form of income, should be diverted to the Treasury. And, finally, some of this increase in value may have to be spent in actually obtaining planning permission, in what has been called premium seeking expenditure, as land owners and would-be developers compete with each other to be the ones who succeed in obtaining permission for the land in which they have an interest. We discuss the position of each of these below, but in a slightly different order.

Central government

The position of central government is the easiest to analyse in part because its reactions to the increasing value of land with planning permission have been the most transparent. At the beginning of the 1970s it had become very apparent, in particular because of the increase in the value of London office buildings during the previous eight or ten years, that substantial fortunes could be made through the operation of the planning system by those for-tunate enough to obtain the right planning permission at the right time. How some of these fortunes were amassed is vividly described by Oliver Marriott (1967). A capital gains tax had been imposed in 1966, with a top rate of 30%, by the then Labour government. In 1974 this was reinforced with respect to property transactions by a Development Gains Tax with a top rate of 60%. This tax was first proposed under the Conservative gov-ernment led by Edward Heath in 1973 but enacted by the Labour govern-ment of Harold Wilson in 1974. Two years later the top rate was increased to 80% and the tax renamed a Development Land Tax. The intention was that the rate would eventually be raised to 100% (Cherry 1996, p. 187). It was recognised that at this rate development would be deterred, but this was accepted since it was also the intention that the role of developer would be taken over by local governments and the profits from development would accrue to them. The Act therefore allowed local authorities to buy land at a price which was net of tax.

One might note that this raises an interesting question. Since they could be expected to buy land cheaply, it should have been expected that they would also use land less intensively than the private developers they were repla-cing. If the high price of land was due to the planning constraints on its use, this implication is odd if it is believed that the constraints are necessary because of the negative externalities arising from urban development in order to preserve rural land and encourage urban land to be used intensively. The illogicality can be explained in that at the time it was generally believed that the price of land was high because of the activities of spec-ulators. Therefore, once speculation was eliminated, the belief was, apparently, that land prices would fall back to more 'normal' levels. It was not realised at the time, in government circles at least, that land prices were high because of planning constraints despite the considerable evidence put together and published by Hall *et al.* as *The Containment of Urban England* in 1973. But then the fact that planning restrictions on the availability of land result in the price of land and housing being higher was only officially accepted following a review of the evidence nearly 20 years later (Eve 1992). As Prest (1981) noted in his discussion of land taxation in the post-war era, political thinking on the economics of land rent has often been simplistic, at best.

In fact, little development was carried out under the Act, and with the election of a Conservative government led by Margaret Thatcher in 1979, the provisions allowing local authorities a share in the profits were repealed. The Development Land Tax remained in existence, however, although the rate of tax was reduced to 60%. It was eventually abolished in 1985 by Nigel Lawson as part of a general process of tax reform, tidying up the tax structure and abolishing taxes with low yields to the Exchequer. As part of this process Lawson had raised the top marginal rate of capital gains tax to 40%, the same rate to which the top marginal rate of income tax had been reduced. This has remained the position since then. Central government may therefore take 40% of any capital gain resulting from the award of planning permission and the subsequent sale of the land. It should be noted that if the sale of the land is delayed then the tax is also delayed, while the Development Land Tax, since it became due at the time of development, not the time of sale, could not be delayed in this way. Moreover the 'taper' relief introduced in 1999 by Gordon Brown means that the capital gains tax liability on assets which have been held for over ten years can be substantially reduced, in effect from 40% to 24%.

Local government

Unlike central government local governments have not been able to impose specific taxes on development. They were therefore in the position of having the power to give planning permission, something which is of value to others but for which they could normally obtain no recompense. The sophistication of the British system of local government finance compounds this situation. Any increase in the tax revenue received by a local authority because of an increase in the value of the property within its area and a consequential increase in the services provided is likely to result in a fully compensating change in the grant from central government. Thus, on the face of it, local authorities have had no financial incentive to award planning permission for any development. In this respect the British system differs significantly from the American where, as we noted in an earlier chapter, city authorities have an incentive to go in for so-called fiscal zoning, trying to zone land uses so as to maximise the difference between the income from taxes from any new development and the cost of the services which consequentially have to be provided.

On the face of it local authorities have therefore had no incentive to grant any form of planning permission. However, in the late 1960s and 1970s they came to realise that they had something of value, which others wanted, and the result was, as an economist might expect, that local authorities tried to appropriate some of the profits for themselves. Specifically they began to exploit a provision of the 1971 Town and Country Planning Act by nego-tiating what came to be called Section 52 agreements with would-be developers. Section 52 of the Act allowed local authorities to require developers to carry out, or pay for, works which were associated with a development for which permission was being granted. The contributions received by the local authorities through these agreements came to be called 'planning gain'. It is now more (politically) correct to say that local authorities 'enter into planning obligations' than that they obtain 'planning gain', but the effect is the same. The term 'planning obligation' is that used in policy guidance by central government. The provision of the Act was interpreted by many authorities with considerable latitude, with the result that developers might find themselves paying for things which were only very loosely associated with the development. The situation was intended to be tidied up by Section 106 of the Town and Country Planning Act 1990, and 'Section 106 agreements' is now the name for what were called Section 52 agreements. It was intended that Section 106 would require that plan-ning gain should be more closely associated with the proposed develop-ments than had seemed to be necessary under Section 52. The development of the idea of planning gain and its application in practice are described by Allinson & Askew (1996) and Rydin (1998, pp. 226–9), and, from a more economic viewpoint by Keogh (1985) and Bowers (1992).

Whatever the legal position may be both would-be developers and local authorities have had financial incentives to reach agreements which would result in generous contributions to the costs of the local authority. The advantage to the developer is obvious. If insufficient is offered then planning permission may be refused completely. If the profits are large, as they may be, it is worthwhile being generous.

The advantage to the local authority depends on the British system of local government finance to which we referred above. Any formal increase in the income of the authority from taxes is likely to be fully compensated by a reduction in the grant received from central government. Planning gain is received on the basis of a one-off agreement, however, and would be difficult if not impossible to incorporate into the kind of formula used to allocate grants and which is supposed to ensure equity between local authorities on a semi-permanent basis, replicable year by year. Even if financial payments could be taken into account, it would be difficult to take into account the provision of goods in kind such as parks. As a result capital improvements in a local planning authority paid for by developers escape the central government compensation mechanism. Road improvements, the provision of parks, capital improvements to local schools, hospitals, or recreational facilities, all of which might properly be the subject of Section 106 agreements, would not result in a reduction in the grant from central government. Any provision over and above that strictly required to provide for the new development therefore represents a real gain to the local authority and its population. For example, a park adjacent to a new residential development will be used by the new residents but will also be visited by other people who live nearby.

Given this situation it is not surprising that a local councillor might express the view, as one did to me, that he was entirely in favour of restricting the amount of land available for development, since this made planning permission more valuable, and so allowed larger contributions towards the costs of local government to be obtained from would-be developers.

It might be thought that it would be possible to apply the basic theory of the firm and, in particular, the theory of monopoly to the analysis of this situation. Such a theory would purport to show how a local authority could act monopolistically to maximise its total revenue from planning gain. For example, it might be assumed that it would extract as planning gain the balance of the available profit after central government had taken its share in the form of taxes, and would so control the availability of planning permissions as to maximise this balance. In fact, such a simple theoretical analysis is not possible, since the shares attributable to other participants also have to be taken into account, and these others have not yet been considered.

The position is further complicated by the fact that others may seek to involve themselves in the negotiations between the would-be developer and the local authority. This can occur because the planning decision, in Britain, is made at the local level by local politicians, and this allows others who have, or think they have, political influence to try to make sure that they benefit from the planning obligations.

In one case of which I have personal knowledge it was put to the party applying for planning permission for residential development of a site, by at least two neighbourhood groups, that although they had no objection in principle to the proposal they felt that they were not getting enough out of it and would therefore object. The leader of one such group 'reminded' the developer that 'in the end it is a political not a planning decision'. Planning obligations which are entered into to benefit such interests may therefore be closer to side payments made to buy off objections and remove opposition at the local, political, level than to strict improvements in the physical plan. Of course, a developer can decide to appeal rather than buy off objectors since, in the end, at an appeal the decision becomes primarily a planning decision rather than a political decision. On the other hand the developer can decide that the cost of going to appeal, even if the appeal is successful, might be greater than the cost of buying off the objectors.

A recent development in the operation of the concept of planning gain has been the use of the system to ensure that housing is provided for low income groups. Although central governments had sometimes discouraged this, it was recommended by the DoE in 1996, under the Conservatives. Local authorities are now encouraged to require that in any large housing development a proportion of the housing built should be 'affordable', whether provided on site or paid for elsewhere (Rydin 1998, p. 227).

This 'formalisation' of the use of planning obligations is peculiar. In the first place it is in the nature of a tax since it reduces proportionately the value of the planning permission given. The fact that payments can be made makes this clear. Second, as a tax it is not obvious why the tax should be imposed on large residential developments but not on small residential developments or on commercial or industrial developments. And third, as pointed out by Crook (1998), it is not only a tax but a hypothecated tax, that is a tax the revenue from which can only be used for a specific purpose. The British Treasury is notorious for its dislike of hypothecated taxes but presumably it did not notice that this is what was being proposed.

Finally, a peculiarity of this hypothecated tax is that it may be imposed on all owners of land who obtained planning permission for development for housing, even if they are otherwise non-tax paying. Thus, a College of Further Education which wishes to sell some land which is surplus to its requirements may have to enter into the same planning obligations as a private developer. But it is not at all clear why money should be transferred in this way from the education budget to the housing budget. This can apply with respect to other forms of planning obligation, for example that a College should provide £70 000 towards the provision of public art. Transfers of this kind outside the planning system would be unheard of.

The land owner and the developer

As has already been pointed out, conventional elementary economic theory would suggest that the balance of any increase in value arising from the award of planning permission should accrue to the owner of the land. But such a conclusion would ignore the risk and uncertainty introduced into the development process by the planning system. It would be largely correct if the owner of the land had obtained planning permission before the sale of the site. Competition should then lead the construction company to be willing to pay the maximum price for the site consistent with making a profit from the development. In the British context, however, a company which may not be the owner of the land will apply for planning permission for a site's development. Of course, the land owner and the developer may be one and the same but they will more usually differ, particularly when the development of rural land is at stake. In urban areas, where what is at issue is the redevelopment of a site with existing buildings, it is more likely that a firm will purchase the site from the previous owners and then apply for planning permission, secure in the knowledge that development of some kind will be permitted. The price paid then depends upon the expectations of the seller and the buyer regarding the kind of development which might be permitted.

In the United States the evidence suggests, in the case of rural land, that three parties become involved (Brown *et al.* 1981). As an urban area expands land likely to be developed in the near future passes out of the hands of users, that is farmers, and into the hands of 'investors', who hold it until it is sold to a construction firm for development. Investors exist because the anticipation of future development means that the capital value of the land is far greater than that of rural land more distant from urban areas so that no farmer would wish to buy it. On the other hand it would not yet be profitable to develop it so no construction firm would wish, yet, to buy it (Evans 2004).

In Britain, however, the restrictiveness and the uncertainty of the system lead to a different role for developers. In many areas the restrictiveness of the system means that agricultural land is unlikely to be given permission to be developed, but if permission is given the land will be worth a fortune. Thus, the eventual development of the land cannot be foreseen and capitalised into its value as it can be in the United States. So, in circumstances where the value of a hectare of land may be less than £5000 without permission or development but more than £1 m with planning permission, the owner of agricultural land is likely to ask from a would-be developer a price substantially greater than £5000 per hectare, but, given the risk, the developer is likely to be unwilling to pay substantially more, since the money would be lost if planning permission were refused.

Because of both the risks and the rewards, a practice of using options has therefore grown up in Britain. A representative description of the situation would be that a firm would approach a land owner and agree to pay a small sum, a few thousand pounds, to purchase an option to buy the land for development, the price of the land to be agreed later. The developer then draws up outline plans and applies for planning permission on the basis of these plans. If permission is refused the firm is likely to appeal against the refusal to the Secretary of State. If the appeal is not successful, the developer bears the cost of the unsuccessful application and the appeal, as well as the cost of the option. The land owner, on the other hand, bears none of these costs, but receives the minimal reward of the price paid for the option.

If planning permission is obtained, however, then the developer will have agreed to buy the land from its owner at a price which will be a percentage of its full market price. This market price will be the price at the time of the actual sale, not the price at the time the option was sold since this may be some years earlier. The market price will take into account the planning permission which now exists, and will have to be agreed between the land owner and the developer, almost certainly with the involvement of professional advisers on each side. There will also be some provision for an appeal to an independent arbitrator if agreement cannot be reached.

In the mid-1980s the percentage of the full market value received by the land owner was nearly 90% but fell towards 60% at the end of the land and housing boom in the early 1990s. Moreover, the cost of planning gain would usually come out of the land owner's share, and since offers under Sections 52 or 106 would have been made by the developer to the local authority during negotiations or during the appeal, these offers would have to be justifiable by the developer to the land owner – the reasons why it was necessary, to obtain planning permission, to pay for this road improvement or that school extension. In the case of some kind of planning gain the land owner necessarily bears the cost directly. For example, if it is agreed that some of the land area under consideration will be given up to the local authority for use as parkland, the land owner loses both the land and the increase in its value which would have occurred if it had been included in the land which could be developed.

So, the land owner receives a percentage of the increase in value, but out of this must pay the cost of planning gain, and capital gains tax on the balance. The developer receives the remaining percentage, which, as has been noted, rose from 10% in the mid-1980s to about 40% ten years later. This percentage includes the firm's profit which may be realised quickly by the sale of some of the land, with planning permission, to construction firms, or it may be realised more slowly if the firm carries out all the construction itself. The percentage accruing to the developer must also cover the cost of trying to obtain planning permission, not only in this case where the application has been successful, but also in the more frequent cases when the applications have been unsuccessful.

It is almost certainly the changing perception of the probability of success during the late 1980s and early 1990s which led to the reduction in the share of the value of the land going to its owner and to an increase in the share going to the developer. As the price of land and housing rose during the 1980s, an increasing number of development applications were made, but an increasing proportion of these applications were refused. As a result, as we have noted, in respect of those pieces of land where applications were successful the percentage of the market value accruing to the land owner fell.

Premium seeking expenditure: consultants, lawyers and others

In 1974 Ann Krueger, in a seminal paper, suggested that profits such as those accruing to developers and land owners will be dissipated in what she called 'rent seeking expenditure'. Bhagwati (1982) suggested that the term 'premium seeking expenditure' would be better, as well as discussing other forms of what he called Directly Unproductive Profit-seeking (DUP) Activities. In discussions of land use where the rent of land can be confused with economic rents, the term 'rent seeking expenditure' can be confusing. Therefore, although 'rent seeking expenditure' has become the customary term in the economics and public choice literature and Bhagwati's terminology is little used, I prefer to use the term 'premium seeking expenditure', to reduce the level of confusion.

Krueger applied her analysis to the allocation of import licences in India and Turkey. The authorities issued only a certain number of such licences in order to restrict imports. The possession of a licence was therefore valuable. People would therefore compete to obtain licences and would be willing to spend real resources in order to obtain them. The expenditure of such resources did not increase economic welfare, however. The same number of licences would be issued whether they were competed for or whether they had been merely distributed as part of a lottery. Since the value of a licence could be described as an economic rent, she called such expenditure rent seeking expenditure and pointed out, first, that it was a deadweight loss as far as the national economies were concerned, and, second, that in theory the whole value of the economic rents could be dissipated in this rent seeking (premium seeking) expenditure.

We can apply Krueger's analysis to the present situation. Suppose that it is known that a local authority is likely to allow land to be developed to provide a certain number of houses in a period. Then, land owners and developers have an incentive to compete to ensure that their land is the land which is given permission. They will do this through lobbying at the time that local authorities are drawing up their plans, formulating planning applications, attempting to persuade local authorities and their officers to give or recommend approval, and going to appeal. In the course of this they will pay for architects, surveyors, and planning consultants, pay the cost of public relations exercises and advertising, pay for lawyers and barristers, and, probably, for other kinds of consultant – transport consultants, environmental consultants, even, occasionally, economic consultants. They will also have to commit considerable amounts of their own time and that of their staff. Two questions follow from this. To what extent do these activities represent a deadweight loss so far as the economy is concerned, and to what extent are the available profits dissipated in this kind of expenditure?

The first of these questions we will return to at the end of the chapter, after we have tried to give an answer to the second. We have already said that it is suggested in the economic literature on rent or premium seeking that competition to obtain these premiums could theoretically lead to all the available premiums being dissipated in premium seeking expenditure. Those economists who would take this view would regard the increase in the percentage accruing to the developer as evidence of progress towards such a position. Whatever the position in this respect, it must also be borne in mind that much of the expenditure by a would-be developer must be matched in some way by local and central government. This is most obvious at the level of the planning appeal when the presence of senior and junior counsel and of expert witnesses on behalf of the applicant will be matched by a similar parade of lawyers and consultants on the part of the local authority, and, sometimes, smaller levels of representation by local action groups.

We noted earlier that the current position would appear to be that up to 40% of the premiums in contention may be dissipated by expenditure on behalf of the developer. Matching expenditure by others suggests that, in fact, up to 80% of the premiums may in practice be dissipated in expenditure by the applicants, government, and others. Moreover, it is conceivable that the amount spent could exceed 100% if the probability of obtaining permission were low enough and the expenditure by others were high enough. This would depend to a large extent, however, on the participants' assessment of the probability of obtaining permission and it is to this question that we now turn.

Planning gain, premium seeking and probability

So far as the developer is concerned there is only a small distinction to be made between what economists and planners might call planning gain and all the other resources expended in order to obtain planning permission. Both expenditure on planning gain and premium seeking expenditure are made in order to persuade government, whether local or central, to grant planning permission. In this respect the difference between the two is solely that planning gain is a transfer of resources to the local authority while premium seeking expenditure is not. The distinction which must be made is, nevertheless, crucial. Expenditure on planning gain has to be made only if planning permission is granted. Premium seeking expenditure is incurred whether the result of the application is successful or not.

To the extent that the allocation of resources between the two is a management problem economics has little, at present, to contribute. The amount volunteered in the form of planning gain will depend upon the negotiating ability of the planning authority or its perceived vulnerability to persuasion by the grant of resources. In some circumstances the developer may think it best to offer large amounts of planning gain. On the other hand, where the local planning authority is perceived to be inflexible, the company may think it best to expend resources in trying to persuade the inspector appointed by central government to adjudicate at the appeal through employing more expensive barristers and more or better consultants and ensuring better publicity.

The allocation of resources by the firm will also depend on the perceived probability of success. In choosing the amounts to be offered as planning gain or actually spent in premium seeking expenditure, the firm will have to take account of the effects of differing levels of expenditure on the probability of success. In the analysis of this economics does have something to contribute.

To analyse the position we have to use some elementary mathematics. Let L_u be the value of a site without planning permission, and let L_p be the value

of this site with planning permission for development. The value of planning permission is V which is equal to $L_p - L_u$. The probability of obtaining
permission, p, can be presumed to be a monotonically increasing function
both of premium seeking expenditure, x, and expenditure on planning gain,
g, that is $p(x,g)$. The expected returns, E, from expenditure on planning gain
or premium seeking are therefore equal to the value of planning permission
multiplied by the probability of obtaining it, less both the cost of planning
gain, multiplied by the probability of having to part with it, and the cost of
premium seeking expenditure, i.e.:

$$E(x,g) = p(x,g)V - p(x,g)g - x \qquad (8.1)$$

Note that the probability of having to hand over planning gain is necessarily
the same as the probability of obtaining planning permission, while premium seeking expenditure, x, is spent whatever happens. The conditions
necessary for the developer's expected profit to be maximised, where p_x is
the first derivative of $p(x,g)$ with respect to x, etc., are:

$$p_x(V - g) = 1 \qquad (8.2)$$

$$p_g(V - g) = p(x,g) \qquad (8.3)$$

provided, of course, that the second order conditions are fulfilled. The first
of these conditions means that, provided that the expected value of an
additional pound of expenditure falls as expenditure increases (the second
order condition), the expected net profit is maximised if expenditure is
incurred up to the point that the increase in the expected value from an
additional pound is equal to one pound (the first order condition). Further
expenditure would be unprofitable since the expected value of an additional
pound would be less than one pound.

The second condition means that, once again, provided that the expected
value of an additional pound of offered planning gain falls as total planning
gain offered increases, then the expected net profit is maximised if planning
gain is offered up to the point that the increase in the expected value from
an additional pound is equal to the expected cost of offering that pound, i.e.
the value of that pound multiplied by the probability of actually having to
part with it.

The first of these conditions is illustrated diagrammatically in Figure 8.3.
On the assumption that g, planning gain, is already fixed, on the vertical
axis we have the expected value $p(x)(V-g)$. Premium seeking expenditure,
x, is indicated on the horizontal axis. The vertical line at $x = V-g$ indicates
the maximum premium seeking expenditure likely to be made by the

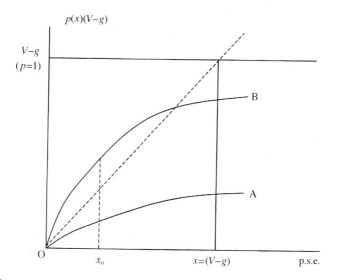

Figure 8.3

developer since this would reduce the firm's profit to zero. In the diagram one can also draw a horizontal line $V-g$ where $p = 1$ and the probability of obtaining planning permission is certain. A curve showing the relationship between the amount of premium seeking expenditure and the expected value of the planning permission is, for obvious reasons, unlikely to reach this level. The diagonal line sloping upwards from the origin shows the points for which $p(x)(V-g) = x$. Points below the diagonal in the figure show combinations of premium seeking expenditure and expected returns which are not profitable.

Thus, if the expected rent function is as indicated by the curve A, the developer will not make an application. It will not be worthwhile incurring any premium seeking expenditure since the probability of obtaining permission is so low. Its expected value, i.e. its value if obtained multiplied by the probability of obtaining it, would be less than the cost of making the application and of incurring any other expenditure supporting it and this would be true however much was spent.

Points in the figure above the diagonal indicate combinations of premium seeking expenditure and expected returns where an application is, given the balance of probabilities, profitable. A plausible relationship between the two is shown by the curve B. The function increases at a decreasing rate. At low levels of expenditure small increases in expenditure disproportionately increase the probability of obtaining planning permission, but the positive effect of increasing expenditure gradually diminishes. That is there are decreasing marginal returns, and at high levels of expenditure the curve moves into the lower, unprofitable, area in the figure.

In respect of curve B the optimal level of premium seeking expenditure is indicated by the point x_0. At this point the first and second order conditions are fulfilled. That is, at this level of expenditure the slope of the curve is equal to one and to the slope of the diagonal. Consequentially, in the figure, the vertical difference between the curve B and the diagonal is greatest, or, in other words, the difference between the expected return and the amount spent in obtaining permission will be maximised. Note that since the curve B still slopes upwards the probability of obtaining permission could still be increased by further expenditure. Nevertheless, this would be unprofitable since the cost would outweigh the increase in the expected value.

Trying to represent graphically the relationship between expenditure on planning gain and the expected value of planning permission would be more difficult and would not necessarily clarify the argument. Similar arguments apply to those used in respect to premium seeking expenditure, with the difference that, although premium seeking expenditure is spent come what may, offers of planning gain are only a cost if planning permission is given, and the profitability of planning gain therefore depends on this probability.

Intuitively it would seem plausible to argue that developers would be more willing to offer planning gain than spend a similar amount in premium seeking expenditure. Mathematically also, since $p(x, g) < 1$, from the first order conditions (8.2) and (8.3) this would also seem likely. General conclusions of this kind are difficult to prove conclusively, however, because developer behaviour depends on the probability functions associated with each kind of expenditure. Nevertheless, it is possible to derive some general conclusions if we make simplifying assumptions. Therefore we assume that

$$p(x,g) = q(x) + q(g) \tag{8.4}$$

so that each kind of expenditure has the same effect on the probability of obtaining permission and that the two probabilities are additive. The curve $q(x) = q(g)$ can then be drawn as in Figure 8.4 with either x or g indicated on the horizontal axis, and with $p(x,g)$ V represented on the vertical axis. From (8.2) and (8.3) above we have the first order conditions:

$$q'(x)(V - g) = 1 \tag{8.5}$$

$$q'(g)(V - g) = q(x) + q(g) = p(x,g) \tag{8.6}$$

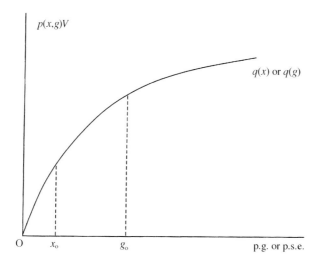

Figure 8.4

Dividing one by the other this means that, at the optimum

$$[q'(g)/q'(x)] = p(x, g) \tag{8.7}$$

Necessarily the value of $p(x, g)$, the probability of obtaining planning permission, lies above zero (impossibility) and below 1 (complete certainty). It
therefore follows that at the optimum $q'(g) < q'(x)$. Moreover, since the
curve $q(x) + q(g) = p(x,g)$ slopes upward at a diminishing rate, it also follows
that at the optimum $x < g$, that is, given an equal persuasive effect of each
kind of expenditure the amount offered as planning gain is likely to be
greater than the amount expended in premium seeking expenditure.
Moreover, the lower is the probability of eventual success, the lower will
be x relative to g.

This seems a plausible representation of likely developer behaviour. The
lower, generally, the probability of obtaining planning permission, the less
willing firms will be to expend real resources in trying to obtain permission, but they will be relatively more willing to make generous offers of
planning gain. On the other hand, the more likely it is that planning permission will actually be granted, the more willing will firms be to expend
real resources in obtaining that permission, although they will be relatively less willing to make generous offers of planning gain to the local
authority, offers which are more likely to be taken up in this case than in
the first case.

Planning gain, premium seeking and welfare

There is, as we indicated earlier, another question with respect to expenditure by developers in order to obtain planning permission, expenditure which we have called premium seeking. The original work on 'rent seeking expenditure', and much of the later work, has regarded it as a deadweight loss so far as the national economy is concerned. In the original study by Krueger, as we said earlier, would-be importers competed for import licences. Since the amount allowed to be imported was fixed by central government, and since it therefore did not matter who had the licences, so far as the national economy was concerned this competition served no useful purpose. It was a waste of resources, a deadweight loss.

With respect to expenditure on obtaining planning permission, therefore, one possibility is that all such premium seeking expenditure is also a deadweight loss, and it is clear that this is so to the extent that the situation is as described by Krueger with respect to import licences. For example, if it is known that planning permission will be given in a period for a certain number of houses, then each of the developers is merely trying to obtain a share of this number. Since the same number of houses will be built, in total, whoever the planning permissions are granted to, it could be argued that such expenditure is certainly a deadweight loss.

Land use, however, and the construction of housing differ in many significant respects from the import of some standard product. Even when permissions will be given for a known number of houses, they have to be given for sites and for houses all of which are in some way different. It could be argued that in making an application each of the developers is providing information about a possible way of providing the houses. While it might be possible to put the names of all the applicants for import licences into a lottery and draw lots, with no welfare loss to the economy, it would not be sensible to put the names of applicants for planning permissions into a similar lottery. The difference is that in the case of property development there is a lack of information about the alternative sites. The processes of lobbying and putting in applications in themselves provide information to the local planning authority about the alternatives available. This information, it could be argued, necessarily improves the quality of planning decisions, as does the information provided at a planning appeal, if the proposal is turned down and the developer appeals.

In practice the truth must lie somewhere between the two extreme positions, premium seeking expenditure is not wholly a deadweight loss because information is generated and provided by the process and this must improve the quality of planning decisions. On the other hand, some of the expenditure is a waste, since some of it is spent on competing with rivals for something that will be granted anyway. The cost of obtaining the information is nevertheless, in most cases, going to be greater than the value of the information to the planning system.

Similar arguments can be put forward with respect to expenditure on planning gain. On the one hand, planning gain may be regarded as the straightforward transfer back to the community of part of the value of the planning permission granted by government on behalf of the community.

The result of this transfer is equitable in that planning gain allows a redistribution of the benefits to the rest of the community, and provides a partial compensation for those likely to suffer from the externalities generated by the proposed development. Looked at positively, the planning gain which is negotiated by the local authority may improve the development, may, at least in part, be reflected in an increase in the value of the development, and may in itself be part of the discovery process, allowing the planning authority to make more informed decisions with respect to the quality of proposed alternatives.

From a negative point of view, however, the offer of planning gain may distort the planning process. Planning authorities may be led to accept proposals that yield the most to them in additional resources, and in doing so may be led to make decisions that are worse than they would be if they were undistorted by offers of planning gain. It is this fear which accounts for the worries expressed by some lawyers and planners. From their point of view the local planning authority is a quasi-judicial body, and legal decisions should not be contaminated in any way by payments of this sort. It is as if judges were to be made offers by plaintiffs and defendants, and to claim that these offers did not in any way affect their decisions. The general public might feel, to put it no more strongly, that such indifference was unlikely and that it would be better if such payments were not made. So, many lawyers would feel that however much it might be protested that planning gain does not distort decisions it would be better if the system were uncontaminated by such payments.

Offers of planning gain may therefore result in the wrong decisions being made. Paradoxically, as we pointed out earlier, the very neutrality of the British system of local government finance may encourage this. Since the system ensures fiscal neutrality in all other respects, the amount of planning gain that can be obtained is one of the few financial benefits that local authorities can obtain for their residents and which will not be cancelled by a compensating reduction in the grant received from central government.

Once again it would seem that the truth lies somewhere in between two extremes. Planning gain may sometimes distort the planning process, but, more usually, planning gain is neutral as regards decision making and beneficial in that it results in some redistribution of the profits made. My own subjective assessment would be that the deadweight loss caused by (a substantial part of) the expenditure by developers to try to obtain planning permission would be a far greater cost to the economy than any distortions caused by offers of planning gain.

Conclusions

In this chapter we have tried to set out the position with respect to the question 'Who receives the benefit from the award of planning permission when it is valuable?'. The number of possible beneficiaries have been many – central government through taxation, local government through offers of planning gain, the owners of the land, the property developers, and the consultants, lawyers and others employed by the development firms to assist them in obtaining permission or by local authorities to resist these applications.

We have also tried to assess the extent to which planning decisions may be distorted by offers of planning gain and by expenditure by developers. Although the latter may not be limitable one possibility with respect to the former is to standardise the amount that has to be paid over to cover infrastructure costs. Then, at least, each applicant would be in the same position with respect to the planning authority, and the possibility of bias would be reduced. In the United States such payments are called impact fees and these are discussed in the next chapter.

9

Impact Fees

'He is well paid that is well satisfied'
(The Merchant of Venice)

Introduction

In the previous chapter we saw that developers seeking planning permission frequently have to negotiate agreements with the local authorities from whom they are requesting planning permission. Under such agreements the developers will agree to pay for the cost of the provision of some infrastructure if planning permission is granted. Apart from the problems which we discussed at the end of the previous chapter – Will such an agreement distort the judgement of the local authority and will the offer distort, and worsen overall, the planning proposal? – there is a further problem which is that the amount is subject to negotiation, so that what is agreed to be paid is dependent on the negotiating abilities of the developer on the one hand and the local authority on the other, or, of course, their representatives.

An alternative approach would be to fix the amount that has to be paid so that it is not subject to negotiation. Where this has been done in some cities in the United States and Canada, these payments have been called impact fees, and this is the term we shall use here. The concept of a fee which is fixed and non-negotiable has been used elsewhere, however. In Italy, for example, such fees are called 'oneri di urbanizzazione' – urbanisation charges, and are not a fixed charge per house but a fixed proportion of the total cost of construction (Ave 1996). They are also used, for example, in Australia (Neutze, 1997). In practice the idea has also been applied in the United Kingdom since the early nineties. When the water utilities were privatised, they were given powers to make a capital charge in respect of any new dwelling for connection to the water mains, a charge intended to cover the cost of reservoir facilities constructed elsewhere.

Impact fees in theory and practice

The empirical evidence of the implementation of impact fees in North America suggests that the amount of the impact fee will be passed on to the purchaser of the new dwelling since the price will be raised by the amount of the fee (see Evans 1999). In the analysis of the English experience in the previous chapter, however, it was argued that the cost of planning gain was likely to fall on the owner of the land, so that it would not be passed on to the purchasers of new houses in the form of higher prices. Indeed, the price of housing would have already been increased as a result of constraints on the availability of land for development.

What happens in practice if impact fees are imposed will depend upon the degree of constraint already existing in the property market in the area at the time. There is some evidence to suggest that impact fees have been imposed in US cities when other forms of growth control have been tried and failed (Gyourko 1991). Impact fees have therefore been imposed when the supply of land for development is relatively unconstrained, i.e. when the elasticity of supply of land for development has been high.

This situation is illustrated in Figure 9.1. Quantity of housing is represented on the horizontal axis, and for simplicity it is assumed that all housing is identical. Costs and prices are indicated on the vertical axis. The absence of constraints on the availability of land for development is indicated by the horizontal line AA', agricultural land can be obtained for development in

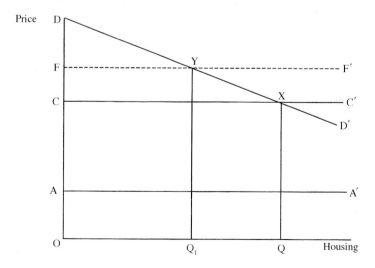

Figure 9.1

the vicinity of the town or city at a cost of OA for each house. The construction cost of a house is represented by AC on the vertical axis, so that the cost of building a house, construction cost plus land cost, is OC on the vertical axis and the unconstrained supply of housing is represented by the horizontal line CC'. The demand for housing is represented by the downward sloping demand curve DD'. This line intersects CC' at X indicating that, in equilibrium, in that period, as indicated on the horizontal axis, OQ houses will be built and sold.

The economic effect of the imposition of an impact fee can be simply represented as an additional cost per house. This raises the horizontal supply curve CC' to a higher level FF'. This intersects the demand curve at Y and so OQ_1 houses will be built and sold. Thus the imposition of the impact fee has resulted in a reduction in the quantity of housing being constructed, one of the possible aims of the tax in some US cities, and raised the cost of housing from OC to OF.

If impact fees were applied in a situation when the supply of land for development, and therefore of housing, was already constrained, as, say, it clearly is in southern England, the position would be as represented in Figure 9.2. The downward sloping demand curve DD' remains, but the amount of housing which can be constructed is fixed at OQ by the planning constraints. In the figure the price of housing is therefore fixed at OP by the intersection of the demand curve with the vertical supply curve, QQ', at P'. The cost of housing construction is indicated on the vertical axis as AC. A

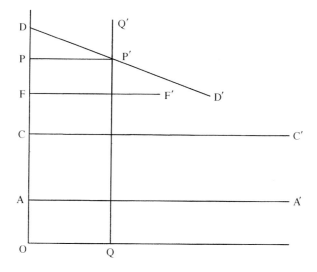

Figure 9.2

developer calculating the amount which could be paid for development land using the residual method would subtract the cost of construction, AC in the figure, from the market price of housing, OP in the figure. The remainder, or residual, OA + CP, indicates the value of the land. Because of the constraints on the availability of land for development this is much, much greater than the price, OA, at which the same land could be bought for agricultural use.

The amount of an impact fee can be represented on the vertical axis by the distance CF. Its imposition serves to reduce the amount which the developer is willing to pay for land to OA + FP. Since this is still substantially greater than OA, it neither affects the amount of development nor the price of housing. Of course, it is possible that the imposition of a large enough impact fee would raise the cost of construction by so much that the amount that the developer would be willing to pay for land would be reduced to a level at or below the price of agricultural land. In these circumstances the quantity of house construction would be affected and the impact fee would be *partially* passed on in higher house prices. In circumstances where the impact fee is not very large and where constraints are tight the normal situation would be, however, that the cost of the impact fee would be borne by the owners of the land in the same way as planning gain.

What the analyses based on Figures 9.1 and 9.2 show is that the economic effect of an impact fee will depend upon the situation. In a small US city, where growth controls have been inoperative or ineffective before the impact fee is imposed, the cost of the fee is likely to be passed on in the form of higher house prices, with the result that housing construction, and hence urban growth, will be slowed. At the opposite end of the planing constraint spectrum, where controls are stringent, operative and effective, as in southern England, neither house prices nor the rate of housing construction would be affected.

Distributional effects

Impact fees will have other economic effects, however, whether in a constrained or an unconstrained situation. In the north American, unconstrained, situation the effect is to favour the existing residents, in particular the existing house owners. As has been shown, when impact fees are introduced in an unconstrained situation they are passed on in the form of higher house prices to the purchasers of new houses. But since existing housing is an almost perfect substitute for new housing, so that the price of the new housing must be competitive with the price of the existing housing, it follows that the imposition of impact fees will result in an increase in the price of existing housing as well as new housing. Existing residents clearly benefit from this since their houses are now worth more, while, of course, new residents do not. There is a further distributional benefit in favour of existing residents. The infrastructure which had to be provided as a consequence of the construction of their homes has been paid for out of general taxation. It is possible, even probable, that some of this infrastructure was loan financed and the loan is still being serviced out of local property taxes. The new residents will therefore not only be paying for the infrastructure associated with their own houses through impact fees but may also be making a contribution to the costs associated with earlier development.

Clearly this redistributional effect in their favour is a reason why existing residents are likely to support the imposition of impact fees if the proposals are put to them. There is a second redistributional reason why existing residents in higher income suburbs and cities are likely to favour impact fees, if the proposal is for a fixed charge per house constructed, as in US cities it frequently is. When the impact fee is passed on in the form of an increase in the price of housing, the result is a greater proportional increase in the price of cheaper, higher density, housing than in the price of more expensive, lower density housing. Thus impact fees will act in a way similar to exclusionary zoning to discourage lower income households from moving into the area. A move to impact fees is in any event regressive since it is a move away from paying for infrastructure through local taxes which are likely to be proportional to property values, and therefore proportional to incomes, and towards the payment of a lump sum per household.

These two redistributive effects will also occur when the supply of land is constrained but, as one might expect, in a much attenuated form. First, although as we have shown, impact fees would not be passed on in the form of higher house prices, nevertheless one result of their imposition would be that the infrastructure costs associated with new housing would be paid for directly, out of the impact fees. The old residents, on the other hand, will still have their share of the infrastructure costs being paid for out of general taxation, and, indeed, if the old infrastructure has been loan financed, the new residents will still find themselves paying towards the cost of servicing the loan.

Second, if the impact fee is a fixed amount per house, the amount paid per acre will be greater when smaller dwellings are to be constructed at a higher density, than when larger dwellings are to be constructed at a low density. As we have shown, if houses are uniform and the supply of land is constrained the imposition of impact fees will reduce the price of land. If houses are not uniform, however, the differential effect outlined above would serve to reduce the price of land for higher density housing by more than the price of land for low density housing. The construction of low density housing would therefore become financially more attractive. If high density development is to remain profitable the price of such housing must rise relative to the price of lower density housing, in order to ensure equality in the prices which developers would pay for different kinds of development. So, although the whole of the cost of the impact fee will not be passed on when land availability is constrained, there will still be a differential effect leading to an increase in the price of smaller dwellings relative to the price of larger. An impact fee would therefore be somewhat regressive in its effects, bearing more on smaller lower income households than on larger, higher income households.

Of course, impact fees do not have to be charged at a fixed rate per house although this happens to be the method used in North American cities. An alternative would be the Italian 'oneri di urbanizzazione' or urbanisation charges, where the charge is approximately proportional to the financial costs of the construction on the site. Clearly this would tend to be less regressive, even possibly slightly progressive, as far as households at different densities are concerned, although it would still tend to favour existing residents over new residents.

Even this effect may be further attenuated if a system of urbanisation charges is applied nationally, as in Italy, rather than by a few cities and suburbs as in the United States. In the latter case the imposition of impact fees raises the costs of new housing in the city relative to other cities where impact fees have not been levied. If fees or charges are imposed on a national basis throughout the whole urban system, then distinctions between old and new residents tend to be less meaningful, if not meaningless. New residents in one town are, after all, likely to be old residents in another. Particularly if there is constraint, so that the price of housing is not affected, the urbanisation charge being borne by the owners of land, any redistributive effect will be negligible. The 'new' residents would have been paying for the infrastructure at their previous residence, so that relocation has relatively little effect.

Nevertheless, it is possible that an urbanisation charge that was proportional to the cost of construction might still be mildly regressive in effect. Housing for poorer households is likely to be built at a higher density so that the cost of construction will be a higher proportion of the final price, and the cost of land a lower proportion. The result will be that the urbanisation charge will still be a higher proportion of their housing cost for poor families, but, of course, the regressive effect would be much, much less than it would be if the charge were the same for all houses, as it is with an impact fee.

Impact fees in the United Kingdom

Should impact fees (or urbanisation charges) be introduced in the United Kingdom? There are certainly strong arguments for replacing the system of negotiated planning obligations by a system in which the amount to be paid is determined and determinate. The strongest is the arbitrary nature of planning gain, the fact that it has to be negotiated with respect to each planning proposal. Moreover, a system similar to the Italian, where the charge is proportional to the cost of construction, would certainly be preferable to a standard impact fee charged in respect of each house, as in North America. Apart from largely eliminating the mildly regressive effects of the latter, set out above, an urbanisation charge can be levied in respect of commercial and industrial development as well as residential. In Italy substantial charges of this kind are levied. For example, Ave (1996, p. 178) cites a charge of 3.5 billion lire (about £1.5 m) as having been made in relation to a retail centre put up outside Turin in 1987.

Certainly an urbanisation charge would ensure that something was paid towards the cost of infrastructure even where the bargaining position of the developer was strong because permission was very likely to be granted. It would, therefore, avoid the problem created by the quasi-voluntary nature of planning gain, in that the amount agreed to be paid depends upon the relative bargaining positions, and abilities, of local authorities and developers. As we showed in Chapter 8 the amount volunteered by the developer is likely to be greatest when the probability of being awarded permission is lowest, and least when the probability is highest.

There are, however, two major problems with changing the current system. The first is a consequence of the system of local government finance operating in the United Kingdom. As we have mentioned before, this system is deliberately set up to ensure that any increase in the revenue accruing to a local government will be balanced by a reduction in the grant from central government. It is also designed to ensure that any decrease in an authority's responsibilities will also be compensated by a reduction in its grant. The laudable intention is that local authorities get larger grants if their resources are lower or the needs of their population perceived to be greater. The effect is to ensure the kind of neutrality which we have noted.

But, again as we have already noted, planning gain is not taken into account in the calculation of the central government grant because it results from free, informal, unregulated negotiation between local authorities and developers. Moreover, the benefits derived from planning gain by a local authority are frequently not even expressed in money terms, but may, for example, be the transfer of the ownership of some land to the local authority to be used as a public park. Because of this, it is impossible to adjust the central government grant to take the income from planning gain into account and any benefits derived from planning gain accrue, gross, without any deduction, to the local authority and its population. But if negotiated planning gain were replaced by a system of impact fees or urbanisation charges, the local authorities would receive financial payments which could be tabulated, accounted for, and even, to some extent predicted. For example, if it is expected, indeed planned, that a local authority will permit 2000 houses to be built in its area in the next year, then it can also be expected, and planned for, that the authority will receive the impact fees associated with these houses. So, central government can also plan to give smaller grants to local authorities receiving larger amounts in impact fees, that is, it can make government grants as neutral with respect to impact fees as they are with respect to every other form of income. It can be easily seen that local authorities will prefer the present situation, while central government might prefer a system of impact fees or urbanisation charges. It follows that any proposal to change over to a system of fixed charges would be fought by the local authorities, particularly those in the more prosperous parts of the country where planning gain may be large.

The second problem is that the situation as regards land prices and planning constraints varies substantially between one part of the United Kingdom and another. A nationally uniform system of urbanisation charges would therefore have different effects in different parts of the country. In most of England, particularly southern England, planning constraints prevail, and an urbanisation charge would primarily be borne by the owners of land. But in parts of northern England, parts of Scotland and Wales, and most of Northern Ireland planning constraints are not tightly enforced, and any charge would tend to be passed on in an increase in the price of buildings, whether residential, commercial, or industrial.

But it is often in these areas that development is being encouraged because incomes are lower and unemployment higher than in the southern part of the country. Indeed, it is because there is a lack of development, and in order to encourage development that the availability of land for development is not constrained. So, while urbanisation charges would have advantages in some areas, there would be political and economic disadvantages in applying them in areas where the demand for development is low, and where development is otherwise to be encouraged. In these areas also one would therefore find that proposals for a uniform system would be opposed.

Developer contributions and environmental impact fees

It is still not impossible that a uniform system of charges might be imposed. It might still be seen as politically advantageous. This appears to have been the situation in Australia where provisions for 'developer contributions' were introduced by individual states. The position with respect to land supply is much closer to the North American than the British in that land use is relatively unconstrained. Nevertheless, the developer charges were introduced in towns and cities in the 1950s and 1960s at a time of rapid urban growth. There is, thus, no similar argument that the contributions were being imposed by, and on behalf of, higher income households in higher income areas to reduce urban growth and to exclude lower income households. What appears to have happened initially is that because governments were unable to pay for the extension of public services to sites, developers offered to pay the cost. In that way the development could be carried out immediately without having to wait for govenment to service the site (Neutze 1977, p. 209; 1997 p. 124).

Developer contributions continued after the rate of urban growth slowed down, largely because it had become a source of funds and it was difficult to turn the clock back. There was, of course, still a redistributive element to the charges when they were introduced. The older generation who already owned their homes gained at the expense of the younger, or at the expense of immigrants in the case of Australia at that time. Of course, the redistributional position is complicated by the probable eventual inheritance of the older generation's now more valuable housing by the younger. The outright losers are therefore likely to be the immigrants from elsewhere and the gainers emigrants to other countries. However, they have now been in operation for many years and the redistributive element has virtually disappeared. Indeed, if developer contributions were now to be dropped the redistributive effects would be reversed. There would then be a redistribution in favour of the new house owners at the expense of the old. Since existing house owners are in a stronger political position this makes it unlikely that they will ever be dropped.

The introduction of developer contributions in Australia, in a relatively egalitarian society, indicates that there are no strong political reasons why a system of charges should not come to the United Kingdom. The main reason, of course, as we have stressed, is that the deliberately resource neutral system of financing local government in Britain means that the local governments have no reason to lobby for any new source of income since this would be removed by central government. On the other hand, given the tendency to central control in Britain, there is a strong possibility that central government might set out to regularise the position. A politically acceptable argument for doing so would be the fact that the main gainers from the current system are local authorities in the more prosperous, and higher income south, while authorities in the less prosperous, and lower income, north are considerably less able to extract substantial planning obligations from developers (Campbell *et al.*, 2000). There is therefore a very strong argument based on equity to bring the system under central control to ensure that the poorer areas are better resourced.

A further argument for a more centralised system was put by the Urban Task Force chaired by the architect Richard Rogers (Urban Task Force 1999). They approached the problem from a somewhat different point of view, however. Rather than being concerned with the infrastructure requirements necessitated by a development they were more concerned with the development's impact on the environment, so that the fees that they suggested were to be called Environmental Impact Fees (Urban Task Force 1999, pp. 221–3).

They indicated that such fees should cover 'wider environmental impacts which are not currently taken into account within the existing system of planning obligations and planning gain'. They suggested that these would include:

    '– loss of countryside and landscape;
    – damage to biodiversity;
    – impacts on historic and cultural resources;
    – soil erosion and loss.' (p. 222).

These are clearly 'once-off' environmental costs resulting from the development and would be suitably covered by an impact fee which was also paid on a once-off basis at the time of the development. Unfortunately also included in the list of environmental impacts given by the Task Force were two which were not 'once-off' and better dealt with in other ways. These were:

    '– increased air pollution caused by increased road traffic use;
    – increases in energy consumption and greenhouse gas emissions.'

These environmental impacts are difficult to predict, continuing, and occur with respect to existing development as well as new development. They should therefore be dealt with, and be being dealt with, through other forms of control and taxation. To make an additional charge for new development in respect of these externalities would therefore be 'double counting' and inefficient.

The same argument applies at least in part to a further environmental impact which the Task Force lists:

'– pressures on waste and waste management systems.'

When such pressures are continuing they would best be dealt with through current taxation or prices. Only the capital cost of constructing additional off-site facilities might be covered by an impact fee, one of a conventional kind which covers the cost of infrastructure.

It is perhaps unfortunate that the Task Force muddled the various kinds of impact together, but then its report is characterised by a certain economic naivety resulting from the fact that there was no economist among its members and virtually none amongst its advisers. Nevertheless, let us suppose that the proposals of the Task Force were suitably refined and implemented. Implementation would raise some interesting questions. The first relates to the distribution of the proceeds. Should they go to local government or to central government? The Task Force suggests that most of the revenue should 'be recycled through the Regional Development Agency to secure further regeneration objectives on behalf of the region'. Apart from the fact that the Task Force was itself concerned with urban regeneration there seems no clear reason why the region should be the area which benefits, rather than the locality or the nation. On the other hand if most of the fee accrued to the local authority it would have an incentive to grant planning permission, while if most accrued to central or regional government it would have almost no incentive.

The second question is more fundamental and goes to the heart of the British planning system. The Task Force appears to envisage environmental impact fees as being an addition to the system of planning constraints which are currently in existence. But if the impact fees covered the costs of the environmental impact of any development and all the infrastructure that it necessitated the question must be raised as to the way in which the system of constraint should then be operated. Planning constraints are imposed, presumably, because it is thought that permitting further development would have an unacceptable environmental impact. As we have shown, the constraints, if demand is high enough, then result in increases in the value of land with planning permission for development. As a result it is used intensively, just as it would be if its cost had been raised by the imposition of an environmental impact fee.

But suppose a charge were levied which covered the full environmental impact of a development. This would imply or herald a shift from a system of planning constraints to control the impact of a development to a system based on taxes. Suppose that the environmental impact was correctly measured by the fee, but that the system of constraints had resulted in the value of land with planning permission being significantly higher, so high that a developer would be able to pay the environmental impact fee, pay the cost of off-site infrastructure, pay a reasonable price for the land to its owner, and still make a profit. What reason would there then be for refusing planning permission? Logically it would be clear that the social benefit exceeded the social cost, and special, overriding reasons would have to be found to refuse permission. Since land values are higher in the south of Britain than in the north, the implication would be that more development would be permitted in the south.

On the other hand, and this raises a third question, the cost of the environmental impact is likely to be more or less the same in the north as in the south. After all, despite a great deal of political noise to suggest the opposite, the southern English regions are less urbanised than some, though not all, northern regions. The implication is then that in many parts of the country where there is low demand the level of the environmental impact fee would be so high as to deter development, since paying it would more than eliminate any profit. Thus, development would be discouraged on environmental grounds in regions where, for political reasons, development has been encouraged.

The implication of this argument is that the land use policies that are in operation are not solely concerned with land use. Both politicians and the electorate are aware, if only at some implicit, subconscious, level, that land use planning policies are used as tools of regional policy to discourage industry in more prosperous regions and encourage it in less prosperous regions, but this is rarely made explicit. When it was made explicit, in the late 1980s, as we shall show in Chapter 11, the disadvantages were also made explicit and the use of land use planning as an *explicit* regional policy disappeared from the agenda.

Summary and conclusions

In this chapter we have discussed ways in which the planning obligations or planning gain discussed in the previous chapter can be formalised into the payment of impact fees or developer contributions. The payment of a fixed amount per dwelling, as occurs in many American cities or suburbs, has been shown to be advantageous to the existing inhabitants, and to raise the price of housing in these cities. It has also been shown to be regressive. Where planning constraints have restricted the supply of development land, as in southern England, the payment of impact fees of this kind would not increase the price of housing and would only have a very weak regressive effect. A fee which was a percentage of the value of the development rather than a fixed amount per dwelling would not even have a regressive effect. We note that the Urban Task Force has suggested that not only should the cost of infrastructure be covered by impact fees or planning obligations, so also should the environmental impact of the development. We show that if this were to happen the planning system would have shifted from a control-based system to a tax-based system of dealing with external diseconomies, and that this would have implications for the way in which it was thought about and operated.

10

The Economic Consequences of Higher Land Values

'Our remedies oft in ourselves do lie,
which we ascribe to heaven'
(All's Well That Ends Well)

Introduction

In previous chapters we have discussed the effects of planning constraints. We have shown that physical planning controls which restrict the availability of land for particular land uses have the economic effect that the price of such land will be higher than it would have been if the land market had operated without intervention. This economic effect has seemed to be unintended, certainly by planners operating in terms of the physical distribution of activities and land uses and regarding differences in land values as not a planning matter.

We showed in earlier chapters that this increase in the value of land may accrue to several economic actors, not just to the owner of the land. Our interest in this chapter, however, is not with the question of who gets the increase in value, but with the effects which this increase in the value of land has on the way that the land is used. If the increase in the value of land was unforeseen and unintended by planners, then these consequential effects will also have been largely unintended and unforeseen. But if land is made more expensive as a factor of production then, from the application of standard economic analysis, we would expect users to respond by trying both to use it more intensively and to substitute for its use other goods and factors of production. Thus the increase in land values will affect the physical use of land. Through the market the unanticipated effects of physical controls will have physical effects which should be a matter of concern to planners.

In Chapter 7, on green belts and growth boundaries, much of the evidence related to South Korea and to the United States, since the economic effects had been reported most fully in these countries. In this chapter most of the evidence relates to Great Britain, and in particular to southern England. Apart from the personal interest of the author in this area, a reason for this is that the increases in land values as a result of planning constraints have probably been greatest here, as the controls laid down in the 1940s and 1950s have been maintained and extended over the years. Most importantly the land use planning system has increasingly come to be seen, over the past 20 or 30 years, as a means of protecting the countryside. Thus, it has not been as though there have been green belts around London and other cities, and that permission could easily be obtained for the development of rural land outside these green belts. Planning policies have been designed by local authorities to try to prevent any development in these rural areas, which are seen as the remnants of the countryside left by the ravages of urban development. In fact, less than 20% of the land even in south-east England is urban but this is not the general perception. The reasons for the difference between perception and rurality are not our concern here, though I have discussed them elsewhere (Evans 1991, 2001). What concerns us here are the consequences of the policies with respect to the towns not the reasons for them in the perceived need to protect the countryside.

Land use policies and land prices

The nature of the land use policies pursued in southern England is indicated in Table 10.1. This is a list of policies in the late 1980s and early 1990s drawn from the structure plans of the counties to the west of London – Berkshire, Buckinghamshire, Hampshire, Oxfordshire and Surrey, and they indicate areas where housing would not usually be permitted. The list is, perhaps, over inclusive, since a policy need only appear in the plan of one county to be included in the list so that not every policy is operative in every county. Nevertheless, as a list, it indicates the strength and inclusiveness of the policies pursued in this part of southern England to restrict the expansion of urban areas, the creation of new ones, or even, indeed particularly, any isolated housing. It is unlikely that any but a very few sites would miss being covered by one or more of these policies, which could then be quoted as a reason for refusing permission for development.

Only in the 1990s did the existence of an overall policy of restricting development on 'green field' sites become explicit, with political parties vying with each other as to which could be more restrictive and which

Table 10.1   Land not available for housing: a typology.

General	Heritage, natural history and countryside
1 Developed land including transport land	17 Agricultural, horticutural and forestry land
2 Land scheduled for other uses	18 Local nature reserves
3 Presumptions against development outside of the existing built-up areas except for infill, rounding off and redevelopment	19 Other sites of natural importance
	20 Historic parks and gardens
	21 Archaeological sites
	22 Landscape features
4 No coalescence of sporadic or dispersed settlements	23 National Trust land
	24 Specific river valleys, canals, etc.
Statutorily designated areas	**Miscellaneous**
5 Green belt	25 Public recreation land
6 Areas of outstanding natural beauty (AONBs)	26 Mineral workings and commitments
	27 Polluted land
7 Sites of special scientific interest (SSSIs)	28 Waste disposal sites
	29 Areas liable to flood
8 National nature reserves	30 Water safeguarding areas
9 Common land	31 Air safeguarding areas
Locally designated areas	**Government land**
10 Areas beyond the green belt	32 Ministry of Defence land
11 Areas of great landscape value	33 Crown land
12 Areas of high ecological importance	
13 Settlements and their setting	
14 Gaps between settlements	
15 Green corridors and spaces	
16 Areas of urban landscape quality	

could therefore ensure that the most housing could be built on 'brown field' sites. By this time also it had been more or less conceded that constraints on the availability of land for development would result in higher land values and higher house prices. Nevertheless, the policies of constraint were put forward with little if any acknowledgement that this would be their effect. Given the current explicit policy of overall constraint, the results of the policies which were put into effect earlier with respect to housing and house prices are of even greater interest, since they had the effect of overall constraint, even if it was not explicitly intended.

The effect on land values of the policies pursued is indicated in Table 10.2. The table, for which the data are taken from Inland Revenue records of land sales, shows the price of land in agricultural use in the south-east of England compared with the price of land for residential and industrial use. It can be seen that the price of land in an urban use is substantially greater than its price in agricultural use. It would appear that obtaining planning permission for housing on a hectare of land held as an agricultural smallholding

Table 10.2   Land values in south-east England (outside London).

Agricultural, mixed farming	£8900
Industrial (from £225 000 to £2 400 000)	Typical: £1 200 000
Residential: regional average for sites in excess of two hectares	£2 490 000

Source: *Property Market Report, Autumn 2003* (London: Valuation Office).

could, theoretically convert the owner into a millionaire (although as we showed in Chapter 8 the million would have, in practice, to be shared with a number of others of which, most importantly, central government would take a large share in taxes).

Care should anyway be exercised in considering figures which represent the price of land since the cost of infrastructure may, or may not, be included and may be substantial so that the true 'price of land' may be difficult to assess. We have referred before to the figures given by Needham (1992) with respect to the Dutch system in the early 1980s. These figures suggest that if the market price of agricultural land were about 2 DFl per square metre, as it was at that time, then this land might be bought from the farmer for about 4 DFl by the local authority, the prime mover under the Dutch system. Once basic infrastructure had been installed the price would rise substantially to about 50 DFl if it were to be sold to a developer, and after further work by the developer the price of a (serviced) site for a house would be about 100 DFl per square metre. Each of these prices could be correctly quoted as the price of land. Nevertheless, the figures suggest that a market price of £100 000 per acre for vacant land but serviced with infrastructure would be compatible with an agricultural price of less than £5000 per acre. But Needham's figures do confirm that prices substantially in excess of £100 000 per acre would appear to be the result of planning constraints on the availability of land.

Further evidence of the effect of the planning system on the price of land is given in Figure 10.1 (Cheshire & Sheppard 2000). This shows an index of the price of land for the construction of housing over a period of more than 100 years. The figures are indicative rather than exact, first because figures from two different sources are put together, and second because the indices are constructed from a possibly biased sample of land price data not from the complete set. However, the graph does indicate that the price of land for housing in England appeared to remain reasonably stable in real terms for nearly a century preceding

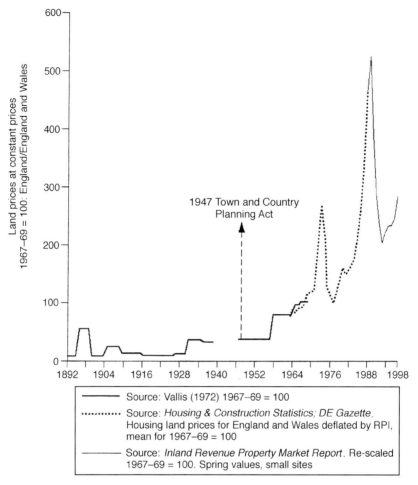

Figure 10.1 Residential building land prices at constant prices: 1892–1998 (Cheshire & Sheppard 2000).

the Town and Country Planning Act 1947, but that prices have risen substantially, if irregularly, since then.

Evidence for the most recent period relating to southern England is given in Figure 10.2. This is drawn from evidence relating to all transactions and published by the Department of the Environment. The figure shows graphs of the indices of the price of housing land, house prices, and incomes for south-east England outside Greater London, as well as the graph of the national retail price index. The figure covers the period from 1969 to 1998 and thus covers the two major house price booms, one in the early 1970s, the other in the late 1980s, as well as the minor boom around 1979/80. Despite the significant price fall after 1989, it can be seen that both land

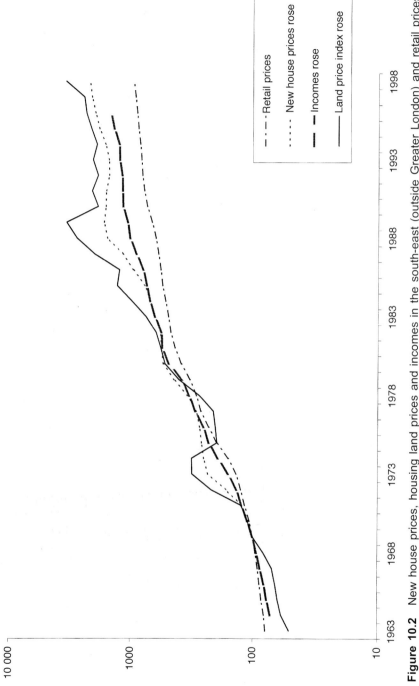

Figure 10.2 New house prices, housing land prices and incomes in the south-east (outside Greater London) and retail prices (national). Source: *Housing & Construction Statistics, Family Expenditure Survey, Economic Trends.*

prices and house prices have risen by more than other prices, that is these prices have risen in real terms. Moreover, they have risen by more than household incomes.

Adjustment in the housing market

The data presented in the figures in the previous section show that the price of land for housing has increased since the introduction of the British planning system in 1947 and has continued to increase. The rate of increase has, of course, been variable, and there were falls in real terms at the end of each boom and a fall even in nominal terms in the early 1990s when the rate of general price inflation was low.

We would expect consumers to react to this substantial increase in the price of housing and in this section we show how they have responded in various ways to the change in circumstances. One reaction to the increase in prices is demonstrated in Table 10.3, which shows on the right-hand side a weighted index of house prices in the rest of the south-east (i.e. the south-east excluding Greater London). This index is constructed in a manner similar to most price indexes that assume that a constant basket of commodities is being purchased. In this case it is assumed that the mix of house types being bought remains the same over time. The left-hand side, on the other hand, shows, again as an index, the average price of houses sold in the area.

If prices remained constant while incomes increased we would expect an income effect to predominate. People would buy larger and more expensive houses, on average, over time, because their increased incomes gave them greater purchasing power. On the other hand, if house prices rose while incomes and prices otherwise remained the same, we would expect a price effect to dominate as people, on average, purchased smaller homes. In the first case the (unweighted) index of the price of houses actually sold would rise faster than the weighted index of house prices. In the second case the reverse would be true, the (unweighted) index of the price of houses sold would fall relative to the weighted index of house prices.

What Table 10.3 shows is that over most of the period, up to the end of the boom in 1989, the price effect dominated. Although people's incomes increased they responded to the even more rapid increase in land and house prices by reducing the size of the houses that they purchased. The position only changed during the 1990s, as house prices fell in both nominal and real terms for the first time for over 40 years, and did so, moreover, over a period

Table 10.3 Weighted and unweighted house price indices (rest of the south-east (1975 = 100)).

Year	Unweighted	Weighted
1975	100	100
1976	106	107
1977	112	114
1978	129	133
1979	168	177
1980	203	214
1981	204	224
1982	202	226
1983	230	256
1984	255	290
1985	276	320
1986	331	378
1987	391	461
1988	495	598
1989	557	691
1990	549	634
1991	539	600
1992	507	558
1993	509	535
1994	530	563
1995	533	568
1996	597	584
1997	647	671
1998	725	754
1999	829	843
2000	974	1006

Source: DoE, *Housing & Construction Statistics*, 1984–1994, Tables 10.8 and 10.9. DTLR, *Housing Statistics 2000*, Tables 5.5 and 5.6.

of years. During the early 1990s, therefore, as prices fell and incomes continued to rise, people could afford to buy larger houses and did so, as the narrowing of the gap between the two indices shows. What one does not see over the period is any evidence that people were able to use their higher incomes to buy bigger houses. The evidence is, in fact, that people were forced to trade down, and that over the period up to 1990 the increase in the price of housing considerably outweighed any income effect. Even after the fall in the price of housing in the 1990s the situation was that the price increase which had occurred over the whole period just outweighed the large income effect which would have otherwise been evident. People could buy, on average, no larger houses at the end of the period than they could at the beginning.

Thus, generally, over most of the period, people responded to the increase in house prices by, in effect, trading down. This resulted in an inter-generational transfer for the owner occupied sector. Once one generation had bought their homes they perceived any increase in house prices as being to their advantage, since the capital at their disposal was now greater. But, of course, later generations could buy less, and the process of trading down occurred over successive generations, the trend being for each to be able to buy a little less than that preceding. Only in the mid-1970s, because house prices rose by less than other prices, and in the early 1990s, because house prices actually fell, was this not true. The process of house price inflation also resulted in a redistribution between those in the rented sector whose costs rose, and those in the owner occupied sector, whose wealth increased.

Builders and developers responded to the increase in land prices by economising in their use of land. The figures in Figure 10.3 show that in 1969 26% of the dwellings mortgaged by building societies in England and Wales were bungalows, while only 3% were flats and apartments. By 1994 the proportions had almost reversed with only 6% of the dwellings mortgaged being bungalows, and 13% being flats.

It might be argued that this change in the pattern of house construction was due to changing demand, in particular an increasing number of small households might be expected to want more flats and apartments. Again, the declining output of the public housing sector during the period, in which large numbers of flats had previously been constructed, might also lead to an increased demand for flats in the private sector. The evidence on price trends for the different types of dwelling tends to refute these hypotheses. If changes in demand had resulted in a higher demand for smaller dwellings then one would have expected that, say, the prices of apartments would have increased more than the prices of larger dwellings. In fact, the reverse is the case. Figure 10.4 shows that the average price of a new bungalow increased by more than the average price of an apartment or a terrace house. The increases in price of these and other types of house appear to show that the larger the land input into the house the greater the price rise (Evans 1988, 1991). Thus, the price changes do not appear to be the result of changes on the demand side, but on the supply side. The increase in land prices seems to have induced changes in relative prices which have led people to switch away from buying housing which uses land extensively and towards buying housing which uses it intensively.

The data in Figure 10.3 and used in the paragraph above relate to the whole of England and Wales since this is the form in which it is available. But as we have said, the constraints on the availability of land were more stringent in southern England where the demand was greatest. The changes in the type of housing which was constructed therefore varied in practice between different parts of the country. Table 10.4 shows figures collected from house

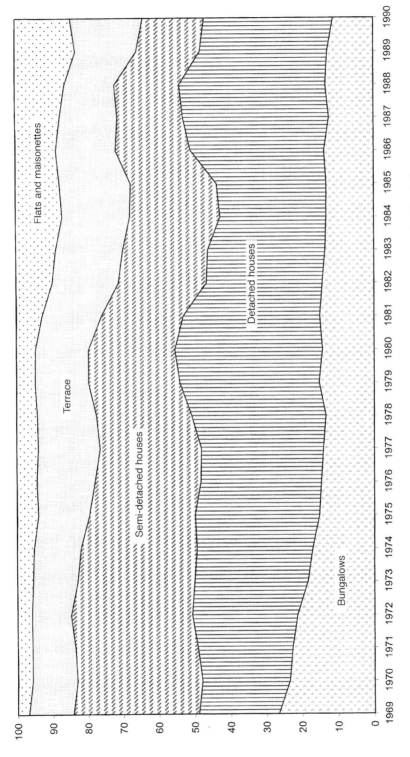

Figure 10.3 Distribution of different types of dwelling mortgaged. Source: *Housing & Construction Statistics.*

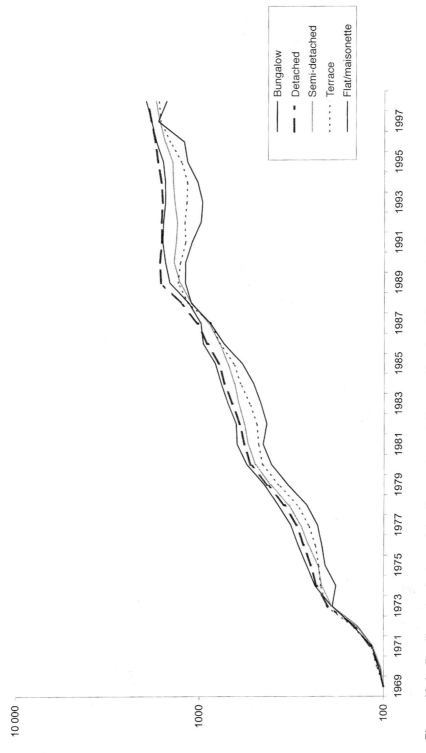

Figure 10.4 Dwelling price by type of dwelling mortgaged. Source: *Housing & Construction Statistics*.

Table 10.4   Dwelling types started in 1990, by region (percentage).

	House type				
	Bungalows	Detached	Semi-detached	Terrace	Flats and maisonettes
North	14	37	16	13	21
North-west	10	45	20	10	15
Yorks and Humberside	20	38	17	12	14
West Midlands	7	38	18	21	16
East Midlands	10	41	25	16	8
East Anglia	11	34	17	27	12
South-west	8	28	14	30	21
South-east (ex-GLA)	5	27	12	25	32
Greater London	3	4	5	22	67

Source: *National House-building Statistics, 1990*, Table 6.

builders by the National House Building Council relating to housing starts in 1990 in different regions. At that date, at the end of the long 1980s housing boom, the difference between land prices in different parts of the country was greatest. The table shows that in the northern regions of England where land prices were lower a substantial proportion of new dwellings were bungalows while relatively few were being built in southern England. On the other hand, in the south, even outside Greater London, a high proportion of the new housing being started was in the form of flats, maisonettes and terraces or town houses, and this was not true in the regions where land prices were lower. This was particularly so in Northern Ireland where, because controls were extremely light (as they also were in the Republic), about a quarter of the houses built were even then single storey bungalows (Adair *et al.*, 1991).

Other changes also occurred in the housing market which can be explained as being induced by increasing land values although the evidence is more anecdotal and less supportable by data because the data are not available. One such change was a reduction in the amount of space allocated to garden or yard space. Just as a greater proportion of flats were constructed relative to houses, to economise on land costs, so a smaller area of land was used for garden space where houses were constructed. It is very noticeable that in southern England the garden space attached to new houses appears to have increased during the first half of the twentieth century, and then gradually decreased during the second half.

Another change which was associated with this one, and also therefore a consequence of the increase in the price of land, has been a tendency to extend suburban houses where this has been possible. Once again this has been a method of using land more intensively, of increasing the capital invested per acre, in other words the substitution of a cheaper factor of production for one that has become more expensive. Once again this trend has been most noticeable in south-east England, in this case particularly in the suburbs of Greater London where the change in land values since the houses were constructed in the 1920s and 1930s has been greatest.

The operation of the economic incentives to extend has often been indirect, however. For example, a household living in an older house might seek to move to a larger one as either income or family or both increased in size. Looking around it would be seen that newer houses of the type that they wanted seemed to have less garden space than they were used to in the house they currently occupied, and which they wanted to continue to enjoy. A calculation would suggest that an older house, probably indeed their existing house, could be extended to increase its size, and that this would not significantly, if at all, reduce the size of the garden. For example, an additional bedroom and possibly an additional bathroom could be built over the adjoining single storey garage.

The extension of an existing house was therefore correctly perceived often to be a cheaper option than moving and buying another house, particularly a new house. For example, a three-bed, one bathroom, house might cost £220 000 but could be extended at a cost of £80 000 to become a four-bed, two-bathroom, house, whereas buying a new four-bed two-bath house would cost at least as much as this and it would have a much smaller garden. As households individually made these calculations and came up with similar answers, whole streets gradually changed as each of the houses, one after another, was extended, and some houses (my own, for example, by myself and an earlier owner) were extended two or three times.

The determination to use space intensively and, in particular, the need to economise on the use of land while at the same time providing what buyers wanted led also to some innovatory ground plans on the part of residential developers. Increasing incomes, associated with increased car ownership, meant that more people wanted detached houses, with garages and garden space, while the economic forces of constraint worked, of course, in the opposite direction. House builders wanted to meet this demand while still economising on land. One method used was to provide three or four houses on a site but with, in effect, a communal driveway. If the open space in front of each of the houses was not fenced off, then the driveway and this open space, being shared in whole or in part, became part of the usable space for all of them. Aesthetically this approach was often pleasing. Less pleasing was the solution occasionally adopted of locating the garage to each house as a separate block in front of it. By putting the garages in front of the houses, instead of between them, the house builder succeeded in supplying detached houses which would otherwise have been, with the garages placed between the houses, terraces or, at best, semi-detached. But the view along a road developed in such a fashion was usually most unattractive since it was dominated by the sides of the garages. Moreover, it could not be said that the view from the house towards the road was attractive either, since it also was dominated by the garage in front of the house.

Another approach which might be adopted was to locate the front of the house close to the road, reducing the front garden to the minimum possible size, but maximising the size of the back garden. In order to allow a car to stand off the road, however, a feature of this design would be that the garage beside the house would be set back from the road, also in this way reducing the appearance of terracing since the frontage of the houses was more broken than it would otherwise have been.

All of these are ways in which the use of land is intensified, but where the way in which market forces are operating is not immediately evident. Of course, there are also more conventional and more obvious ways. Houses with large gardens may be bought up and demolished to be replaced by apartment blocks or a row of town houses. When it is physically possible because of its location the owners of a house with a large garden may sell it off for development keeping the house themselves, or, more probably, selling it and moving away to avoid the opprobrium of their neighbours. Of course, developers will themselves seek out and painstakingly acquire and put together pieces of land which can be developed. For example, a developer over many years may acquire the ends of a number of long gardens in order to put together a large enough site. At the end of the 1980s, when land values were at their highest some developers rented helicopters to allow them to fly over suburban areas in order to identify possible development sites.

In seeking out sites the pressure to intensify the use of land has not only applied to land which has already been developed for housing. At the end of the 1980s, particularly, the owners of playing fields or of garden allotments might be asked to sell their land for development and might often do so. Here the undesirable physical results caused by economic forces set in motion by physical planning controls are at their most evident. The protection of open space outside the urban area in the form of controls preventing development in the countryside causes, paradoxically, the building over of open space within the urban area where it is in short supply.

Commercial and other uses

The economic forces leading to the intensification of land use operate with respect to uses other than housing, as the price of land and of space is raised for commercial, leisure, and industrial uses. Table 10.5 presents evidence on the cost of land in various parts of the United Kingdom. Once again the price of land is particularly high in the south, but the prices of land for different uses do not vary uniformly in the same way. So, the price of land for industrial development falls to lower levels in northern England than its price in other uses, and this is probably due to differences in attitudes towards new industrial development. Cheshire *et al.* (1985) found that in the early 1980s the price of land for industrial use in north-east England was also low and appeared to be close to the level that would represent the cost of agricultural land plus the cost of infrastructure. This was because a policy of advance construction of factory space in the area was pursued, one of several policies intended to reduce unemployment in the area. The price of land may also vary not only because of differences in the degree of constraint on the supply side but also because of differences on the demand side. So, Cheshire *et al.* found that the price of land for offices in Darlington, in the north-east, was very low, but this was not surprising given that there seemed to be no demand for offices in the town and none were being constructed at the time.

Table 10.5   Typical land values by region, autumn 1998.

	Industrial and warehouse (£'000)	Offices, R&D and light industry (Class B.1)[1] (£'000)	Residential (large sites) (£'000)
North-east	140	193	1 010
North-west and Merseyside	304	527	1 010[2]
Yorkshire and Humberside	330	600	870
East Midlands	464	586	1 260
West Midlands	468	613	1 440
South-west	557	650	1 720
Eastern	834	821	2 660
South-east	1 194	1 660	2 490
Wales	201	319	980
Scotland	204	494	920

Source: *Property Market Report, Autumn 2002* (London: Valuation Office).

[1] Class B.1 is, strictly, land for a building for use as an office other than for financial and professional services, for research and development of products or processes or for an industrial process which can be carried out in a residential area without detriment to the amenity of that area.
[2] This is an average of the figure for the North-west (£1 180 000) and that for Merseyside (£840 000).

The identification of the effects of the higher cost of land and space in England and in different parts of England is more difficult in the case of industrial and commercial uses because other policies may also affect land uses, and also because significant changes occur on the demand side that do not similarly occur with respect to housing. So the cost of land may change and vary over time because conditions change, and social or technological changes cause demand or supply to alter. For example, during the 1980s it was evident that constraints on the availability of shopping space, in particular supermarkets, led to the space which was available being used far more intensively than in France or the USA. Cheshire *et al.* (1985) found that in the early 1980s the price of land for retail use was £2.5 million per acre in Reading, England, but only about £100 000 per acre in what they regarded as an equivalent town, Stockton, in California. Not surprisingly the effects of such substantial price differences could be seen in the way space was used in England – queues were longer at the checkouts, car parking was more congested, aisles were narrower and there was more congestion within the stores. In effect, in order to pay the higher rent, turnover per square foot had to be higher. The position changed, sharply in some cases, at the beginning of the 1990s for two entirely different reasons. In the first place, a number of planning applications for large supermarkets were approved, some of which had been in the pipeline for many years. At more or less the same time moral and legal opposition to late night opening and to Sunday opening collapsed and the major supermarket chains kept their stores open for far longer. The result was that the increased supply of space and the fact that the same turnover could be achieved in a longer period of time led to a considerable reduction in the level of congestion in British stores. The major difference between Britain and France became the physical one that aisles remained narrower in Britain.

The intensification of land use may be most evident, as with housing, in the way that more intensive uses may take over space from less intensive uses, but, once again, it may be difficult to distinguish the effects of changes in demand from the consequences of economic forces since, anyway, the two may work together. During the 1960s and 1970s both could be seen to operate with respect to the use of land for leisure activities. For example, greyhound racing tracks and large cinemas are an extensive use of land and during the 1960s and 1970s one use was virtually eliminated and the other declined in number with those that remained being turned into multi-screen operations. But then multiplex cinemas were being built at that time in the United States, as they were in the 1990s in the UK so the changes could simply be attributed to social changes. This was not so evident, however, with respect to the frequent newspaper stories of schemes to redevelop the grounds of well known football teams such as Queens Park

Rangers or Fulham (both in west London), and, with rather less publicity, the actual redevelopment of lesser known clubs whether League, such as Brighton, or non-League, such as Wealdstone. Given the increasing popularity of football as a spectator sport during the period these schemes could not be seen as driven by declining demand, except to the extent that the demand was not sufficient to cover the increasing opportunity cost of the clubs' grounds.

With respect to some space-using activities demand has increased and a switch to a less intensive use has not been possible so that the result is an increase in the price. This is most obvious with respect to restaurants and hotels. It is evident, on any comparison, that the price of a meal and the price of a hotel room will both tend to be higher in England than across the Channel or the Atlantic. A major cause of this is that the cost of space is greater in England and part of the payment for the room or the meal is a payment for this space, which therefore has to be higher than elsewhere.

With respect to manufacturing, the evidence has again to be based on casual empiricism. What appears to have happened, and which was particularly evident in the late 1980s, has been the displacement of a less intensive use like manufacturing by other uses. Thus as the price of land for housing rose faster than the price of land for manufacturing local authorities in the south seemed usually to be willing to give permission for a change in the use of the land to residential, or, sometimes, commercial use. This was, of course, logical, if manufacturing as a land use was perceived as creating greater diseconomies than residential or office use. The redevelopment of a manufacturing site adjacent to housing would seem to be clearly beneficial from a planning point of view. Thus, manufacturing uses were displaced, particularly from southern England, with production being shifted elsewhere, if the site were operated by a large firm, or resulting in the firm's closure if it was occupied by a small firm. In both cases, of course, production was anyway transferred to another location whether within the same firm's operations or outside it, and either elsewhere in the UK or abroad.

The problems caused to manufacturing firms in southern England because of both a shortage of land for their own use and a shortage of housing for their employees was at one point in the late 1980s mentioned as being a sort of regional policy, expected to encourage employment away from southern England to other parts of the UK where land and housing were cheaper and unemployment was higher. So, in 1987 Nicholas Ridley, then Secretary of State for the Environment, wrote in *The Guardian* of 20 March 1987 that:

because we and the local planning authorities are maintaining tighter planning controls in the South East, fully aware of the political pressures, development land prices in the South East have risen to very high levels. Industry and commerce not only face high prices if they want to build and develop on land; they also face high prices and a shortage of labour as housing costs are high and housing is in short supply. So there is already a strong cost incentive for businesses to look outside the prosperous points of the South East to locate elsewhere and the signs are that this is exactly what they are doing.

Margaret Thatcher, the Prime Minister, made a similar statement in an interview on BBC television on 24 July 1987, concentrating, in her case, on house price differences, and saying that 'you will find differences in house prices between north and south will be the thing which persuades more companies to move north'.

The period during which statements of this kind were made was very brief. In November 1987 Lord Young, Secretary of State for Trade and Industry, denied that there was any policy of using land and house prices to encourage companies to move north. Presumably the government's economic advisers had pointed out that any relocation of jobs or firms away from southern England would not necessarily be to somewhere else in the UK but could equally well be to a location on the other side of the Channel, which would be as close, if not closer, and where the cost of space and of housing would be even cheaper.

In recent years planning policy has again become a kind of regional policy, once again unacknowledged. This is because the aim, since the late 1990s, has been to ensure that most new housing is built on 'brownfield' land, not on greenfield sites. The problem is that the demand is for housing in the south while most of the derelict and vacant land which the policy focuses upon is located in the north (Kivell 1993, p. 152). While the aim may be laudable, the policy has been set out solely in physical terms, with little understanding or interest in the economic means through which the policy can be effected. The implication of the policy is that unsatisfied demand will cause house prices and land prices to rise in the south. As house prices rise, immigration will be deterred and, possibly, some employment will shift. The result will be some increase in demand in the north leading to the development of the derelict land there. What also happens, of course, is that the increase in land and house prices makes it worthwhile demolishing existing housing in the south and rebuilding on the land at a higher density. Development is then occurring on what are 'brownfield' sites in planning terms, even if not on derelict or vacant land.

Factor price equalisation

Empirical evidence on the displacement of commercial and manufacturing activities is, as has been said, not available in the same way that it is available with respect to housing, since comprehensive data are not collected in the same way. Such displacement would be in line with the theoretical analyses that have been developed to explain the nature of international and interregional trade. So, the Hecksher–Ohlin theory of international trade would suggest that countries and regions would tend to import goods that use factors of production which are in relatively short supply there and would tend to export goods that largely use factors with which, relative to other countries and regions, they are well endowed. There are, of course, many other determinants of the nature of international trade – distance, language and culture, excise duties, technology, etc., so that relative factor endowments are only a part of the explanation. What the theory suggests, however, is that factors that are in relatively short supply in a country will therefore be relatively expensive and so it will tend to be cheaper for consumers to import from elsewhere products a large part of the cost of which derives from the use of these factors in their production.

As has been made clear, planning controls and constraints are intended to limit the availability of land for urban uses, in effect the system ensures that land as a factor of production is in relatively short supply in southern England. The price of land in urban uses therefore rises, since it is made relatively scarce and is accordingly relatively expensive. The price signals sent through the market lead consumers to purchase articles using these factors made elsewhere. The result is a displacement of uses, sometimes to other parts of the UK, sometimes to other parts of the world. That the displacement is occurring because of factor endowment effects will not be obvious, however, since the process is so indirect. Sometimes, it is true, a large firm will sell off the site of a factory in the south, and open another elsewhere. More usually, however, the economic forces operating are disguised as a firm or plant operating at a location finds it difficult to compete with factories elsewhere and either does not grow with the market or closes down entirely. Production has been transferred elsewhere but indirectly rather than directly.

These changes will induce a narrowing of the price differences. In theory, in a perfectly competitive economic setting the displacement of activities using the scarce factor of production to elsewhere should be so great as to lead to the price of the relatively scarce factor falling because of the fall in demand. On the other hand, as production using the factor in surplus shifts to an area the price of that factor would rise because of increased demand. In the end, in theory, 'factor price equalisation' would occur as the displacement of activities became so great as to lead to each factor having the same price in each country or region. In the case in point the price of land in southern England would theoretically fall to the level elsewhere, but only activities that used land intensively would be located there. This is, of course, in theory, as has been stressed. Nevertheless one would expect some tendency towards factor price equalisation. This tendency must, however, be limited by the fact that many goods and, particularly, services are not traded internationally or even interregionally. Moreover, markets do not tend to adjust to any new long-run equilibrium at any great speed, particularly where international trade is concerned, and the inertia is considerable.

One of the chief activities that one would think could not be traded is housing. If people are working in one country it is difficult and inconvenient to live in another. Of course, it is sometimes possible. For example, one could work in Geneva in Switzerland but live only a few miles away in France. With respect to the island of Great Britain, cross-Channel commuting is both expensive and time consuming, even after the construction of the Channel Tunnel. Some cross-Channel commuting does take place, however, because the difference between house prices north and south of the Channel makes it potentially worthwhile. Nevertheless the 'import' of housing services has been most evident, not with first homes, but with second homes which can be, and are, at some distance from workplace and family home. So, many British families have purchased second homes, not in England, where prices are seen to be high, but across the Channel in France, or in Spain or Italy. Of course, to a large degree the purchase of a second home abroad is not only just that but also represents a demand for a different culture or a different climate, or both. Nevertheless, the price difference may be substantial. For example, amongst many other properties, *The Sunday Times* of 8 May 1988 advertised a four-bedroom, two-bathroom, converted farmhouse in four acres south of Caen at £95 000, while on the other side of the Channel it advertised a three-bedroom, one-bathroom lodge in two acres in West Sussex for £180 000. Or, for a more recent example, *The Sunday Times* of 30 November 2003 advertised an eight-bedroom, two-living room, completely renovated old school, with courtyard and outbuildings 35 miles south of Calais at £213 000. On the English side of the Channel one could instead buy a four-bedroom cottage with stables, paddock, and six acres of woodland in West Sussex, near Haslemere, at £795 000. Such substantial price differences make the purchase of a second home more feasible, and the lower purchase price helps to compensate for the potentially high cost of travel, and for worries about differing legal systems. So, although one would have thought that housing would be an area where it would be dif-ficult to see these economic forces working, in fact, in the second homes market, the position is clear, and helps to account for the wave of house purchases south of the Channel in the late 1980s, purchases which have continued but at a steadier rate, and have spread further afield as cheap airlines such as Ryanair and Easyjet reduce the cost of travel to southern France, Spain and Italy.

Conclusions

We have pointed out in this book that many planners do not see the workings of the economic system as relevant to physical planning. Their view, and it is a tenable view, is that their concern is with physical plan-ning, with the way in which land is used. That the operation of the system results in increases in the price of some land and property and decreases in the price of other pieces of land and property is not their concern. Indeed, some would hold that these changes should definitely be excluded from their consideration because otherwise they might become biased by the knowledge that A will do well or that B will do badly. There is a lot to be said for such a point of view, but what we are concerned with in this chapter cannot be ignored in the same way. What is argued here is that the system not only causes changes in prices, which can perhaps be put out of mind and ignored, but that these changes in prices, operating through the market, affect the way in which land is used, and these consequential effects cannot be ignored in the same way without illogicality. If the use of land is the sole interest of the planner then economic forces resulting from planning which then further affect the use of land cannot be ignored.

What we have shown in this chapter is that the physical constraints on urban development in the UK, in particular in southern England, have clearly resulted, through the operation of the market, in changes in the kind of housing that is built. The rise in the price of land has led to land being used more intensively as fewer bungalows and more apartments have been built. Successive generations have not been able to afford the larger houses that their higher incomes might be thought to have entitled them to; indeed during most of the post-war period they have been forced to trade down. Similar changes are less easy to document with respect to commercial and industrial uses, both because similar data are not available and because it is less easy to distinguish social changes affecting demand from changes affecting the cost of land and therefore supply. Nevertheless they appear to have been at work.

11

The Macroeconomic Effects of Planning Constraints

'Striving to better, oft we mar what's well'
(King Lear)

Introduction

In the previous chapter of this book we looked at the way in which physical constraints on the availability of land for development, and the resultant higher land prices, affect the development which does take place and where it is located. The concern there was with the physical effects of the constraints, effects which were not necessarily anticipated when the controls were imposed. In this chapter we examine the economic effects of the constraints. Just as the constraints have unanticipated impacts on physical development so they also have unanticipated impacts on the economy, its stability and its growth. Some of these effects are supported by both argument and hard empirical data, such as the effect of the planning system in making the supply of housing very inelastic, but other effects can be supported by argument alone since the evidence is difficult if not impossible to obtain, for example the negative impact of the constraints on the development of land on the growth of the economy.

The elasticity of supply of housing and economic booms and slumps

Planning restrictions and constraints are put in place at a point in time and tend to remain unchanged, or to change very slowly relative to changes in the national economy. This is nowhere more obvious than in the responsiveness, or rather the lack of it, of the land and property market to the cyclical changes which occur in any economy as variations in demand occur. The planning system is a physical planning system. It is explicitly assumed in planning physical resources that changes in demand over time will occur gradually and consistently and that land can be allocated to cope with these changes in demand. The land use planning system tends to be concerned with long-run changes, for example, with changes in the number of households in the economy. But most variations in demand are short-run changes, the result of fluctuations in the economy, changes in interest rates, etc. The long-run trend, even if correctly predicted within the planning system, will usually be out of line with short-run fluctuations around the trend. We shall show in the next section of this chapter that the way in which the British system operates in allocating land for housing tends to ensure such differences, and even to exacerbate them. In this section, however, we start by showing why the impact of a land use planning system on the elasticity of supply is important and has significant consequences.

In economic terms the consequence of the tight controls on the availability of land is that the price elasticity of supply of property, of housing in particular, is considerably lower, both in the short run and in the long run, than it would be, or is, in an economy where the supply is less tightly controlled. In the latter, increases in the price of housing will quickly lead to increases in the number of houses being built as construction firms respond to the economic signal that house building is more profitable. In an economy in which the supply of land for housing is restricted, construction firms will not be able to respond to the perceived price signals because the land will not be made available. The consequence is that as prices rise but no significant increase in supply occurs, the increase in price is not damped down by any increased supply, and the price rise is consequently greater than it would have been with a less controlled housing market.

The position is represented diagrammatically in Figure 11.1. The quantity of housing supplied in a period is indicated on the horizontal axis and price on the vertical axis. The initial demand for housing is shown by the curve DD'. The initial price and quantity of housing are given by OP on the vertical axis and OQ on the horizontal axis. Two possible supply curves consistent with the initial price, quantity, and demand curve are shown as S_L and S_H, where S_L indicates a lower elasticity of supply than S_H, which indicates a higher elasticity of supply.

Suppose that the demand for housing now increases as incomes rise and employment increases during the upswing of the business cycle, so that the demand curve shifts to D_1D_1'. In the economy in which the elasticity of supply is low and represented by S_L, the price of housing rises sharply to OP_1, and the quantity of housing constructed increases to OQ_1. In the

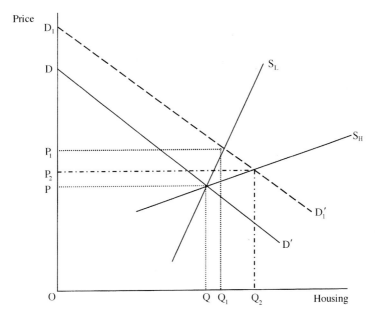

Figure 11.1

economy in which the elasticity of supply is higher, however, the rise in price is considerably less, rising only to OP_2, while the increase in the quantity of housing constructed is much greater, represented in Figure 11.1 by an increase to OQ_2.

The extent of the possible differences between countries in their elasticities of supply of housing is indicated by the results of research into the housing markets in the US and UK economies. Thus, Topel & Rosen (1988) found that the long-run, that is five-year, elasticity of supply for the US economy was very high, at about 24, a figure near to complete elasticity. Tsoukis & Westaway (1994) found, on the other hand, that the long-run supply elasticity for the UK was about one, about the same as the short-run elasticity for the US. With respect to other economies with major differences in their planning systems, Malpezzi & Mayo (1997) found the price elasticity of supply to be low in South Korea and in Malaysia, where constraints are also tight, when compared with the elasticity of supply in Thailand and the USA.

A low elasticity of supply not only means that the price of housing will rise faster than it otherwise would have done, and that the increase in the amount of construction will be less; it also means that when demand does fall at the end of the business cycle, the price of housing will fall faster and further than it would have done otherwise, and, of course, the amount of housing constructed will not fall as far as it otherwise would have done.

In the British case, the extent of the falls in real house prices at the end of economic booms in the mid-1970s and the early 1980s were masked by the high rates of inflation prevailing in each of those periods – double digit inflation as it has been called. Real house prices fell but with rates of inflation of 20% or more, nominal house prices did not actually fall substantially, if they fell at all. Only in the early 1990s, when the rate of general price inflation had been brought down to relatively low levels did nominal house prices fall substantially at the end of a boom. Indeed, in some parts of the country house prices fell by a third or more, with consequential problems for those who had bought their property near the height of the boom, and whose house was now worth less than the amount borrowed on mortgage on the security of the house (Reilly & Witt 1994). Many people were unable to move because it would have been necessary to pay off their loan in order to do so and this was not possible. Many others were ruined as the bank or building society foreclosed when they were unable to keep up the repayments on their loan.

Sharp variations in house prices have a further destabilising effect in that interest rates are affected. When house prices rise there is concern over inflationary presure. Interest rates may then be maintained at a higher level than they otherwise would be solely in order to damp down the housing market. Industrial investment is then deterred; after one increase in the UK Minimum Lending Rate it was remarked that manufacturing workers in northern England were being laid off because of rising house prices in southern England.

If Britain were to join the eurozone one problem would be that the interest rate would be determined in respect to the whole eurozone economy and the behaviour of the British housing market would be of little consequence in determining European (and therefore British) interest rates. Concern over this problem led the Chancellor of the Exchequer, Gordon Brown, to appoint Kate Barker in early 2003 to review the supply of housing in the UK. Her interim report, acknowledging the impact of the planning system, was published in December 2003.

Housing land availability in Britain

The problem of price instability would exist anyway, but is increased and exacerbated by the fact that land use planning is carried out in physical rather than economic terms. Economic effects, prices, etc., are not regarded as relevant to what is consequently dealt with as a physical problem. In Britain planning for land for housing is seen as solely a question of the physical availability of land for a predicted number of dwelling units. The British system is, indeed, remarkable in its continued use of what elsewhere might be discarded as a Soviet-style central planning system.

As the system operates, the statisticians at the Department of the Environment project the expected number of households likely to be formed over the following years, using population projections and taking into account demographic and social changes. These projections are refined down to regional level and, within each region, the different counties are informed how many additional households will have to be accommodated within their area within the period. The process of allocation inevitably involves bargaining and argument as each county suggests that fewer households need to be accommodated within its area than have been suggested, and that more houses could be built elsewhere. For example, in south-east England, it is inevitably argued by the more rural counties that more dwellings could be constructed within London.

Discussions then take place within each county with representatives of the house building industry as to where the proposed number of dwellings could be built, and, again after some discussion and bargaining, agreement will be reached that the land which has been allocated for development in the next five-year period could indeed be used to build the requisite number of dwellings. Inevitably, since agreement must be reached, the conclusion drawn from this consultation process is that there is no shortage of land for house building since the amount of land likely to be made available is equal to the amount of land necessary. And it is at this point that a divergence appears between a conclusion drawn from central planning principles and one drawn from the operation of market forces. For as we have shown earlier in this book, from the evidence of the high price of land for urban use it is very clear that there is, in fact, a shortage of land in the sense that the price of land for house building in most of the country is significantly higher than the price of land for agricultural use.

The truth is, of course, that the market ensures that supply equals demand at some price. The whole land availability discussion is in this respect almost a pretence. If the total amount of land made available were actually too great, then it is true that it would be obvious since large areas of land allocated for housing would not be used. If the land made available is too little, however, there will be no similar evidence of unsatisfied demand, for if the demand for land is greater than the supply the price rises to choke off the demand and ensure equilibrium.

Moreover, the way the land market operates is such that, as we showed in Chapter 7, although a local authority may indicate that land would be permitted to be developed, the owners have a choice, and cannot be compelled to sell their land for development. Even when price differences indicate a shortage there will therefore always be some land which remains undeveloped. Bramley (1993a, b) in his empirical studies of the operation of the system calls this an 'implementation gap'.

Conversely it has been found by local authorities that developers will find sites for development the existence of which had not been appreciated by the staff of the local authority. Thus, the land allocated as available for development in a period is only an approximation to the land which is actually developed, and the central planning mechanism only partially brings supply into line with demand. In practice equilibrium is achieved through the market.

Moreover, as one might possibly expect, just as the central planning mechanism is misleading in its pretence that demand in the long run is being planned for, so also, with its concentration on the long run to the neglect of the short, the system helps to exacerbate fluctuations in prices. Evidence of this is provided in a study by Monk *et al.* (1996) of house building in three county districts to the north of London (north Hertfordshire, south Cambridgeshire and Fenland). They found that as the price of housing rose through the 1980s the number of planning applications also increased, as one would expect. Also as one would expect, it was found that this resulted in a greater number of developments being permitted, at least in the earlier part of the period. The districts then realised that if the rate at which permissions were granted remained as high, they would at the end of the period have permitted more development to take place than they had agreed to during the consultation process. As a result the local authorities reduced the number of developments they permitted so that they did not exceed the amount required under the five-year plan. The effect was, of course, to exacerbate the price boom. As prices rose later in the period the local authorities actually reduced the supply of housing coming to the market with the result that the price rise was not damped down by an increased supply but fuelled by a greater shortage.

Obviously the evidence relates only to these three districts, but there is no reason to suppose that they were unrepresentative and so that this kind of dis-equilibrating response was exceptional. Certainly it helps to provide a further explanation for the low price elasticity of supply of housing in the UK. The quantity of housing provided does not increase as the price increases because the planning system tries to ensure that it does not. Instead it tries to ensure a more constant supply of housing over time. The costs of this were borne, as we pointed out at the end of the previous section, by those who bought at the higher prices and were financially ruined in the ensuing fall.

The change in the system in the early 1990s to one where development was 'plan led' helped to reduce the price elasticity of supply still further. Before that developers could respond to increases in house prices by bringing forward additional proposals, as they had done in the 1980s, and if necessary appealing against a refusal by the local authority with a fair chance of success. After this change it became difficult to do this because the plan, as approved, was less flexible. Either a site was in the plan as being suitable for housing development, or it was not. If not, then this was an important 'material factor' in any appeal and the appeal was not likely to be successful. So, in the late 1990s, as house prices rose the number of houses built did not increase. (The median selling price of new homes sold in England in 1995 was £69 000. By 2002 it had more than doubled to £145 000. But the number of homes completed in England peaked in 1995 at 161 800 and then fell to average about 150 000 p.a. over the ensuing years (NHBC *Private House Building Statistics* 1996, 2003).)

A further shift in the system in the late 1990s from what had been called 'predict and provide' to what was called 'plan, monitor, and manage' represented a further toughening of the policy of constraint. In effect, if too much housing land was predicted to be required, local authorities should manage the situation by increasing densities and ensuring that smaller dwellings were built than developers might wish to provide.

The rate of saving and the price of housing and property

In the first two sections of this chapter the discussion was concerned with fluctuations in demand and their interaction with the inflexiblity of the planning system. It was argued that the result was to exacerbate the normal fluctuations in property prices over the cycle affecting people's financial position as well as the economy as a whole. The effects of these price variations will be short-term, however, but the economy as a whole may also be affected in the long run by the increase in property prices which has taken place, particularly the increase in the price of housing. As we showed in Figure 10.2, the rise in house prices in the UK has been virtually continuous since reasonably accurate data became available in the 1960s. Only in the 1990s did house prices fall in nominal terms. The data relating to land values which are available showed in Figure 10.1 that land values had increased, if more unevenly, since the 1940s. It can be presumed that the increases in land values were derived from increases in house prices, so that house prices rose more or less continuously for nearly half a century. And, for most of this period it came to be accepted in the UK that the purchase of a house was a virtually risk-free investment and that house values could not fall.

Government policies towards house purchase encouraged people into owner occupation. The strong and continuing rise in house prices created wealth for house owners in the longer run, although the high interest rates prevalent in the 1970s and 1980s, because of high levels of inflation, meant that this increase in wealth was often obtained by some belt tightening in the early years of house ownership. It would be expected that this continued increase in their main asset would affect people's attitudes to saving. It appeared to be, and was, better to purchase the largest possible house with the largest possible mortgage than to save. The real value of money saved and put into securities or lent at fixed interest rates would be eroded by inflation while the price of a house would rise, on average, faster than the general price level. Thus the continuing increase in house prices, and the favourable tax treatment of housing would have encouraged investment in housing by owner occupiers rather than saving for investment elsewhere. This would appear to have been one factor behind the low rate of saving out of income in this period. It is notable that the rate of saving rose in the early 1990s when house prices fell, so that the increase in wealth which people might have expected from this source did not occur. It then fell again in the late 1990s as house prices began to rise rapidly again.

It should be noted that a long-run increase in house prices because of planning constraints need not necessarily lead to low rates of saving. In South Korea the rate of saving during this period was exceptionally high, even though, as we pointed out in Chapter 6, controls on the availability of land for housing were as tight there as in the UK. Moreover, this high rate of saving has also been attributed to the long-run rise in house prices resulting from planning constraints. The paradoxical difference appears to be due to the differing systems of housing finance. In Britain a system of financing the purchase of housing had developed with the building societies in the nineteenth century. This allowed people to deposit money and also to borrow money and was extremely efficient. As a result it was relatively easy in Britain to borrow a high proportion of the cost of purchase of a house, sometimes more than 90%. In South Korea, on the other hand, an equivalent system of financing house purchase had not developed. Similar loans were not available. Korean households therefore had to rent because they could not afford to buy. While they were renting they had also to save until much later in life than was the case in Britain to buy a house, often without a loan. It can be seen that, paradoxically, an inefficient system of housing finance, coupled with rising house prices encouraged high levels of saving as people attempted to save more and more in order to attain a receding target. On the other hand an efficient system of housing finance, and rising house prices, encourages people to borrow rather than save, to achieve the objective of house purchase as early in life as possible (Hannah *et al.*, 1993).

The differences in saving rates then impact on the growth of the economy. Certainly a factor in the low rate of growth of the UK economy was the low rate of saving, while the high rate of saving in Korea could finance the development of manufacturing industry at a rate which would not otherwise have been possible.

Cities, growth and agglomeration economies

The impact of policies of constraint on the efficiency and the growth of the economy may be less direct and even more difficult to prove than their impact on the rate of saving and investment. Nevertheless it can certainly be argued that constraint will have negative effects of this kind. The question is only whether these negative effects are justified by the positive benefits. One kind of negative effect results from controlling the growth and size of cities.

As we noted in the introductory chapter of this book, the early town planners regarded the city in geographical or architectural terms, as an exercise in civic design. To the extent that they were concerned with economics they regarded the economic forces creating cities as malign since they encouraged high densities, pollution, congestion and the spread of disease. And to some extent, of course, they were right since, as we observed in Chapter 2, the external diseconomies of pollution, congestion, etc., are greater when people are crowded together, as they are in cities in a way they are not elsewhere. These problems were then seen as physical problems that could be dealt with by physical solutions. In the case of London what was proposed and carried through was the creation of a green belt, density controls, and the dispersal of the population to new and other towns beyond the green belt.

What was neglected was an understanding of the city as an economic organism, of the economic forces that bring cities into existence. There is some justification for this in that economists themselves paid little attention to the economic analysis of towns and cities, but since the 1950s, and the development of urban economics as a separate sub-discipline, we have a better understanding of the economic costs and benefits of cities. In brief, it is clear that urban concentration is associated with high land values, that house and property prices tend to be higher at the centre of cities than elsewhere, that employment densities are highest near the centre so that journeys to work are longer. And, of course, congestion and pollution tend to be greater in large cities.

Since firms which are located in these cities manage to compete effectively with firms located elsewhere, however, the implication is that there are some advantages to an urban location which, for some firms and for some industries, more than compensates the firms for the higher costs. If this were not so the firms would move elsewhere or be driven out of business by firms at cheaper locations. These advantages have come to be called agglomeration economies, and although they are less visible, and less self-evident, than the economic disadvantages, nevertheless, for the reason stated, they must exist.

The nature of these agglomeration economies are discussed in any urban economics text and we do not need to do more here than indicate their nature (see, for example, McCann 2001). This is most easily done with respect to commercial, office-based activities. If offices are located close to each other in a city centre this proximity allows communication between people to take place easily, especially through face-to-face meetings which become necessary when nuances of expression, body language, and other forms of feedback are thought to be important, for example, in negotiations. Further, because of this proximity information is more freely and quickly available. This need for proximity is most obvious in the way financial activities concentrate together, a concentration indicated by the use of the names of physical locations – Wall Street, the City, as names for the financial groupings.

As well as the financial services, other kinds of specialist business service will also choose to locate in the central city – accountants, lawyers, advertising agencies, etc. since their main market will be there. The size of this market allows them to specialise and the economies of scale that they gain from this specialisation will make their services cheaper or more reliable than those obtainable from a less specialist firm in a small town. In turn, of course, the existence and availability of these services provide a further encouragement for offices of all kinds to locate in the city, including the head offices or regional offices of manufacturing and retailing firms.

The number of people who have to work in the city centre may, in fact, be quite small, but the workforce is multiplied several fold because professionals and executives have to be supported by clerks, assistants and other support staff. In turn the population of the city is further increased by the fact that the needs of this working population have to be served both where they live and where they work. Retail and service activities therefore have to locate there. Again the existence of this major market will also support and attract the manufacturing industry.

What has been put forward above is a static interpretation of the nature of agglomeration activities. The economic advantages of cities can also be given a more dynamic interpretation. So Jane Jacobs (1969) and Ben Chinitz (1961), in different ways, argued that the economies of large cities allowed continuing innovation and development in a way that small towns did not. In more recent work, authors such as Romer (1986) and, in particular, Krugman (1991) have argued that past mainstream economic analyses of economic growth have ignored the dynamic economies of scale available in cities, particularly the economies available through the division of labour. It should also be noted, in case it is thought that the work is only theoretical, that over the past 20 years or so numerous empirical studies have demonstrated the existence of these agglomeration economies as researchers have attempted to categorise them.

The position is therefore as follows. Agglomeration economies exist and are the primary reason for the existence of cities. The growth of cities is limited, however, by the fact that as they grow the costs of location there also rise as the cost of space and of housing rises, as wages and salaries rise to compensate workers for the higher housing costs and longer journeys to work. An economic analysis of the urban system would suggest that the largest cities would grow to a point where the diseconomies balanced the economies.

Planning constraints on urban growth affect this balance, as, indeed, they are intended to. As we showed in Chapter 6 the effect of a constraint such as a green belt is to raise housing costs and space costs and to increase the length of journeys to work; in turn this increase in living costs is passed on in higher wage costs. Economically, therefore, the effect is that the costs associated with location in a city such as London are much greater than they would have been in the absence of the constraint, for a city of that size. Looked at in the opposite way, the attainment of greater agglomeration economies is prevented by the costs that deter firms from moving to the city or expanding there. Economically, therefore, the agglomeration economies associated with those costs are less than they would have been if the city had been allowed to expand.

The issue in question is therefore one which particularly relates to London. The physical constraints on its physical growth have clearly restricted that growth over the last 50 years. This has clearly affected the agglomeration economies available. The higher costs and lower benefits derived from a location in Britain's largest city will also therefore have affected the British economy as whole, since, at the least, the London region is a large part of that economy and could have been a larger part. And so two, perhaps three, questions have to be asked. Has the lower economic growth and lower level of income resulting from this constraint been fully compensated nationally by the preservation of unspoiled countryside in the London Green Belt? And, for the present and the future, in a situation which could not have been foreseen in 1947, now that London is one of the cities, albeit currently still the largest, competing with each other in the European Union, is it handicapped in this competition by the physical constraints on its growth? And for the third question, if Britain is part of a Union in which nationalist interests are submerged, does this matter?

Competitiveness

The possible negative effects of the land use planning system on economic growth and development have recently been highlighted by neutral observers of the British economy. In 1998 the McKinsey Global Institute published a report entitled *Driving Productivity and Growth in the British Economy*. In it product market and land use regulations are identified as the two most important factors explaining large differences in GDP per capita between the United States and European countries and, in particular, in explaining relatively low labour productivity in the United Kingdom economy.

The report's conclusions result from looking at a number of industries in some detail. One of them was the hotel industry in which they note that 'regulations governing land use, planning and building mean that the cost of building or refurbishing a hotel in the United Kingdom is up to 40 per cent higher than in the United States' with the result that the 'UK break even occupancy was close to 80 per cent, compared to just 50 per cent for a similar type of hotel in the United States' (p. 14). This meant that much investment, even by British hotel companies, went abroad, and British hotels remained uncompetitive and expensive. The report notes that nearly half the UK's stock of hotel rooms in 1998 were over a century old, compared with 3% of the US stock and 14% of that in France.

With respect to the computer software industry, the report argues that 'planning regulations have even constrained the growth of new high technology sectors in the IT industry', since these sectors benefit from clusters, and the development of such clusters 'has been slowed or even prevented by local planning restrictions' (p. 16). With respect to retailing, the report points out that 'land use and planning regulations make it difficult for large-format operators to develop new sites or expand existing ones. Leading operators are prevented from achieving their full productive potential, while new operators are discouraged from entering the market' (p. 14).

It is interesting to note that when the report came out the President of the Royal Town Planning Institute dismissed the criticisms, first, as having been voiced before, in the 1980s (see, for example, Evans 1988). The implication appeared to be that having been made, and ignored, before they could now be ignored again. His second response was that the leading firms in industries such as retailing supported the present system. But this was to ignore the substance of the criticism that the system restricted entry and competition. The planning system can operate to ensure that firms already in operation will not face new competition and so can behave monopolistically. At its most obvious, the retailer that has received planning permission for an out of town supermarket can rest assured that the local authority will protect his market position since they will not give permission for a second, competing, supermarket.

The McKinsey report argues that there should be a comprehensive reform of land use regulations, and that 'what is needed is new regulatory framework that finds a balance between economic and social objectives' (p. 24). It also draws attention to the way in which the neutrality of the UK's system of local government finance discourages development. The report points out that 'unlike many other countries, the current balance of central and local government funding means that local communities derive limited financial benefits from new investment' (p. 24). This means that if 'local planners are to implement a more growth-oriented regulatory regime' their communities would have to derive some direct benefit from granting planning permission. This line of argument suggests a way in which loosening up the UK planning system could be made more acceptable to local communities, indeed probably the only politically acceptable way.

Conclusions

In this chapter we have been explicitly concerned with the macro-economic effects of planning constraints. It can also be argued that economic growth may also be affected by the kind of planning system which is in operation – whether it is flexible or inflexible, whether decision making is quick or dilatory, whether the system is slow and expensive and whether the decisions that are made are economically correct or not. We shall discuss this question in the final chapter since before we can do so we need to examine the characteristics of different planning systems and their political nature.

What we have tried to show in this chapter is that planning constraints can and do impact on the macro-economy. Constraints on the responses of the house building industry to economic changes can exacerbate the price fluctuations to which the industry is liable, even while smoothing out fluctuations in the rate of house construction. These price fluctuations can have disastrous financial consequences for those who buy near the top of the cycle, in particular for those who buy their first house and who may find themselves owing more than their house is worth.

We have also argued that the rising property values caused by planning constraints can significantly affect the rate of saving although the effect is not immediately predictable. In the United Kingdom, with an efficient system of financing house purchases, the effect appears to have been to lead to lower savings rates as people have been able to buy their house early and to sit back and allow it to appreciate in value. In South Korea, on the other hand, the lack of a similar system for obtaining loans for house purchase has meant that households have had to rent for long periods while they saved the money to buy a house without a loan. The result has been a high rate of saving.

Finally, we have argued that the system can affect economic growth directly. First, constraints such as a green belt will affect the economy of a large city such as London. Costs are raised, firms are deterred from expanding there or locating there, and the agglomeration economies that might be available in a larger city with the same costs are not there. Given the level of agglomeration economies available in the city, the costs are relatively high. The same level of agglomeration economies might be obtained in a city of the same size elsewhere where costs are lower. It is open to question whether the social gains derived from the imposition of the green belt fully compensate for the lower economic growth and lower income levels resulting from the existence of the green belt.

Second, the system can affect the competitiveness of the economy by raising the cost of entry and of operation. Firms that are already in operation are protected from competition by the need of new entrants to obtain planning permission which may be costly and time consuming and which may never be granted. Thus the system can protect the inefficient and the monopolistic.

12

Methods of Planning

Glendower. *I can call spirits from the vasty deep.*
Hotspur. *Why, so can I, and so can any man;*
But will they come when you do call for them'
(Henry IV, Pt 1)

Introduction

In this book we have primarily been concerned with a system in which physical controls have been used to regulate land use. Further, we have been concerned mainly with the British system which requires an application to be made for permission for virtually any and every development proposal, however small it may be. In this chapter we consider alternatives. First, we consider the reasons why planning systems tend to be based on controls rather than taxes, and, indeed, why taxation is considered to have no implications for land use planning, this despite the fact that much of welfare economics is based on analyses of the use of taxes to correct externalities. Second, we look at the differences between American-style zoning systems and British-style non-zoning systems, and the economic implications of the differences. And third, we look at the implications of the methods of planning used in Sweden, The Netherlands and Hong Kong where central or local governments are much more involved in the land market and in ensuring that what is planned actually happens in practice than they are under the Anglo-American systems – positive planning as it has been called, rather than negative planning.

Controls and taxes

In Chapter 2 of this book we discussed the various reasons which welfare economic analysis would suggest justified intervention in the market. The main reason for intervening in the land use system was perceived to be the existence of external diseconomies. It was argued that both external economies and diseconomies were pervasive in urban areas, since the close proximity of activities meant that an activity on one site tended to affect, for better or worse, activities on neighbouring sites. The reader may remember that the economic analysis of intervention to ameliorate the negative effects of external diseconomies began with the analysis of the use of taxes and subsidies and their optimum level.

Following this opening discussion, however, the reader will certainly have noticed that the ensuing discussion of the economics of land use planning in practice was notable, with two exceptions, for the absence of discussion of taxes or of evidence of their use. The exceptions were impact fees, which, in the USA, anyway appear to have been imposed because physical controls had not restrained growth, and Development Land Tax, which was imposed to cream off the profits from development which were high because of controls and which were perceived to be excessive. The preferred tools of planning have been land use controls, taxation has never been the first thing to be used. It is evident that physical planning has been seen to be one thing and taxation and fiscal policy another. In government circles the one has not been thought to have much relevance to the other.

Nevertheless, as we sought to show in the previous chapter, land use planning can, and does, impact on the macro-economy, and these effects ought not to be neglected. What has also been ignored has been the impact of economic policy, in particular fiscal policy, on land use. Nowhere has this been more evident than in government policy towards owner occupation. Because the two have not been seen to have anything to do with each other, in Britain, at least, taxation has not merely been neglected as a planning instrument, it has been used in a way entirely counter to land use policy. In part this has been accidental, it is true, but whether accidental or not, while land use planning has sought to restrict land use, taxes have been used to encourage more land to be used by subsidising housing, and in particular by the favourable tax treatment of owner occupation.

In part this situation arose out of an historical accident. Until about 1960 owner occupiers were assessed for income tax (called Schedule A) on the imputed rent of their home, i.e. the rent they would have had to pay for such a property. In this way the tax system was meant to be neutral between renters, their landlords and owner occupiers. Both the landlord and the owner occupier could deduct the cost of maintaining their properties from the rent on which they were taxed. This system worked so long as the owner occupiers were a small minority of the population, and so long as the imputed rent was reasonably accurate, and both these conditions held up to about the middle of the century. Inflation during the Second World War and afterwards meant, however, that the costs of maintenance, and the cost of borrowing, increased considerably in monetary terms, while the imputed rent remained fixed. At the end of the 1950s the position had been reached where many taxpayers were keeping elaborate records of the cost of maintenance and using these costs to show that they were, in fact, liable for little or no tax under Schedule A. Either, therefore, the imputed rents had to be revalued, and substantially increased, which would have led to a political outcry by the now more substantial body of owner occupiers, or Schedule A had to be abolished. The Conservative government of the time, not surprisingly, took the second option, but continued to allow the full amount of mortgage interest paid to be tax deductible, aiming, it was said, to create a nation of owner occupiers. It might, of course, be noted that neither Australia nor Canada has allowed mortgage interest to be tax deductible but the levels of owner occupation have been as high as, or higher than, in Britain. Nevertheless, at the point when the constraints on the availability of land for development were starting to be really effective, governments heavily subsidised the cost of house purchase encouraging people to buy the largest houses that they could.

A favourable attitude towards home ownership continued under succeeding governments. When a Labour government introduced a Capital Gains Tax in the mid-1960s, the 'principal place of residence' was not affected, only second homes. Again, when a Value Added Tax was introduced by the Conservative government in the early 1970s, housing was exempted. A shift in policy only started to occur in 1976 when the Labour government limited tax relief on mortgage interest to that on the first £25 000 of any loan. Since the average loan at the time was less than half this amount, this was, at the time, more of a political gesture than a significant change in fiscal policy. It became important fiscally as inflation continued and house prices increased so that by the early 1980s there was substantial political pressure to increase the figure of £25 000. This was resisted by the Treasury since the level of owner occupation was by then substantial, as therefore was the cost of mortgage tax relief. In the event the figure was raised to £30 000, reportedly at the personal insistence of the Prime Minister, Mrs Thatcher, and there it remained.

It will be seen that the argument over the level of relief was conducted solely in terms of fiscal policy, equity and the cost to the Treasury. At that time, the mid-1980s, there were therefore two contradictory policies. Fiscal policy was intended to encourage owner occupation by reducing the cost of home ownership; it therefore served to increase the demand for housing and for land. At the same time, land use policy was intended to constrain the amount of land available for housing and other urban uses. The economic effect of the two together was that the tax incentives were largely translated into higher house prices to keep the demand for housing and land down to the level which physical planning constraints made available. There was, however, a failure to understand the position because, to reiterate the point, fiscal policy was not seen as having anything to do with land use policy, and vice versa. Thus, it was argued at the time that the limit for tax relief should be raised because the price of housing was high, indicating a failure to realise that any reduction in the cost of house purchase would be reflected in an increase in demand which would result in still higher house prices, largely wiping out any advantage to house buyers.

Only from 1988 onwards was a serious attempt made to cut back the level of mortgage tax relief, in part for reasons of equity, but primarily to cut the cost to the Treasury. The proportion of the interest rate for which relief was given, i.e. which was in effect paid by central government, was progressively reduced from a maximum of 40% to zero when it was finally abolished in 2000. This reduction took place over a period during which house prices were falling, but without any apparent recognition by any Chancellor that the withdrawal of tax relief would have any effect on the housing market. At one point in the early 1990s, a minor change to the level of stamp duty was made, on a temporary basis, and this was explicitly stated as being intended to help the housing market to recover, but the much greater effect that the gradual, and anticipated, withdrawal of mortgage tax relief was having went unremarked by any Chancellor and presumably unnoticed within the Treasury.

Even while tax relief on mortgage interest was being phased out another conflict between fiscal policy and planning policy was introduced. The Domestic Rate, a tax on housing more or less proportional to its value, was abolished by the Thatcher government at the end of the 1980s. It was replaced by the Community Charge or 'poll tax' which was unrelated to housing consumption. The anticipated abolition of the rates helped to fuel the house price boom which was occurring at that time. Because of the political unpopularity of the Community Charge, however, a factor in Mrs Thatcher's downfall, John Major's government sought a replacement. This was the Council Tax which incorporated elements of both the Community Charge and the Domestic Rates. Thus, the tax payable does increase with the value of a house, but it does so in a series of eight steps, and the increases in the tax at each step are proportionately less than the increase in the value of the house. Thus, the larger is the house and the higher is its value, the lower is the tax as a proportion of its value. So, for example, in the London

Borough of Harrow in 2003/2004 a tax of £817 had to be paid on properties valued (in 1991) at less than £40000 but the tax on any dwelling valued at over £320000 (again, in 1991) was only three times as great at £2451, whatever the size or value of the house.

So, while planning policy at the turn of the century was to encourage higher density housing, the tax system actually encouraged larger, land extensive housing, and served to discourage high density housing. A further feature of the Council Tax, and another legacy of the 'poll tax', was that the tax on second homes could be only half that on the primary residence. It follows that not only would someone buying up two adjoining cottages in a rural area pay less tax in total on the new, larger, dwelling but if they then used it as a second home that total tax payable could be halved. Thus, while planning policy might aim to encourage affordable housing in rural areas, the tax system discourages its continued existence.

This brief history of the relationship between tax policy and land policy is a paradigm example of the lack of any recognition of the impact of taxes on land use. Even when mortgage tax relief was being gradually withdrawn in the early 1990s, no politician attempted to claim, as they might well have done, that this was to reduce the demand for land. Changes were instead put through with little comment and as part of the budgetary process, for fiscal rather than environmental reasons.

Given the lack of any politically recognised connection between changes in existing taxes and land use, the lack of use of taxes and subsidies in the operation of land use planning is to be expected. If those responsible for taxes do not recognise that they affect the use of land, why should those planning the use of land think of using taxes to assist in this? So, while economic analysis might suggest that if a land use imposes an externality on others a tax might be imposed to correct the situation, this is almost never done. Instead, planning seeks to rearrange or segregate land uses to minimise the effects of the externalities, or to contain or reduce the area allocated to this land use. In the latter case, as we have shown, the result will often be that the value of the land where this use is permitted will rise. Even if the effect were the same so far as economic efficiency is concerned, it nevertheless seems odd, at first sight, that the preferred solution should be one that makes better off the owners of the land where the land use causing the negative externality already exists. A tax, on the other hand, would have the effect of reducing the extent of the externality, would make those already imposing the externality no better off, and possibly worse off, while yielding an income to government that could be used to compensate those suffering from the externality.

One suggested explanation for the preference for controls has been that it is politically easier to introduce controls. A control allows those activities that are already in existence to continue, but limits the extent to which new activities can be introduced in the area. Such a proposal will tend to be supported by those owning the activities, and in the case of commercial activities, by those working for them, since such a control puts the activities in a quasi-monopolistic position. On the other hand, a tax would be opposed both by the owners, and, after the negative effects on employment had been explained by their employers, also by the employees. Those suffering from the externality would support either proposal. Further, while they might prefer a tax if some of it reached them in compensation, if this is unlikely, as it is, they will be indifferent between the two proposals. The result is that it will be considerably easier politically to introduce controls and more difficult to impose taxes (Fischel 1995, p. 327f; Webster 1998).

However, the effect of controls is, as we have demonstrated earlier, that the value of land is liable to be highest when it is most constrained. The paradox is that those land uses which are regarded as socially beneficial such as agriculture have a low land value, while those land uses that are seen as imposing social costs have high land values. The consequence is, as we showed in Chapter 8, that the price signals given to land owners suggest that it would be profitable to try to convert the use of their land from one to another by obtaining planning permission to do so. As a result resources will be expended in trying to achieve this. Thus, the use of controls sets in train market behaviour which seeks to undermine the effect of the controls. A tax, on the other hand, would have the reverse effect in discouraging people from converting land from a use on which no tax is paid to one on which no tax would have to be paid.

Again, while there may be political or public choice reasons why controls may be preferred to taxes, the use of controls prevents the compensation of those suffering from external effects, and can reinforce the non-optimising nature of the system. For example, at the present time in Britain most proposed developments will be objected to by those living in the vicinity, and they will seek to ensure, by lobbying planning officials and political representatives, that permission is not given. Fischel (2001) shows that this is also the position in the United States. As he points out people, particularly home owners, will object even when the possible damage to their own interests is very small, since they have something to gain by objecting and nothing to lose. On the other hand, if the system were more financially based, payments could be made, either directly or out of tax revenues, which would compensate these objectors. If side payments could be made, for example, any developer would have to balance the costs of doing so against the profits from the development, and would go ahead if it still seemed profitable. In this way the costs and benefits could be balanced against each other.

Of course, the use of controls rather than taxes and other financially based methods may not be solely due to political choice, or to inertia in the planning system. There is an economic argument for the use of controls rather than taxes under some circumstances (Weitzmann 1974). The economic theory on which the use of taxes rests assumes that the costs and the benefits of an externality are known and fixed. If, on the other hand, the costs or the benefits are uncertain and vary, then the fixing of the tax at some average level would be misleading. It would discourage the activity on some occasions when the tax is too high, and allow the activity on other occasions when the tax is too low.

If the social cost may on some rare occasions be extremely high it may be thought best to use a control in order to avoid even the remote possibility that the worst possible scenario happens. Better to have a ban on all river pollution than a tax. Although a tax would prevent anyone polluting the river in most circumstances it might make them think it worthwhile on some very exceptional occasion. This kind of argument is reinforced by other considerations. While one may be aware of the nature of the effects of some activity, a precise costing may be difficult to obtain, and the precise balancing implied by the theory may be more than adequately replaced by a physical control.

The argument for controls is reinforced by the irreversible nature of land development. The economic analysis of externalities uses as an example an externality like smoke pollution where the effects of the smoke are more or less concurrent with its emission, and the smoke then disperses. A tax which is found to be too low or too high at first can be corrected later. This is not possible in the case of land development. Construction now cannot, except at great cost, be pulled down later. It affects those in the vicinity now, and those who may be in the vicinity later. Better possibly to err on the safe side and use controls to be sure.

A further reason for the use of controls rather than taxes is distributional. Controls do have distributional effects, as we have shown, in that some land owners benefit as their property increases in value. Nevertheless, the use of taxes rather than controls would also have distributional effects, but on the consumption rather than the production side. The use of taxes would allow some to buy their way in at the expense of others. Thus, it might be felt that in an unspoilt and beautiful area of countryside such as the English Lake

District there should be no development such as isolated houses. With a tax system this would imply that a very high but not infinite tax would be imposed. But no matter how high the tax was, since it is less than infinite, and therefore a tax rather than a control, it would be possible for some multi-millionaire to pay the tax and build a house there. However, this would mean imposing the costs, the presence of the house, on the rest of the population. In most people's view this would be inequitable and the tax should therefore be set infinitely high, i.e. should be a control, to prevent the wealthy imposing spatial externalities on the rest of the world.

These economic and political arguments explain the widespread use of controls in land use planning, and, to a lesser extent, the absence of any use of taxes. On the other hand, economic analysis would suggest that controls and taxes (or subsidies) should, if they are both used, at the least work together. The thesis of this book is that land use planning cannot be considered solely as a system of land use controls, as a system only affecting the allocation of land uses, it will also have economic effects. And the opposite is also true, as the brief outline above of the history of owner occupation and taxation in the UK illustrates. Fiscal policy, tax decisions, will have an impact on the demand and supply of land and so will affect land use. They too cannot be considered in isolation. Fiscal policy and physical policy have to be considered together and to work together, the tax and subsidy system should be supportive of land use planning and vice versa. For them to work against each other as they have done for many years in the UK is an absurdity.

The degree of control of detail

Methods of controlling land use could be ranked in terms of the degree of control and intervention by government, and, what is more or less the same thing, the level of detail for which permission has to be sought. The British method of control is one of the most restrictive, in terms of this ranking, since an application has to be made for almost any development, however small, and because permission may be refused on almost any grounds, including, in particular, aesthetic reasons. Since one person's good taste may be another's bad taste, this can, and does, introduce an element of arbitrariness into the planning process.

The method of controlling land use used in most of the rest of the world is 'zoning', where the use to which an area of land can be put is stated and a development which conforms with the stated zoning policy is permissible and permitted. The only direct application which may be necessary may be one relating to the conformity of the proposed development with building regulations. Obviously, with a zoning system, no detailed control of the style and design of buildings is thought to be necessary; control is limited simply to the type of use.

Between these two extremes a number of variations is possible, depending on the degree of intervention and the level of detail which is controlled and controllable. It is also possible, though rare, for there to be no government control, even in a developed economy. As we noted in Chapter 5, the metropolitan area of Houston, Texas, is notable for the fact that much of it is not subject to any system of zoning regulation. Instead the owners of property enter into legal agreements – covenants, as to the land use or uses that are permitted. Some of the Houston area is actually unregulated and development is uncontrolled, being neither zoned nor subject to agreed covenants.

What we are concerned with in this section are the consequences, particularly the costs, of increasing the level of detail which is controlled. In particular, we shall show that the high level of detailed control evident in the British system has economic and other consequences not evident with the lighter touch of the zoning system.

The advantage of the British system of land use planning is precisely the greater control over land use and development that is given by the system to planning officers, the local councillors who are the members of development control committees, and, in the event of an appeal against a rejection, the inspector 'appointed' by the Secretary of State and the Secretary of State himself. Control can be at a finer level than with a zoning system. The system need not create a degree of uniformity of use, since it is not true that only one use will be permitted within an area. In theory any use can be applied for and permitted or refused, although, of course, planning decisions have to be justifiable and defensible at any planning appeal. The greater level of control should therefore produce a better physical environment, albeit with the control over the degree of permitted individual variation leading to a more homogeneous landscape.

One advantage of any system of land use planning is intended to be that it reduces uncertainty. Land owners and property developers will know from the published plans for the development of the area what it is planned will happen on other sites. With this knowledge they will be able to plan the development of the sites that they own with greater security and with a better idea as to the nature of the most profitable, permitted, development. The system should make it impossible that developments will be started which would be incompatible with other land uses in the area, and which might therefore fail leaving behind an idle and derelict building. Certainty and security will also be increased if the published plans for the area clearly state the kind of development that is, or would be, permitted. Obviously a zoning system does this and therefore increases certainty in this sense. A system for which permission for any development has to be obtained does so in the sense that a plan for the area is published. On the other hand, it then increases the level of uncertainty in a different form since permission still has to be obtained for a development even if it is in line with stated planning policies and permission may be refused. While in the complete absence of planning, land owners would know that anything could occur on other sites but that they have complete control over their own sites, with the British system they gain security and certainty with respect to the other sites but have greater uncertainty about what can be done on their own.

The high level of uncertainty which this creates for would-be developers means that various stratagems have had to be developed to reduce it, and, consequently, to avoid delays and unnecessary expense. The main method has been to negotiate with the planning officers, the professional planners employed by the local authority, as to what precisely is likely to be permitted and whether what is being proposed is likely to be permitted.

Negotiations of this kind do not eliminate uncertainty. Negotiations will take place with the planning officers, not with the elected councillors who are the members of the development control committee who will actually make the decision to give planning permission or not. Having acceded to all the suggestions made by the officers, the developer may still put in an application and have it refused. Applications will usually be put to the development control committee with some form of recommendation from the officers, to permit or to refuse, although a few will be put up with no recommendation. Even though the professional planners may suggest that an application should be permitted, permission may still be refused by the committee. The applicant must then decide whether to appeal to the Secretary of State, which will be costly and will certainly cause delay, or to try a further application taking into account the reasons for refusal given by the committee which may be more successful, although, of course, success is not guaranteed.

It can easily be seen that one cost of the system, a cost that is associated with the high level of uncertainty, is the increased risk of delay. Legally, the planning authority is supposed to give a decision within eight weeks of receiving an application, but there is no penalty to the authority if it does not do this. After eight weeks the developer can regard the proposal 'deemed refused' and appeal against this deemed refusal, but, if anything, this dis-advantages the developer rather than the local authority. It will certainly take some months before an appeal is heard. If the developer takes this route it therefore certainly does not shorten the time before a decision is obtained and most applicants will usually accept that it is best to wait on the deci-sion of the local authority's Development Control Committee even if this takes longer than eight weeks.

One tactic that has been adopted is to submit two applications which are virtually identical – the 'twin track' approach. After eight weeks one can be 'deemed refused' and the appeal process set in motion. The other can con-tinue to be discussed with the planning officers. In this way any delay if the application is refused by the development control committee is minimised since the appeal process has already been set in motion, and some pressure is put on the committee since it is made aware that a negative decision will be appealed against, so putting the authority to some cost in defending its refusal.

Planning delays may be costly to the developer, although the costs may be minimised by trying to ensure, if possible, that the planning application is not on 'the critical path'. For example, an application can be made and detailed design work can continue while the application is being con-sidered. Nevertheless, if the application is refused, this design work may be wasted. Thus, there are certainly private costs caused by delay and uncer-tainty. There is a further question, however, as to whether there are social costs.

If the consideration of the planning application is an accurate balancing of the social costs and benefits of the proposed development, and on balance the authority decides that the costs exceed the benefits and refuses per-mission, then that decision has avoided imposing social costs on the population, and any delay in making it is immaterial. Moreover, if the decisions which are made quickly are those where the costs greatly exceed the benefits or the benefits greatly exceed the costs so that the decision that must be made by the committee is clear, then the costs of delay in these cases will be minimal since the delays will be short. Finally, if the cases that go to appeal or that are subject to long drawn out negotiations are those where social costs and social benefits are finely balanced, then, given that the net social benefit of a development that is finally permitted is small, the social cost of delay will therefore also be small. Indeed, the delay may be regarded as beneficial from society's point of view if the inquiry process that causes the delay results in a better development than would have been built otherwise (Keogh & Evans 1992).

This argument depends upon the acceptance of the view that planning decisions are themselves optimal and that the consideration of planning applications is a balancing of the costs and benefits. If this is so then the social cost of delay is minimal. If, however, planning decisions do not optimise in this way, then the social costs of delay will magnify the cost of this economic inefficiency. So, if the system delays the construction of a development in respect of which the social benefits substantially outweigh the social costs, then the social costs of the delay are themselves high. However, the social costs of delay will be completely outweighed by the social cost incurred if an application is refused that should have been per-mitted, since the social benefits would outweigh the costs. The delay in this case is permanent. And the costs of delay are also eclipsed by the social cost of allowing an application where the costs outweigh the benefits, and which should therefore be refused. Whether the planning system is optimal in this sense is questionable and we will return to the problem in the final chapter.

It can be seen that as well as causing delay and increasing uncertainty the process of seeking planning permission lends itself to strategic thinking and behaviour. Moreover, the strategy adopted may be different for different kinds of developer. A small firm working mainly within one or two local authorities may seek a good working relationship, and so may not wish to appeal against refusals. On the other hand, a volume house builder, operating on a national scale would be more likely to appeal since a good relationship with any single authority is of relatively little value.

A further consequence of the lack of certainty created by a 'non-zoning' system is that it encourages the possession by large developers such as volume house builders of land banks, land on which planning permission has been obtained and which can be developed at some future time. A developer such as a volume house builder will seek to ensure continuity in the supply of sites for development so as to ensure that management, equipment and labour can be used efficiently, being transferred from one site to another without being laid off or idle. Commentary on the financial pages of newspapers would suggest that a land bank of at least three years' supply seems to be regarded as necessary for the financial health of a house builder. To maintain such a land bank in a 'non-zoning' context requires that rather more applications are made and they are made somewhat earlier than would be the case if there was more certainty about the outcome. The number of applications actually made will depend upon the perceived probability of success, and the length of time it is expected that it will take to carry through each application to a final decision. It is evident that there is an incentive to make more applications than the minimum in order to be absolutely sure that the minimum necessary number of sites will be available in the future. A site with planning permission can be kept to a later date, in the company's land bank, or it can be sold, and the cost of making the application recouped. On the other hand, not having a site available for development at the right time can mean that an exorbitant price will have to be paid to buy one, in order to keep the firm in business (White 1986).

It can be seen that the planning system is not neutral with respect to the process of construction and development but affects its character and operation. In the British 'non-zoning' system, obtaining planning permission becomes an important part of the business. It is likely, particularly in areas of planning constraint where planning permission is itself worth a considerable sum, that the planning side will contribute far more to the profits of the business than the construction side. Indeed, one consequence is that some firms in the UK have concentrated solely on this side of the business, selling the land once permission has been obtained for the actual building to be done by some other firm.

It can also be seen that the system will tend to favour the large development and the large developer over the small. The cost of making an application, and in particular the cost of going to appeal will not increase in proportion with the size of the development. Further, it is possible for the large developer to employ the staff and advisers to carry through a number of applications at the same time. For a small firm this may be uneconomic because of the cost. The result as White (1986) notes, is that small firms are the ones likely to be forced into making 'suicidal' bids to try to obtain land for development.

In favouring the large over the small, the system will also have aesthetic consequences, favouring large-scale development over small and uniformity over variety. For example, a normal process in France or the United States would be for a would-be buyer to select a design from a house builder's portfolio, the design only being settled at the time that building is about to start. This would be more difficult in Britain where planning permission is given on the basis of the design submitted, and a change in the design would require planning permission to be sought again. It is easier for everybody if, for example, a housing development is large, and with relatively few differences between the planned houses. Bland uniformity is more likely to be acceptable without question than variety and variousness. If virtually all the houses are the same, this minimises the time that the developer and the development control committee have to spend on matters of design.

The supply of land by government

The zoning and non-zoning systems of planning currently practised in the USA and the UK have one thing in common. In both cases the planning systems attempt to control the use to which a piece of land can be put by its owner, but they take no steps to compel the land to be developed and used in this way. In a US city agricultural land may be zoned for development for single family housing but no government will make this happen. Government powers for planning the use of land held in the private sector are negative not positive, things can be prevented from happening but they cannot be made to happen. The systems are reactive. Obviously with respect to activities in the public sector the position is different; there is, of course, expected to be some internal consistency in what one arm of government plans and another arm of government does, road building being the most obvious example.

This was not expected to be the case when the modern British planning system was initiated in 1947. At that time it was expected that things would so turn out that all property development would be carried out in the public sector and none, or virtually none, in the private sector. This view was sanctioned by the existence of a 100% Betterment Levy which made private sector property development unprofitable, and was intended to do so. The idea fell by the wayside with the return of the Conservatives to power in 1951, and although two attempts to revive it were made, in the creation of the Land Commission in the 1960s and through the Community Land Act in the 1970s, these creations of Labour governments were repealed by the Conservative governments that succeeded them. They were never seriously operated, although it may be noted that the Welsh Land Agency, created in the 1970s, continued to exist.

The position in some other countries has been very different from that existing in Britain and the USA. Local and central governments have been active in ensuring that what is planned takes place, and in an ordered fashion. So, in The Netherlands it has been normal for a local authority to buy up land which is zoned for development in the ensuing period, if necessary using its powers of compulsory purchase to ensure acquiescence on the part of land owners, to lay out and service the land with infrastructure, and to sell the serviced sites on to construction firms for development. The process is described by a number of authors and in some detail by Needham (1992). It was referred to in earlier chapters because the system provides information on the price of land at various stages on the path to development.

A similar kind of policy has been pursued in Sweden (Duncan 1985; Kalbro & Mattsson 1995) although there the local authorities have not been so involved in buying up land as in The Netherlands, so that a larger proportion has been developed without passing through government hands. Furthermore the Swedish local authorities appear to have attempted to buy further ahead in time, in anticipation of future development, rather than to facilitate immediate development.

Another example of this in practice was the development of the city of Canberra as the capital of Australia. All the land in the area which was designated as that of the Australian Capital Territory was acquired from the pastoralists who farmed it and grazed stock on it. As the city was built, land was progressively released for development, as and when it was thought that new housing, shops, etc., should be provided. The Commonwealth government retained the freehold of all the land, however, selling only leasehold rights. Although the policy has not been as comprehensive as in Canberra, the Australian States have operated policies of buying up land ahead of development, although only in South Australia did the State's role become significant (Neutze 1977, p. 212).

For historical reasons a policy somewhat similar to that pursued in Canberra has been operated in Hong Kong. In the Crown Colony all the land was owned by the Crown. Partly as a result of this situation an idiosyncratic system of planning and controlling land development came into existence. The government of the Crown Colony sold land for development with the requirements as to how the land should be developed, in effect the planning conditions, attached as conditions relating to the sale (Bristow 1987; Staley 1994).

The policies of controlling the land to be released for development pursued in these various countries are significantly different from the policies pursued elsewhere, and, it might be thought, confer some significant advantages. From a planning point of view the systems are 'positive' rather than 'negative'. From an economic point of view the effect is to alter the supply of land, affecting both its price and the pattern of development. This is most obvious at the urban fringe. Suppose that expansion at the urban fringe is relatively uncontrolled, except through zoning of the development which occurs. Some land will be sold by its owner for development, but other land will not be sold. The owners will prefer to wait for the kind of reasons we discussed in Chapter 7, attachment to the location, speculation and uncertainty about the future. The result is that the pattern of development will be haphazard and what has come to be called urban sprawl will occur. The price of land will be higher than it otherwise would have been since the margin of urban development is some distance further from the city centre than it might have been if development had been more compact.

This more compact development can be achieved by methods of 'positive planning'. The authority buying and supplying the land can ensure that land which is closer to the city is developed first, and land prices will, if anything, tend to be lower because of the compactness of the pattern of development of the city. On the other hand, if methods of 'negative planning' are to be used then the only way to try to achieve similar compactness is by imposing an urban growth boundary or green belt around the city. As we demonstrated in Chapter 6, the effect of such a boundary is to limit the supply of land for development and to cause land and property values to rise. The higher land values are expected to induce land owners to sell, where development is permitted, although of course, for speculative and other reasons, some land may still be left undeveloped.

The economic argument can be illustrated diagrammatically, although the diagrammatic analysis fails to take into account the effects of compactness on land values. Figure 12.1 is a version of a diagram used in Chapter 7. Land is represented along the horizontal axis and OQ is an area of land lying outside the built up area of a city. Prices are indicated on the vertical axes. OA is the price of land for agriculture both here and elsewhere. SXS' is the supply of land to the market in the period representing the preferences of the owners of land. Some would be willing to sell, would be in the market, at the going (agricultural) market price, OA. The others would be unwilling to sell at that price but would be willing to sell for a higher price, the range

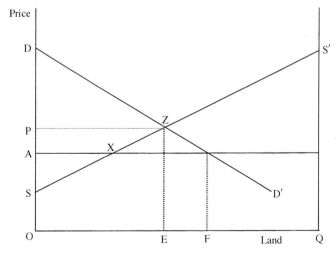

Figure 12.1

of prices which would be acceptable being indicated by the upward sloping line XS'. The demand for land for urban use, i.e. housing, is represented by the downward sloping demand curve DD'. The figure shows that in the absence of any government intervention equilibrium in the demand and supply of land for development would be indicated by the intersection of the demand and supply curve at Z. The price would be OP on the vertical axis and on the horizontal axis OE is sold for urban development. The price of land for housing, OP, will be higher than its price for agriculture, OA. It should also be noticed that the land sold for development will be randomly scattered through the area since there is no presumption that the land owners who are most willing to sell are those owning land close to the urban area.

Government intervention in the land market would enable it to buy up a similar area of land equal to OE, but adjacent to the existing urban area. The price paid could be equal to OA if its powers of compulsory purchase were fully exercised. It could then sell it on at a price OP taking a profit. It could alternatively buy more land at this price, up to OF in the figure, leading to the price of housing being lower. Since Needham (1992) reports that the Dutch local authorities pay a price well above agricultural use price, the option chosen seems to be that of paying OP or more for the land, to compensate the land owners for having to sell their land, but giving the advantage to the city of a more compact and ordered development.

The economic situation if a government tries to achieve compactness using 'negative planning' methods such as an urban growth boundary was demonstrated in Chapter 7 and was represented there in Figure 7.6. We showed there that limiting the area of land available for development will result in higher land prices. Since there are fewer land owners able to sell, developers have to bid more to persuade the unwilling owners that it would be best to sell. With less land available, less is developed and the price is higher. What is sold, however, lies wholly within the boundary and the development is more compact (Evans 2004, Ch. 12).

But intervention through negative planning methods to achieve compact-ness and prevent urban sprawl does so only by causing the price of land and housing to be higher than it otherwise would be. Intervention using positive planning methods, as in The Netherlands, will tend both to achieve com-pactness *and* to reduce the price of land and housing. The sole cost arises from the fact that the land has to be acquired using at least the threat of compulsory purchase. Many of the original land owners will therefore receive a price that is lower than they might have achieved in the market, or will have to sell earlier than they would have wished to have done. Some would regard this as an infringement of individual liberty. An extreme expression of this view is presented by Cobin (1997), who holds that land owners should not be subject to any responsibilities to the state. Nevertheless, it might be argued on the other side that negative planning methods result in a large number of people having to pay more for their houses than they might otherwise have had to, and this may conversely be regarded as an infringement suffered by them. In The Netherlands it would appear that it is expected that development will occur in this way so that land owners can anticipate that they may have to sell out at some point. Knowledge, rather than uncertainty, about this almost certainly makes it easier to accept and to plan for (Evans 2004, Ch. 13).

Conclusions

In this chapter we have looked at three ways in which planning systems may differ. First, it seems that planning systems generally use controls instead of taxes and the reasons why this might be were examined. Although there would be good political reasons and some economic reasons why controls will be preferred, it still seems odd that the influence of taxation on land use is generally ignored – indeed politicians seem to take the view that taxes affect land use only when they say they do, if the relationship between taxation and the demand for housing in Britain is a guide.

Second, planning systems can differ in the level of detail which they consider and the extent to which development proposals are submitted to examination. The British 'non-zoning' system requires virtually all proposals to be put forward for permission or refusal. This contrasts with 'zoning' systems where a proposal is deemed acceptable if it is in accord with the zoning plan. It is argued that the British system affects the way in which development is carried out, favouring large scale and more uniform developments. It is also clear that it causes delay in the construction of those buildings which are approved, and also creates a level of risk and uncertainty since with any application there is the possibility it may be rejected.

Third, planning systems vary in the extent to which governments involve themselves in the bringing forward of land for development. Most, whether using zoning or non-zoning methods do not do so. Rather they lay down in greater or less detail how they expect the land to be used and refuse permission for land to be developed in ways which are not in accordance with their plans. It is then up to the private sector. Land owners may choose to keep their land in its existing use if they so wish. This can lead to urban sprawl at the urban fringe as the owners of different pieces of land take differing decisions. In some countries, of which The Netherlands is the most notable example, governments will acquire land for development and bring it forward in an ordered manner, leading to more compact patterns of development. It can be shown that this kind of procedure will achieve as much or more compactness with lower land prices than would be obtained using methods such an urban growth boundary to limit the extent of development.

13

Politics, Public Choice and Political Economy

'How now, how now! What say the citizens!'
(Richard III)

Introduction

In the preceding chapters we initially applied welfare economic analysis to understand, from an economic point of view, what planning might be about and how it might be evaluated. Then we went on to show that the use of physical controls to determine land use, the means of controlling land use usually adopted, has particular consequences in that it creates differences in land values, most obviously resulting in much increased land values where use is most constrained. We have then shown how these land value differences, in themselves, have affected the planning system, the physical layout and structure of areas, and people's behaviour. And finally we have explored alternative approaches to land use planning looking at their advantages and disadvantages.

In the course of the analysis we have tended to assume, have had to assume, that the purpose of land use planning is the maximisation of economic welfare. This had to be assumed in the first place because otherwise we could not use welfare economic analysis which is based on this assumption. Moreover, it seemed sensible to start off with this presumption in order to find out, at the least, how far the land use planning system lived up to this expectation. It would seem odd to start with the assumption that the aim is not to maximise welfare.

Nevertheless, this is not the explicit objective of the planners and the planning system. It is only an objective identified by economists as to what the objective ought to be. It is also possible to try to see in what ways the system, qua system, does not operate to achieve this objective. In other words we come back to the crucial difference between an 'ought' and an 'is'. This is well defined in economics. It marks the difference between normative or welfare economics and positive economics, the analysis of how the economic system ought to operate and what ought to be done to increase welfare, and the analysis of what actually happens and why.

To a large extent in the preceding chapters we have been concerned with the positive economic side of planning, for example in the discussions of the consequences of increased land values. There still remains a further 'positive' question, however, as to why the planning system is as it is, why it may not set out to maximise welfare and what happens instead.

The process of planning, the planning system, is made up from a very large number of decisions being made by professional planners, elected councillors, and officials and ministers of central government. The decisions which they make are not made, of that we can be absolutely sure, in the light of whether economic welfare will be increased by what they decide, but in response to government policies, physical planning principles, and, last but not least, electoral pressure. How then does the system operate? It will certainly be true that decisions will be made that do not increase welfare, no system is perfect, but is there any systematic way in which planning decisions diverge from the optimum.

What we will suggest is that decisions are heavily influenced by political pressures, and by the assessment of politicians, whether local or national, as to the relative importance of these pressures. In economics the view that the actions of governments are primarily determined, not by the views of politicians and officials as to what would be best for society, but by their views as to what would be best for them has come to be called public choice theory, and associated with the work of James Buchanan. The application of public choice theory as a positive theory of planning has been suggested by Poulton (1991a, 1991b) and its application discussed by Poulton (1997), Pennington (2000), and Webster (1998). We start, however, with an alternative economic approach, the application of the economics of regulation.

Economics, the regulator and the regulated

The economics of regulation was developed originally by George Stigler and largely derived from United States' experience in the regulation of public utilities such as electricity supply. It suggests that the operations of industry regulators and regulatory systems are likely to be 'captured' by the industry that is regulated (Stigler 1973). Since the consumers of the product in whose interests regulation is meant to take place are many, dispersed, and unorganised, while the representatives of the regulated industry are few and organised, it is inevitable, it is argued, that an amicable relationship will be built up between the regulator and the regulated. This close relationship will be assisted by the fact that in order to regulate an industry the regulator must obtain information from the industry, being in consequence both indebted to the industry for the data provided and dependent on the accuracy of the industry's own information, as to, for example, their costs and profitability.

An example of this close relationship between regulator and regulated in the UK is the cosy relationship which existed over the years between the farming industry and the former Ministry of Agriculture Fisheries and Food. It has often been remarked that MAFF has more often seen itself as a defender of the industry than as its controller and regulator, and that any change, whether it is to increase production or preserve the environment by reducing production, seems to mean greater subsidies to the industry than before (Bowers & Cheshire 1983; Pennington 1996).

Is the regulatory relationship within the planning system of this kind? Certainly there are occasions when this is a possibility. So, as we noted in Chapter 11, representatives of the house builders are supposed to meet with local planners to discuss and agree the availability of land for development. At the Enquiry in Public which is now required prior to approval of any area Structure Plan, representatives of major developers and land owners will appear to put the case for their land to be designated in the plan as suitable for development (Adams 1994). The position of each developer or land owner is, however, somewhat ambivalent. Each wishes their land to be so designated but has little interest in any general relaxation of constraint. In this way are their profits maximised. Developers and land owners are unlikely to argue for any substantial relaxation of a strict control on the availability of land since the tighter the control the higher the price that can be obtained for their product.

But the resemblance of this situation to that of a regulated industry is not close, since planners and politicians do not seek to regulate the profits of property development The planning authorities do not see it as their responsibility to keep down or reduce the price of land or the profits of developers and builders. Certainly a close relationship exists but the analogy breaks down because the planning authorities themselves have an interest in restricting the supply of land for development. If anything it could be said that it is not that the interests of the 'regulators' have come to coincide with the interests of the 'regulated', rather, in this industry, the interests of the 'regulated', the builders, have come to coincide with the interests of the 'regulators', the planners. The planning authorities have a greater interest in constraint. The developers and builders have sought some relaxation in the strictness of control, even if in their own interest. The reasons for the constraint on the availability of land have therefore to be sought elsewhere.

The farming industry and the rural population

While the planning system does not appear to be operated in the interests of the building industry, there is at least some evidence that it has been run in the interests, initially of the farming industry, more recently in the interests of rural residents.

In Britain there has been for many years a strong political lobby defending the interests of farming and rural communities. We mentioned above the way in which MAFF appears to operate, not to regulate farming but as a lobby for support from government and the Treasury in particular. This is associated with a strong popular prejudice in favour of the countryside. As I have argued elsewhere, this prejudice appears often irrational, and some-times seems based, albeit subconsciously, on a folk memory of the Second World War, and hence on a view that Britain should import as little food as possible (Evans 2001). If Americans are automatically in favour of 'motherhood and apple pie', then the British equivalent would be the countryside, the defence of which is led by the Council for the Protection of Rural England.

It is relevant to note that when the Town and Country Planning Act 1947 came into force, it was, despite its name, primarily a town planning act rather than a country planning act. Farm buildings and farm activities were not subject to planning control. Farmers could erect factory buildings for factory farming and did not need permission to do so. Any other kind of factory at any location whether urban or rural did require permission. One can see evidence here of the MAFF lobby mentioned above. The overt reason for this omission at the time would appear to be that farmers were then being encouraged to produce as much as possible and no bureaucratic obstacles were to be put in their way. There was a view also, promoted and supported by the farming industry itself, that the farmers were in some sense the 'trustees' or 'guardians of the countryside' and that it could safely be left in their hands. From a political viewpoint one may also note that about 10% of the working population was employed in agriculture at that time so that it constituted a formidable lobby. From an economic point of view it might also be argued that since rural areas were thinly populated the effects of bad buildings were felt by fewer people than in towns, although this argument runs counter to the general prejudice against any other type of building in the countryside.

The years since the passing of that Act have seen considerable changes in the countryside as the farming industry, helped by large subsidies, strove to increase output – building factory farms, grubbing up hedge-rows, and increasingly engaging in monoculture over large areas. As output and productivity rose the proportion of the total working population employed in agriculture fell to below 2%. Further, as employment in agriculture fell, and car ownership rose, so the villages and rural areas that had formerly only housed farmers and rural labourers increasingly became dominated by people who lived there, or had their second home there, but worked in an urban area. This new rural population was not concerned with agricultural output but with maintaining the 'rurality' of the villages and the areas to which they had moved. A significant indication of the shift in the balance of power was a change in the law. Since 1995 new farm buildings or changes to existing farm buildings have required planning permission if they were located within 400 metres of any residential buildings (Department of the Environment 1997). The people occupying these residential buildings, to whom the power to object to an agricultural building was now given, would, of course, tend to be precisely the new rural population of urban workers. Further, since the rurality of the area is capitalised into the value of the homes they have bought, in a way that it is not capitalised into the value of a farm, these former town dwellers, the new residents in the rural areas, have become the strongest defenders of the countryside, and those most strongly opposed to any further development.

Thus, if the planning system can be said to generally favour any class or group, it is the farming industry on the one hand and the residents of rural areas who would seem the main beneficiaries. The fact that the British political system is based on MPs and other political representatives being elected to represent particular residential areas assists by giving political weight to their interests since they are spatially defined. And, as Pennington demonstrates, the political system then gives greater weight to their special interest. He found that MPs from metropolitan constituencies were significantly under represented on the House of Commons Select Committees for both Environment and Agriculture (Pennington 2000, p. 135–7). However, this explains only one aspect of the planning system. We still have to look further.

Public participation, public choice

A feature of the British planning system, since 1968 at least, is the deliberate involvement of the general public. As we have already mentioned in Chapter 12, planning applications are considered by planning officers who are professional planners who submit them for decision to a Development Control Committee of locally elected politicians, with or without a recommendation. The public participate by sending comments on applications to the local authority, the points in their letters being summarised by planning officers and passed on to the Committee. If they feel strongly, of course, members of the public can write directly to their elected representatives or lobby them. In some authorities those objecting can ask to address the committee.

The peculiarity of this system is that it gives weight to objections, to lobbying against a proposal. The position can be illustrated if we return to the diagram which we used in Chapter 2 to analyse the economics of external diseconomies. In Figure 13.1 prices and costs are represented on the vertical axis. Suppose that a series of developments are proposed which will provide a quantity of housing, OS, and this is represented on the horizontal axis. The social value of the housing can be represented by the marginal profit to the developer and starts as OA on the left-hand vertical axis, falling as the amount of housing built increases. If all the proposals were accepted then the profit from the last house would be SB on the right-hand vertical axis. Suppose also that construction of this housing would impact on the environment of those living in the area if more than OE, on the horizontal axis is built, and the social cost of each additional house increases, as indicated by the upward sloping line EG. It is evident that the socially

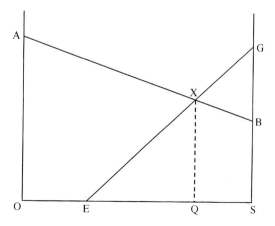

Figure 13.1

optimal level of development is given by the point at which the marginal social cost equals the marginal social benefit. In the figure this is X and the socially optimal level of development is therefore OQ.

The marginal cost is not borne by the same people as those who gain the benefit, however. Those gaining the benefit are the owner of the land, the developer and the builder, and the future occupants of the houses. One of the first three will be the applicant whose case is, in effect, the application. The future residents are usually unidentified and unidentifiable, and so have no say. Those suffering the costs are, however, not only identifiable but are current residents in the area of the local authority making the decision, and, more importantly, voters in the next election. The elected councillors on the Committee, as politicians who hope to be re-elected, will pay more attention to the objections of their current electors than they will to the views of a the single applicant who may or may not be a voter, or to the possible views of any putative future resident who will not even have a vote in the area if permission is refused. It would be surprising if the committee did not err on the side of safety and restrict the amount of development it allowed. In Figure 13.1 the amount of housing permitted could be expected to be restricted to a level below the optimum OQ, and to be much closer to OE, the output in respect of which no objections would be received. Thus, in terms of public choice theory the system is designed so as to support a no-change position.

Whether it is a good idea to set up a system which will resist change is open to question. Economists tend to assume that people's preferences are given, stable and rational. There is, however, experimental evidence to suggest that people's choices are biased in that they will tend to prefer what they have to what they might have. The phenomenon has been thoroughly studied and is variously called the Inertia, Endowment, or Status Quo effect (Kahneman *et al.* 1991). For example, to simplify one such study, Kahneman *et al.* (1990) divided a group of Cornell University students into two sets, one set being given a Cornell mug, its current price being also indicated, the other set being given money which they could use to buy the mugs if they wished, the others being likewise allowed to sell. Generally those who received the mug preferred to keep the mug and those who received the money preferred the money. Thus, although those who received the mugs had no sentimental or other previous attachment to them, they generally wanted to keep them.

Let us put this into planning terms. If it was proposed that a new village be built on some open land, then people would prefer that it were not built and would object to the proposal. Supposing on the other hand that the village already existed and it was proposed that it should be demolished to create more open countryside, then people would prefer that it was not demolished and would object to this proposal. An actual example, to which I have referred elsewhere (Evans 1991), is the Ribblehead Viaduct in Yorkshire. A proposal that this rail viaduct across a valley in the North Yorkshire countryside should be demolished was opposed by a group pressing for its preservation. But had there been no viaduct, and it was proposed that one should be built, there is no doubt that this too would have been vociferously opposed. We expect that people will object to change, because they have become attached, for sentimental or historical reasons, to what they are familiar with. The laboratory experiments indicate that even without any familiarity with the existing situation, there would be a preference for the status quo. It follows that this preference will only be strengthened if there is a history which provides some justification for it.

What has been set up by the British planning system is a system which allows this preference for the status quo to be expressed through the political system. The politicians who operate the system have strong incentives to listen to the objections expressed by voters to any proposal, and to give them weight. They are not going to try to calculate and take into account the benefits which might be gained by those who stand to benefit, who are not necessarily voters.

It is, I confess, difficult to give hard statistical evidence of this of the kind preferred by economists. Experience and involvement in the system over many years on both the development and the objecting side has led me to this view. One example will be given, chosen from many that could be given because it is clearest. In 1989 the University of Reading wished to increase the size of one of its catered Halls of Residence by building a new block for a hundred students. In doing so it proposed to construct the new building so that a pedestrian quadrangle was formed at the centre for the Hall. To achieve this it was proposed that a new vehicular entry to the Hall should be built, from the end of an adjacent road, to allow access for lorries bringing catering supplies to the kitchens, so that they did not need to drive into the central quadrangle. Although the new entry was some distance from any houses, and the vehicles would not pass their houses, the 24 households living on this road lobbied strongly against the proposal which, as a result, was refused. Permission would only be given if the lorries continued to drive into the central quadrangle.

Since the sole diseconomy is the noise and disruption caused by the lorries, it would seem obvious on any evaluation of relative social costs that the costs would be lower when only some 24 houses, say 60 people, were affected by them passing at some distance, than they would be if 350 students plus other residents were affected by them driving through the centre of their Hall. Thus, the decision of the local authority clearly did not maximise net social welfare. On the other hand, it may be perceived that from an electoral viewpoint the nearby residents had more power than the students since they would still be there and voting at the next election. Current students, on the other hand, were indifferent since they would not be there when the building was finished, and future students would be unaware of the events of two or three years before. The decision of the local authority was therefore in line with a public choice assessment of the situation.

At an altogether different level of the political system it is well known that during the period of the Thatcher administration the political ideology was in favour of the market and a relaxation of controls. But although moves were made in the direction of relaxing planning constraints, in particular by stating that there should be a 'presumption in favour of development', in practice there would seem to have been little actual relaxation of the degree of constraint. The votes to be lost by allowing development were usually perceived as greater than the votes to be gained. So politicians like Nicholas Ridley gave speeches in favour of the system of control, although it is evident that their political ideology was against it. The experience of Consortium Developments Ltd, a firm that was set up by a group of volume house builders to try to obtain permission for a new medium-sized town somewhere in the London region is relevant. Although it was set up on the basis that some form of private new town of this kind would be favoured, in practice they were unsuccessful in obtaining permission. Three major proposals were made and the nearest to success was reached with one called 'Foxley Wood' to the south-west of London and beyond the green belt. The application was unprecedentedly supported at the planning appeal (the application was, of course, refused by the local authority), by a statement by the Department of Trade and Industry as to the need for new housing to accommodate the labour that was required in the area by firms facing severe labour shortages. The Inspector initially supported the local authority and refused the appeal, but the decision was called in by the then Secretary of State, Nicholas Ridley, and the proposal approved. Shortly afterwards his successor, Chris Patten, reversed this decision and the application was, in the end, refused. It is clear that the political disturbance created by the possibility that the development would be approved was in the end a deciding factor, particularly for a politician like Patten less in favour of the market than Ridley.

Economic welfare and the planning system

Does it matter if the system operates in a way which does not maximise economic welfare, in some sense, but in a way designed to maximise the electoral position of politicians? If we are solely concerned with explaining how the system works, with creating a 'positive theory of planning' as Poulton suggests, then the answer is no. But if we wish to take a more normative viewpoint, to suggest that the way the system operates significantly reduces welfare, then the answer is yes.

In the first place we have argued earlier that there is a significant distortion because the values of the farming community and of rural dwellers are given a considerably greater weight in the system because of the way that it is set up and operates. The results, in terms of the costs imposed on those living in cities, have been documented in earlier chapters, in particular Chapters 6, 10 and 11. To take one point from these. One effect of urban constraint is the building over of open spaces such as allotments and playing fields within urban areas. It seems odd to sacrifice open space in urban areas, where it is in short supply, in order to preserve rural open space, which is plentiful. On the other hand, the distortion of the political system serves to explain it (if it does not excuse it).

More important than the bias against the towns built into the system is the negative bias of the system and its impact on the whole economy. The negative impact on the system occurs in a number of ways. One such is the effect of delays built into the system. It was argued in the previous chapter that the social cost of delay was low if the delays occurred because of the difficulty of balancing the costs and the benefits. In effect the delay was part of the cost of making the right decision and of acquiring the information to do so. But, if the correct decisions are not being made in that costs and benefits are not being carefully balanced, then delay becomes a more important problem. If developments where the benefits substantially out-weigh the costs are also delayed, then delays will impose a substantial drag on the economic system. Such delays may occur if politicians play the system. For example, if it is expected that a proposal would be approved on appeal to the Secretary of State, the politicians on the Committee may impose conditions which delay development but may not actually refuse the application. In this way they can indicate to voters that they have done their best, and could do no more, citing the fact that they would lose an appeal.

Clearly these delays reduce economic growth since investment occurs later than it otherwise would. A more important cost to the system will be the fact that the negative bias in the system will ensure that developments which would increase economic growth and economic welfare are refused. Sometimes the fact that growth will be delayed and reduced is admitted and made explicit. For example, the revised Oxfordshire Structure Plan for the early 1990s stated that 'the Council does not wish to restrict unduly the development of small firms, or the expansion of [existing] firms' in Oxfordshire, as industrial development and housing is concentrated in a few locations and footloose firms are discouraged from moving to the county (Oxfordshire County Council 1990). But the implication of this statement is that it was intended to restrict the growth of firms in Oxfordshire, even if 'not unduly'. But how much is 'not unduly'. Even if the effect were only equal to one half of 1% per annum the cumulative effect is not negligible. After half a century, the period the current system has been in operation, incomes in Oxfordshire, on average, would be 25% less than they might otherwise have been. The effects in any one year are so small as to be able to be neglected, but the cumulative effect of a restraint on growth may be considerable.

The prevention of development, the negative effect of the system, becomes in the end accepted and, indeed, a matter for self-congratulation for politicians, who are, after all, doing what their constituents want, and feel that they are therefore entitled to some credit. For example, the chairman of the Reading planning committee, on leaving the post in 1989, said that he thought that his period of office had been very successful – because of the number of proposals which had been refused – 'Not one new major office development has been approved in Reading ... We managed to keep development down' (*Reading Chronicle* (12 May) 1989).

Sometimes the costs of delay become obvious. The extreme example is the saga of Terminal 5 at Heathrow. It was first proposed in 1981, but the application was turned down by an inspector who concluded, nevertheless, that a fifth terminal would be needed. A second application was made in 1993, and this went to a public inquiry which opened in 1995, and took four years, hearing 730 witnesses and costing £83m. The inspector's report took 18 months to write and the government considered it for 11 months before, finally, in November 2001 approving construction of the proposed terminal. When fully completed it will be nearly a quarter of a century since it was first proposed. Given that rival airports such as Amsterdam Schiphol, Paris Charles de Gaulle, and Frankfurt had been able to propose, design and construct major improvements in much shorter periods of time it was obvious that the costs of delay arising from the British procedure far outweighed any possible gain. A result was a set of government proposals to speed up the planning process in the case of major infrastructure projects (Department of Transport, Local Government and the Regions 2001).

The implication is that the planning system has had a significant economic impact on the UK economy since it came into effect 50 years ago, and that as a result the British GNP per capita is lower than it would otherwise have been. The gain has been a tidier physical environment than is observable in many other countries, particularly those with more rapid rates of economic growth. This negative impact is not usually noted by economists seeking reasons for the low rate of growth of the British economy, but that is because few economists have any interest whatsoever in planning. Their whole training leads them to ignore matters related to land and location, so they tend to consider only those factors conventionally considered 'economic' – investment, training, labour relations, management, etc. But since the planning system is designed to restrain physical development, it would be strange indeed if it did not restrain economic development as well. Moreover, as we noted in Chapter 11, the possible anti-competitive effects of the planning system have now been noted by at least one group of 'non-spatially oriented' economists in the McKinsey Global Institute's 1998 report on productivity and growth in the British economy.

Sustainability

Of course, it could be, and is, argued that at the moment economic growth should be tempered and controlled in the interests of global sustainability. In Britain over the past ten years 'sustainability' has increasingly been called in aid as the reason for planning constraints and controls. It was first evident in the planning guidance given by central government to local authorities on the subject of planning for transport in 1994 (Department of the Environment 1994). There physical planning methods were outlined as a means of reducing the use of the private car. The problem is that no change in existing planning policies was, in practice, suggested. The usual policies of constraint on any development outside existing urban areas were restated and justified by the need for 'sustainability', despite some empirical evidence that they could actually result in increased car use (Headicar & Curtis 1994). There was no consideration of, indeed no mention of, the impact of green belts on the use of transport in causing people to live beyond the green belts and to have to commute across them to work. Any serious consideration of planning policies in relation to the concept of sustainability would suggest that development might be permitted on the inner edge of green belts so that journeys to work could be shortened and car use reduced. The empirical research quoted earlier by Headicar & Curtis (1994) on car use in new housing developments in Oxfordshire drew attention to the way in which the green belts around Oxford and London appeared to cause people to live further away from their work and to use cars, noting that those living in new developments close to Oxford used their cars less and had shorter journeys to work.

The Rogers Report (Urban Task Force 1999), a White Paper (DETR 2000a) and subsequent planning guidance on housing (PPG3) and transport (PPG13), however, marked a lightening of the policy of constraint in the interests of sustainability (DETR 2000b). The one argued that the density of new development should be increased. The other that car use was to be discouraged, by, for example, limiting the amount of off-road car parking space which might be provided in any new development.

From an economic viewpoint, there are a number of problems with taking the concept of sustainability as the prime motivator for the planning system. First, it is sometimes not obvious what is meant by 'sustainable', but let us assume that what is meant is the limitation of fossil fuel use and carbon dioxide emissions in the interest of global sustainability. Then if one accepts, and I do, that something needs to be done urgently to control emissions and limit global warming, first, it is not obvious that this is best done through the planning system. Planning controls can deal with local externalities, as we showed earlier. It is not at all clear that they can deal with global externalities.

Second, it should be transparently obvious that if only 1% or 2% of the urbanised areas are built or redeveloped each year, then it will take 50 years or more to have a noticeable effect on fuel use, operating through the planning system. If the problem is believed to be serious then other measures which operate more quickly should be taken. If it is not believed to be serious then making it the primary motivation for planning controls is at best misleading.

Third, if the use of fossil fuel is the problem, then taxes on fossil fuels have an immediate effect on consumption and on use. People adapt by using less, and this is so even if no new building takes place. But they may do so by using smaller, more fuel efficient cars, as well as making shorter journeys. Operating through the planning system allows the continued use of less fuel efficient vehicles.

Fourth, the policy of encouraging increased housing density is based on the fact that, across the cities of the world, there is a negative correlation between fossil fuel use and housing density. This is cited both in the Rogers

Report and in the White Paper. But high fuel use in the USA and Australia coincides with low densities and low fuel prices. Lower fuel consumption in Europe coincides with higher densities and higher fuel prices. The relationship between fuel use and density can be explained primarily by differences in the price of fuel. Thus, simply increasing density may not have the intended effect, indeed the effect may be the opposite of that intended, as the research by Headicar & Curtis, quoted earlier, demonstrated.

In conclusion

The analysis in this chapter has concentrated on the position in Great Britain. Any analysis depends upon the political situation in that country and it is difficult for an outsider to appreciate the nuances. The situation in Japan, for example, where use of powers of compulsory purchase is regarded as generally politically unacceptable, obviously differs significantly from that in The Netherlands where the possible use of powers of compulsory purchase is, at the least, a valid threat. Again, the purchase of land ahead of development is politically acceptable in The Netherlands, while three attempts to try to institute such a system in Britain have been swiftly abolished.

The Fifth Amendment to the US Constitution which, among other things, restricts the 'taking of land' without full compensation effectively dissuades city and state authorities from any form of development control which might be construed as 'taking'. This considerably distinguishes the US from most other countries where central governments at least have greater power. Nevertheless, a considerable amount of empirical evidence suggests that there too electoral and public choice considerations are probably more important than any attempt to maximise social welfare. We have mentioned in Chapter 5 that zoning is characterised as not only externality zoning but also fiscal zoning and exclusionary zoning. In both the latter two cases the prime motives are regarded as the benefit of the existing residents of the town, implicitly at the cost of others elsewhere. Other examples can be cited. For example, there is some evidence that when an urban area is governed by relatively few local authorities then they can be more restrictive, in effect can act in a cartel-like fashion, and house prices are then higher (Thorson 1996). Lenon *et al.* (1996) found considerable interdependence between zoning, taxing and spending for towns in Connecticut, both within towns and, apparently as a result of competition, between nearby towns. Competition with other nearby towns appears to have also affected the spread of growth controls in northern California.

But political influences can have different effects in different countries. Public choice does not necessarily lead to constraint. It has been argued that in Australia, particularly in New South Wales, developers have had the greatest influence. As a result, politicians have favoured development so that environmental safeguards and controls have been weakened if not dismantled (Gleeson & Hanley 1998). Again, in Italy, control over development has been so weak, for various reasons, social as well as political, that a third of the houses built have been put up without planning permission. Amnesties have then been declared so that on payment of a small fine, past illegal development can be legalised (Evans 2003).

Political influence on planning decisions is not then limited to the United Kingdom. Evidently the planning system is generally as affected by electoral influences as by the desire to maximise social welfare which is the economic justification for intervention in the land use system. The economist can therefore merely accept that this is so and set about analysing the way the system works, a positive economic or a public choice approach. In much of this book this has been the approach which has been adopted. But as was said above, the economic justification for planning is that intervention in the market can increase welfare. The early chapters of this book set out the way in which planning instruments and policies can be justified in these terms.

But the implication of the discussion in this chapter is that although welfare economics can justify intervention, the intervention which does occur is not of the kind justifiable in this way. Therefore, an altogether more difficult problem faces the economist analysing planning – to indicate the way in which the intervention that does take place actually reduces welfare. It is a more difficult task since, however correct may be the arguments marshalled by the economist it has to be recognised that the intervention that does occur is electorally popular and, for that reason, unlikely to be changed. To point out the costs of the policies pursued, and that they benefit the vocal few at the cost of the many, is therefore an unpopular course for an economist but one which is very necessary, in the hope, but not the expectation, that some improvement can be made.

References

Abercrombie, Patrick (1959) in: D. Rigby Childs (ed.) *Town and Country Planning*, 3rd edn. Oxford University Press, London.

Adair, A.S., J.N. Berry & W.S. McGreal (1991) Land availability, housing demand and the property market, *Journal of Property Research*, Vol. 8: 59–67.

Adams, D. (1994) *Urban Planning and the Development Process*. UCL Press, London.

Adams, J.G.U. (1974) ... and how much for your grandmother? *Environment and Planning A*, Vol. 6(6): 619–626.

Allinson, John & Janet Askew (1996) Planning gain, in: Clara Greed (ed.) *Implementing Town Planning*: 62–72. Longman, Harlow.

Ave, G. (1996) *Urban Land and Property Markets in Italy*. UCL Press, London.

Ball, Michael J. (1973) Recent empirical work on the determinants of relative house prices, *Urban Studies*, Vol. 10(2): 213–233.

Barker, Kate (2003) *Review of Housing Supply, Securing our Future Housing Needs: Interim Report – Analysis*. HMSO, Norwich.

Bhagwati, Jagdish N. (1982) Directly unproductive, profit-seeking (DUP) activities, *Journal of Political Economy*, Vol. 90(5): 988–1002.

Blair, Thomas L. (1973) *The Poverty of Planning: Crisis in the Urban Environment*. Macdonald, London.

Bliss, Barbara (1945) *The New Planning*. Faber and Faber, London.

Bowers, John (1992) The economics of planning gain: a reappraisal, *Urban Studies*, Vol. 29(8): 1329–1339.

Bowers, J.K. & Paul Cheshire (1983) *Agriculture, the Countryside and Land Use*. Methuen, London.

Bramley, G. (1993a) The impact of land use planning and tax subsidies on the supply and price of housing in Britain, *Urban Studies*, Vol. 30: 5–30.

Bramley, G. (1993b) Land use planning and the housing market in Britain: the impact on housebuilding and house prices, *Environment and Planning A*, Vol. 25: 1021–1051.

Breheny, M. (1999) People, households and houses: the basis to the 'great housing debate' in England, *Town Planning Review*, Vol. 70(3): 275–293.

Bristow, Roger (1987) *Land-use Planning in Hong Kong*. Oxford University Press, Hong Kong.

Brown, H.J., R.S. Phillips & N.A. Roberts (1981) Land markets at the urban fringe, *Journal of the American Planning Association*, Vol. 47(2): 131–144.

Buchanan, C.D. (1958) *Mixed Blessing: the Motor in Britain*. Leonard Hill, London.

Buchanan, D.H. (1929) The historical approach to rent and price theory, *Economica*, Vol. 9 (June): 123–155. Reprinted in: William Fellner & Bernard F. Haley (eds) (1957): *Readings in the Theory of Income Distribution*. Allen & Unwin, London.

Buckley, M. (1988) Multicriteria evaluation: measures, manipulation and meaning, *Environment and Planning B: Planning and Design*, Vol. 15(1): 55–64.

Campbell, Heather, Hugh Ellis, Caroline Gladwell & John Henneberry (2000) Planning obligations, planning practice, and land-use outcomes, *Environment and Planning B: Planning and Design*, Vol. 27(5): 759–775.

Cherry, Gordon E. (1996) *Town Planning in Britain since 1900: the Rise and Fall of the Planning Ideal*. Blackwell, Oxford.

Cheshire, Paul C. & Stephen Sheppard (2000) Building on brown fields: the price we pay, *Planning in London*, Vol. 33, April/June: 34–36.

Cheshire, Paul C., Stephen Sheppard & Alan Hooper (1985) The economic consequences of the British planning system: some empirical results, *Discussion Paper in Urban and Regional Economics*, No. 29, Department of Economics, University of Reading.

Chinitz, Ben (1961) Contrasts in agglomeration: New York and Pittsburgh, *American Economic Review*, Vol. 51(2): 279–289.

Clawson, M. & J.L. Knetsch (1966) *The Economics of Outdoor Recreation*. Johns Hopkins UP, Baltimore.

Coase, Ronald (1960) The problem of social cost, *Journal of Law and Economics*, Vol. 3(1): 1–44.

Cobin, John M. (1997) *Building Regulations, Market Alternatives, and Allodial Policy*. Avebury, Aldershot.

Crecine, J.P., O.A. Davis & J.E. Jackson (1967) Urban property markets: some empirical results and their implications for municipal zoning, *Journal of Law and Economics*, Vol. 10, 79–100.

Crook, A.D.H. (1998) Fiscal austerity, affordable housing and the planning system: betterment tax and hypothecation, *Town Planning Review*, Vol. 69(4): iii–vii.

Cullingworth, J.B. (1997) British land-use planning, *Urban Studies*, Vol. 34(5/6): 945–960.

Department of the Environment (1994) *Planning Policy Guidance Notes 13: Transport*. HMSO, London.

Department of the Environment (1995) *Planning Policy Guidance Notes 2: Green Belts*. HMSO, London.

Department of the Environment (1997) *Planning Policy Guidance: 7 (revised) – The Countryside*. Department of the Environment, London.

Department of the Environment, Transport, and the Regions (2000a) *Our Towns and Cities: the Future*. The Stationery Office, London.

Department of the Environment, Transport, and the Regions (2000b) *Planning Policy Guidance No 3: Housing*. The Stationery Office, London.

Department of the Environment, Transport, and the Regions (2000c) *Planning Policy Guidance No 13: Transport*. The Stationery Office, London.

Department of Transport, Local Government and the Regions (2001) *Major Infrastructure Projects: Delivering a Fundamental Change*. The Stationery Office, London.

Diamond, Derek R. (1991) The City, the 'Big Bang' and office development, in: Keith Haggard & David R. Green (eds), *London: A New Metropolitan Geography*. Ch. 5. Edward Arnold, London.

Douglas, Norman (1915/1983) *Old Calabria*. Century, London.

Duncan, S. (1985) Land policy in Sweden: separating ownership from development, in: S. Barrett & P. Healey (eds) *Land Policy: Problems and Alternatives*, Ch. 15: 308–344. Gower, Aldershot.

Evans, Alan W. (1973) *The Economics of Residential Location*. Macmillan, London.

Evans, Alan W. (1974a) Economics and planning, in: Jean Forbes (ed.) *Studies in Social Science and Planning*. Scottish Academic Press, Edinburgh.

Evans, Alan W. (1974b) Planning for offices: the economics of plot ratio control, in: Jean Forbes (ed.), *Studies in Social Science and Planning*, 81–99. Scottish Academic Press, Edinburgh.

Evans, Alan W. (1983) The determination of the price of land, *Urban Studies*, Vol. 20: 119–139.

Evans, Alan W. (1985) *Urban Economics*. Basil Blackwell, Oxford.

Evans, A.W. (1987) *House Prices and Land Prices in the South East: A Review*. House Builders Federation, London.

Evans, A.W. (1988) *No Room! No Room! The Costs of the British Town and Country Planning System*. Institute of Economic Affairs, London.

Evans, Alan W. (1990) The assumption of equilibrium in the analysis of migration and interregional differences: a review of some recent research, *Journal of Regional Science*, Vol. 30(4): 515–531.

Evans, Alan W. (1991) Rabbit hutches on postage stamps: planning, development and political economy, *Urban Studies*, Vol. 28(6): 853–870.

Evans, Alan W. (1998) Dr Pangloss finds his profession: sustainability, transport and land use planning in Britain, *Journal of Planning Education and Research*, Vol. 18: 137–144.

Evans, Alan W. (1999) The land market and government intervention, in: Paul C. Cheshire & Edwin S. Mills (eds) *Handbook of Regional and Urban Economics* 1637–1669. Elsevier Science, North Holland.

Evans, Alan W. (2001) *Challenging the Myth: What is the Countryside for?* Lecture, Royal Society of Arts, 4 December 2001. [www.rsalectures.org.uk].

Evans, Alan W. (2003) Shouting very loudly: economics, planning and politics, *Town Planning Review*, Vol. 74(2): 195–212.

Evans, Alan W. (2004) *Economics, Real Property and the Supply of Land*. Blackwell, Oxford.

Eve, Gerald (1992) *The Relationship between House Prices and Land Supply*. Department of the Environment Planning Research Programme. HMSO, London.

Fischel, W.A. (1989) What do economists know about growth controls? A research review, in: D.J. Brower, D.R. Godschalk & D.R. Porter (eds), *Understanding Growth Management*. The Urban Land Institute, Washington, DC.

Fischel, W.A. (1990) *Do Growth Controls Matter?* Lincoln Institute of Land Policy, Cambridge, MA.

Fischel, W.A. (1995) *Regulatory Takings: Law, Economics, and Politics*. Harvard University Press, Cambridge, MA.

Fischel, W.A. (2001) Why are there NIMBYs? *Land Economics*, Vol. 77(1): 144–153.

Foster, C.D. & C.M.E. Whitehead (1973) The Layfield Report on the Greater London Development Plan, *Economica*, Vol. 40(60).

GB Commission on the Third London Airport (1970) *Papers and Proceedings*, Vol. VII. HMSO, London.

GB Commission for the Third London Airport (1971) *Report*. HMSO, London.

Glaser, R., P. Haberzettl & R.P.D. Walsh (1991) Land reclamation in Singapore, Hong Kong and Macau, *Geo Journal*, Vol. 24, No. 4: 365–373.

Gleeson, Brendon & Penny Hanley (eds) (1998) *Renewing Australian Planning? New Challenges, New Agendas*. Urban Research Program, Australian National University, Canberra.

Greffe, Xavier (1990) *La Valeur Economique du Patrimoine*. Anthropos-Economica, Paris.

Grigson, W. (1986) *House Prices in Perspective: A Review of South-East Evidence*. SERPLAN, London.

Gyourko, J. (1991) Impact fees, exclusionary zoning, and the density of new development, *Journal of Urban Economics*, Vol. 30, pp. 242–256.

Hall, Peter (1980) *Great Planning Disasters*. Weidenfeld & Nicolson, London.

Hall, Peter (1982) *Urban and Regional Planning*, 2nd edn. Penguin Books, Harmondsworth.

Hall, Peter (1997) The future of the metropolis and its form, *Regional Studies*, Vol. 31(3) (May): 211–220.

Hall, Peter, H. Gracey, X. Drewett & R. Thomas (1973) *The Containment of Urban England*. Allen & Unwin, London.

Hannah, Lawrence M., Kyung-Hwan Kim & Edwin S. Mills (1993) Land-use controls and housing prices in Korea, *Urban Studies*, Vol. 30(1): 147–156.

Harrison, A.J. (1977) *Economics and Land Use Planning*. Croom Helm, London.

Hausman, Daniel M. & Michael S. McPherson (1996) *Economic Analysis and Moral Philosophy*. Cambridge University Press, Cambridge.

Headicar, P. & C. Curtis (1994) Residential development and car-based travel: does location make a difference? Paper presented at PTRC European Transport Forum, School of Planning, Oxford Brookes University, September.

Hibbert, Christopher (1977) *London: The Biography of a City*, 3rd edn. Penguin Books, Harmondsworth.

Hill, Morris (1968) A goals-achievement matrix in evaluating alternative plans, *Journal of the American Institute of Planners*, Vol. 34(1): 19–28.

Huh, Serim & Seung-Jun Kwak (1997) The choice of functional form and variables in the hedonic price model in Seoul, *Urban Studies*, Vol. 34, (7): 989–998.

Inwood, Stephen (1998) *A History of London*. Macmillan, London.

Jacobs, Jane (1969) *The Economy of Cities*. Jonathan Cape, London.

Kahneman, Daniel, Jack L. Knetsch & Michael H. Thaler (1990) Experimental tests of the endowment effect and the Coase theorem, *Journal of Political Economy*, Vol. 98(6): 1325–1348.

Kahneman, Daniel, Jack L. Knetsch & Michael H. Thaler (1991) The endowment effect, loss aversion and status quo bias, *Journal of Economic Perspectives*, Vol. 5, No. 1 (Winter): 193–206.

Kalbro, Thomas & Hans Mattsson (1995) *Urban Land and Property Markets in Sweden*. UCL Press, London.

Keogh, Geoffrey T. (1985) The economics of planning gain, in: S. Barrett & P. Healey (eds) *Land Policy: Problems and Alternatives*, 203–228. Gower, London.

Keogh, G. & A.W. Evans (1992) The private and social costs of planning delay, *Urban Studies*, Vol. 29, No. 5, 687–699.

Kim, Kyung-Hwan (1993) Housing policies, affordability and government policy: Korea, *Journal of Real Estate Finance and Economics*, Vol. 6(1): 55–71.

Kim, Kyung-Hwan (1994) Controlled developments and densification: the case of Seoul: Korea. Discussion Paper, Department of Economics, Sogang University, Korea.

Kim, Chung-Ho & Kyung-Hwan Kim (2000) The political economy of Korean government policies on real estate, *Urban Studies*, Vol. 37(7): 1157–1169.

Kivell, Philip (1993) *Land and the City*. Routledge, London.

Knaap, Gerrit, J. (1985) The price effects of urban growth boundaries in Metropolitan Portland, Oregon, *Land Economics*, Vol. 61, 28–35.

Kostof, Spiro (1991) *The City Shaped: Urban Patterns and Meaning through History*. Thames & Hudson, London.

Kostof, Spiro (1992) *The City Assembled: the Elements of Urban Form through History*. Thames & Hudson, London.

Krueger, Anne D. (1974) The political economy of the rent-seeking society, *American Economic Review*, Vol. 71(1): 171–178.

Krugman, Paul (1991) Increasing returns and economic geography, *Journal of Political Economy*, Vol. 99(3): 483–499.

Lai, W.C.L. (1994) The economics of land use zoning: a literature review and analysis of the work of Coase, *Town Planning Review*, Vol. 65(1): 77–99.

Lee, Jim S. (1997) An ordo-liberal perspective on land problems in Korea, *Urban Studies*, Vol. 34(7): 1071–1084.

Lenon, M., S.K. Chattopadhyay & D.R. Heffley (1996) Zoning and fiscal inter-dependencies, *Journal of Real Estate Finance and Economics*, Vol. 12: 221–234.

Leven, Charles L., James T. Little, Hugh O. Nourse & R.B. Read (1976) *Neighbourhood Change: Lessons in the Dynamics of Urban Decay*. Praeger, New York.

Levine, Ned (1999) The effects of local growth controls on regional housing production and population redistribution in California, *Urban Studies*, Vol. 36(12): 2047–2068.

Li, M.M. & H.J. Brown (1980) Micro-neighbourhood externalities and hedonic housing prices, *Land Economics*, Vol. 56: 125–141.

Lichfield, N. (1956) *Economics of Planned Development*. Estates Gazette, London.

Lichfield, N. (1988) *Economics in Urban Conservation*. Cambridge University Press, Cambridge.

Lichfield, N. (1996) *Community Impact Evaluation*. UCL Press, London.

Lombardi, P. & G. Sirchia (1990) *Il quartiere 16 IACF di Torino*, in: R. Roscelli (ed.) *Misurare nell'incertezza*. Celid, Turin.

London County Council (1951) *Administrative County of London Development Plan 1951*. London County Council, London.

Malpezzi, S. & S.K. Mayo (1997) Getting housing incentives right: a case study of the effects of regulation, taxes, and subsidies on housing supply in Malaysia, *Land Economics*, Vol. 73: 372–391.

Marriott, Oliver (1967) *The Property Boom*. Hamish Hamilton, London.

McCann, Philip (2001) *Urban and Regional Economics*. Oxford University Press, Oxford.

McDonald, J.F. (1995) Houston remains unzoned, *Land Economics*, Vol. 71: 137–140.

McMillen, D.P. & J.F. McDonald (1991) Urban land value functions with endo-genous zoning, *Journal of Urban Economics*, Vol. 29: 14–27.

McMillen, D.P. & J.F. McDonald (1993) Could zoning have increased land values in Chicago? *Journal of Urban Economics*, Vol. 33: 167–188.

Meeks, Thomas J. (1990) The economic efficiency and equity of abortion, *Economics and Philosophy*, Vol. 6: 95–138.

✗ Mildner, Gerard C.S. (2001) Regionalism and the growth management movement, in: Randall G. Holcombe & Samuel R. Staley (eds) *Smarter Growth: Market-Based Strategies for Land Use Planning in the 21st Century*. Greenwood Press, Westport, CT.

• Monk, S., B.J. Pearce & C.M.E. Whitehead (1996) Land-use planning, land supply and house prices, *Environment and Planning A*, Vol. 28: 495–511.

• Munton, Richard (1983) *London's Green Belt: Containment in Practice*. George Allen & Unwin, London.

Needham, B. (1992) A theory of land prices when land is supplied publicly: the case of The Netherlands, *Urban Studies*, Vol. 29(5): 669–686.

Nelson, Julianne (1993) Persuasion and economic efficiency: the cost–benefit analysis of banning abortion, *Economics and Philosophy*, Vol. 9: 229–252.

Nelson, Arthur C. (1985) Demand, segmentation, and timing effects of an urban containment program on urban fringe land values, *Urban Studies*, Vol. 22(5): 439–443.

Nelson, Arthur C. (1988) An empirical note of how regional urban containment policy influences an interaction between greenbelt and ex-urban land markets, *Land Economics*, Vol. 54: 78–184.

Neutze, Max (1977) *Urban Development in Australia*. George Allen & Unwin, Sydney.

Neutze, Max (1987) The supply of land for a particular use, *Urban Studies*, Vol. 25(5): 379–388.

Neutze, Max (1997) *Funding Urban Services*. Allen & Unwin, Sydney.

NHBC (1996, 2003) *NHBC Private House Building Statistics*.

Oxfordshire County Council (1990) *Oxfordshire 2001: Oxfordshire Structure Plan Proposed Alterations No 4*. Oxford County Council, Oxford.

Oxley, M.J. (1975) Economic theory and urban planning, *Environment and Planning A*, Vol. 7: 497–508.

Pargal, Sheoli & David Wheeler (1996) Informed regulation of industrial pollution in developing countries: evidence for Indonesia, *Journal of Political Economy*, Vol. 104(6): 1314–1337.

Pearce, David W. (1978) *The Valuation of Social Cost*. George Allen & Unwin, London.

Pennington, Mark (1996) *Conservation and the Countryside*. Institute of Economic Affairs Environment Unit, London.

Pennington, Mark (2000) *Planning and the Political Market*. Athlone Press, London.

Pogodzinski, J.M. & T.R. Sass (1991) Measuring the effects of municipal zoning regulations: a survey, *Urban Studies*, Vol. 28(4): 596–621.

Posner, Richard (1992) *Sex and Reason*. Harvard UP, Cambridge, MA.

Poulton, Michael C. (1991a) The case for a positive theory of planning. Part 1, What is wrong with planning theory, *Environment and Planning B*, Vol. 18(2): 225–232.

Poulton, Michael C. (1991b) The case for a positive theory of planning. Part 2: A positive theory of planning, *Environment and Planning B*, Vol. 18: 263–275.

Poulton, Michael C. (1997) Externalities, transaction costs, public choice and the appeal of zoning, *Town Planning Review*, Vol. 68: 81–92.

Prest, A.R. (1981) *The Taxation of Urban Land*. Manchester University Press, Manchester.

Reilly, Barry & Robert Witt (1994) Regional house prices and repossessions in England and Wales: an empirical analysis, *Regional Studies*, Vol. 28, No. 5 (August): 475–481.

Ricardo, David (1815) *The Principles of Political Economy and Taxation*, Everyman Library. Dent, London.

Romer, Paul M. (1986) Increasing returns and long-run growth, *Journal of Political Economy*, Vol. 94, No. 5: 1002–1037.

Roscelli, R. & Zorzi, F. (1990) Valutazione di progetti di riqualificazione urbana, in: R. Roscelli (ed.) *Misurare nell'Incertezza*. Celid, Turin.

Rosen, S. (1974) Hedonic prices and implicit markets: production differentiation in pure competition, *Journal of Political Economy*, 82(1): 34–55.

Rydin, Yvonne (1998) *Urban and Environmental Planning in the UK*. Macmillan, London.

Saaty, T.L. (1980) *The Analytic Hierarchy Process*. McGraw-Hill, New York.

Schaeffer, P.V. & C.A. Millerick (1991) The impact of historic district designation on property values: an empirical study, *Economic Development Quarterly*, Vol. 5, pp. 301–312.

Siegan, Bernard, H. (1972) *Land Use Without Zoning*. Heath-Lexington, Lexington, MA.

Smith, Adam (1776/1960) *The Wealth of Nations*. Dent, London.

Smith, V. Kerry (1993) Nonmarket valuation of environmental resources: an interpretative appraisal, *Land Economics*, Vol. 69(1) (February): 1–26.

Speyrer, J.F. (1989) The effect of land-use restrictions on market values of single-family houses in Houston, *Journal of Real Estate Finance and Economics*, Vol. 2: 107–113.

Staley, Samuel R. (1994) *Planning Rules and Urban Economic Performance: The Case of Hong Kong*. Chinese University Press, Hong Kong.

Stigler, George J. (1973) The theory of economic regulation, *Bell Journal of Economics and Management Science*, Vol. 2: 3–21.

Taylor, A.J.P. (1965) *English History 1914–1945*. Oxford University Press, Oxford.

Thorson, J.A. (1996) An examination of the monopoly zoning hypothesis, *Land Economics*, Vol. 72: 43–55.

Titman, S. (1985) Urban land prices under uncertainty, *American Economc Review*, Vol. 75, No. 3 (June): 505–514.

Topel, R. & S. Rosen (1988) Housing investment in the United States, *Journal of Political Economy*, Vol. 96, No. 4: 718–40.

Tsoukis, C. & P. Westaway (1994) A forward looking model of housing construction in the UK, *Economic Modelling*, Vol. 11(2): 266–279.

Urban Task Force (1999) *Towards an Urban Renaissance*. E & FN Spon, London.

Wabe, J.S. (1971) A study of house prices as a means of establishing the value of journey time, the rate of time preference and the valuation of some aspects of environment in the London metropolitan region, *Applied Economics*, Vol. 3(4): 247–255.

Wallace, N.E. (1988) The market effects of zoning undeveloped land: does zoning follow the market? *Journal of Urban Economics*, Vol. 23: 307–326.

Webster, Christopher J. (1998) Public choice, Pigouvian and Coasian planning theory, *Urban Studies*, Vol. 35(1): 53–75.

Webster, Chris & Lawrence Wai-Chung Lai (2003) *Property Rights, Planning and Markets*. Edward Elgar, Cheltenham.

Weitzman, Martin L. (1974) Prices vs Quantities, *The Review of Economic Studies*, Vol. 41(4): 477–491.

White, P. (1986) Land availability, land banking and the price of land for housing, *Land Development Studies*, Vol. 3: 101–111.

Willis, K.G. (1980) *The Economics of Town and Country Planning*. Granada, London.

Willis, K.G. (1982) Green belts: an economic appraisal of a physical planning policy, *Planning Outlook*, Vol. 25: 62–69.

Willis, K.G. & M.C. Whitby (1985) The value of green belt land, *Journal of Rural Studies*, Vol. 1(2): 147–162.

Willis, Ken (1994) Paying for heritage: what price for Durham Cathedral? *Journal of Environmental Planning and Management*, Vol. 37(3): 267–278.

Zahedi, F. (1986) The analytic hierarchy process: a survey of the method and its application, *Interfaces*, Vol. 16: 96–108.

Index